PORTRAIT

Adlai E. Stevenson:
Politician, Diplomat,
Friend

PORTRAIT

Adlai E. Stevenson:

Politician, Diplomat,

Friend

by

Alden Whitman and *The New York Times*

HARPER & ROW, PUBLISHERS

NEW YORK

CONTENTS

Illustrations follow page 116.

FOREWORD

The day that Adlai Stevenson died he was appraised by James Reston of *The New York Times* as "the right man at the wrong time," implying that a man of such grace, dedication and reason might have fared better as a Presidential candidate in the 1960's than he did in the witch-hunting, cold war fifties. It can also be argued, I believe, that Stevenson was the right man at the right time because the United States in the fifties badly needed the voice of reason that Stevenson so eloquently provided, and that election to office was not the measure of his stature.

Whatever the ultimate evaluation of Stevenson, he was in his own lifetime both a symbol of intelligence in politics and an example of perplexity in personal attitudes—a combination not readily understood. His hesitations were often taken for weakness; whereas in fact they usually reflected a stubborn adherence to his values. He thought his principles important, himself not; so that public adulation did not inflate him. "Fame," he once remarked, "is fine, provided you don't inhale."

Stevenson's keeping his head to size, his lack of pomposity and side, and his delight in humorous situations endeared him to his friends and invited the confidence of statesmen. Once, on a trip to the Ivory Coast (now Ghana) in 1955 Stevenson was visited by Dr. Kwame Nkrumah bearing a beautiful golden cloth as a gift.

Nkrumah tried to show Stevenson how to don the garment, swinging it over his shoulder like a Roman toga. But Stevenson could not get the hang of it. Every time Nkrumah draped it on, it slipped off again until, weak with laughter, the two of them clowned up and down the room making Roman gestures with the cloth. Then, over dinner, the mood changed, and Stevenson and Nkrumah had a long and candid discussion of Ivory Coast politics, all the more open because of its unforced companionship.

Another reflection of Stevenson's refusal to "inhale" flattery and fame was his indifference to titles. At the United Nations he held the rank of ambassador, yet he always seemed uncomfortable when he was addressed as "Mr. Ambassador" or was introduced at a public gathering as "the Honorable Adlai E. Stevenson." He preferred to be called "Governor" or even "Guv," these dating from his governorship of Illinois; and, of course, he was "Adlai" or "Ad" to his intimates.

Stevenson's urbane temper, his wit, his courtesy were in the style of the eighteenth century, as were his rationalist and Deist beliefs and his emphasis on striving for perfection in society. There was even an eighteenth-century look to his face, which would not have seemed out of place under a wig.

About his political ideas there is much that can be traced to John Locke, to John Stuart Mill and to Thomas Jefferson. There is a dash of Woodrow Wilson, too. Stevenson's views were not expressed systematically, but, as his speeches and his actions suggest, they were perfused with humanity and democracy. His concept of democracy was directly from Lincoln: "of the people, by the people and for the people"; and he took the words to mean what they said.

Stevenson was so unusual a political and personal phenomenon that he raised many questions about himself: Was he a tragic candidate for the Presidency, born to lose? Was he a modern Hamlet? Was he all words and no substance? Was he a crusading liberal, eclipsed by Kennedy? Did he make a genuine contribution to American public life and to the world?

This book does not pretend to offer all the answers or final truths, for it is a portrait, not a definitive biography. It aims to show Stevenson as his contemporaries viewed him, sometimes harshly, sometimes with mellowness, sometimes with dispassion. The portrait is drawn from the record as Stevenson made it and as observers read it.

The principal source is *The New York Times*, whose reporters covered Stevenson assiduously from early 1952 to his death in 1965. Without these reporters (and the editors who shaped their copy for publication) this book would not have been possible. Where dispatches are quoted without attribution they are from *The Times*. Sources other than *The Times* have also been drawn upon with appropriate acknowledgment. But of course neither *The Times* nor these ancillary sources are responsible for any editorial judgments expressed in this book, or for any errors of fact that may have been unwittingly introduced in writing it. For any errors of fact there is but one word: *Peccavi*.

Portrait has been a joint effort. Editorial contributions have been made by John Corry of *The Times*'s National News Desk and by Bernard Weinraub, a reporter on that paper's Metropolitan Desk. Richard Rustin, also of *The Times*, provided research assistance. The whole was overseen by John G. Stewart of *The Times* Book Division.

ALDEN WHITMAN

PORTRAIT

———◦∞◦———

Adlai E. Stevenson:

Politician, Diplomat,

Friend

CHAPTER I

---◆◇◆---

"WE WANT STEVENSON . . ."

I

T WAS NOW almost forty-six minutes into Wednesday, November 5, 1952, by the clock in the ballroom of the Leland Hotel in Springfield, Illinois. The temperature outside was suitably crisp, but inside it was hot, for the ballroom was jammed with hopeful and earnest campaign workers assembled there since the previous midafternoon to watch election returns that they had firmly persuaded themselves would place Adlai Stevenson in the White House. In the course of the long evening the crowd's cheerfulness had dwindled, although, oddly, their fervor had not; nor had their desire to hear yet another word from their candidate.

So the television cameras, peering into the crowd, caught the moment of expectancy as a middling-size, partly bald man in a dark blue suit, white shirt and a red-figured tie emerged into the second-floor room from a freight elevator. A small police escort parted a path for him and his sons, Borden and John Fell, as they made their way to a microphone-festooned platform at the far end of the room. The organist played the University of Illinois fight song and, as its notes receded, there was a chant that started nowhere and came from everywhere at once: "We want Stevenson! We want Stevenson!" Finally Stevenson reached the dais, and the television lights bounced off his high, freckled forehead as he began to recite, in a sudden hush, a statement that the crowd dreaded to hear.

"I have a statement that I should like to make," he began and proceeded to read his concession of victory to Dwight D. Eisenhower for the Presidency of the United States. This is a ritual going far back into our political history, and it requires the defeated candidate, when he is certain that the voters have rejected him, to thank his friends for their efforts in his behalf and to send a telegram of congratulations to the victor. Few such occasions are memorable, nor do the bland words uttered there linger.

But with Stevenson there were few banalities. His concession of defeat was different, as were many things about him. In his formal statement he sought to assuage the feeling of many of his supporters that the country could not be the same with Eisenhower's victory.

"We vote as many," he said, "but we pray as one. With a united people, with faith in democracy, with common concern for others less fortunate around the globe, we shall move forward with God's guidance toward the time when His children shall grow in freedom and dignity in a world at peace."

When he had finished reading his telegram to Eisenhower in New York, Stevenson paused. Then, spontaneously, he went on:

"Someone asked me, as I came in, down on the street, how I felt and I was reminded of a story that a fellow townsman of ours used to tell—Abraham Lincoln. They asked him how

[2]

he felt once after an unsuccessful election. He said he felt like a little boy who had stubbed his toe in the dark. He said that he was too old to cry but it hurt too much to laugh."

As he spoke men and women wept and there were cries of "No! No!" And afterward, one woman fought her way to the platform and grasped Stevenson's hand. "Governor, we're with you always!" she exclaimed. He reached out, patted her cheek and said, "Bless you."

Then, as quickly as he decently could, he extricated himself from the throng and returned by car with his sons and a few close political supporters to the big white Executive Mansion two blocks away. He looked momentarily drained, the jauntiness with which he had stepped into the hotel gone.

The Stevenson workers, most of them volunteers, and the party faithful, still stunned, still gloomy, still tearful but still, amazingly, undefeated in spirit, drifted out of the ball-room. Reporters and television crews departed. And the lights went off on a surrealistic room of twisted chairs, strewn coffee containers, chewed cigar butts and crushed cigarette stubs.

It was the conclusion of a long campaign, and a hopeless one, albeit a sparkling one. Stevenson had not wanted to run. He had, in fact, been blackjacked into it. As late as the night before the Democratic nominating convention in Chicago he had sat up until 2 A.M. in the kitchen of Jacob M. Arvey, the Illinois party leader, proposing other names and insisting that he wanted only to run for re-election as Governor.

Stevenson realized that he couldn't win. "You know," he told a friend at the time, "you really can't beat a household commodity—the catsup bottle on the kitchen table."

"To run as a Democrat in 1952 was hopeless, let alone

against the Number One war hero," he said years later. Yet he had run out of loyalty to his party, an abiding sense of obligation and duty. "And finally," as he explained afterward, "could anyone in good health and already in public life refuse the greatest honor and greatest opportunity in our political system?"

Not only did Stevenson run, and run hard, but he also mounted a campaign singular in its literateness, grace and humor. And one, moreover, that, despite almost solid opposition from the country's editorial pages, gathered him 27 million votes, 3 million more votes than Harry S. Truman had polled in winning in 1948. However, it was not the votes that Stevenson polled but the voters whom he aroused that set his campaign apart. They were the young, the idealistic, the passionate, to whom Stevenson was both a cause and the vehicle for a just and better America. That was not a thing precisely defined; it was more a longing, a yearning; but something nonetheless worth working for. And work they did, in droves, as volunteers, as amateurs out to demonstrate the muscle of goodwill.

Stevenson himself caught that spirit, and he molded it by the remarkable directness with which he discussed public issues. The substructure of his thinking he elaborated in this way:

For years I have listened to the nauseous nonsense, the pie-in-the-sky appeals to cupidity and greed, the cynical trifling with passion and prejudice and fear; the slander, fraudulent promises and the all-things-to-all-men demagoguery that are too much a part of our political campaigns. Sometimes in the deafening clamor of political salesmanship, I've thought that people might be better served if a party purchased a half-hour of radio and TV silence during which the audience would be asked to think quietly for themselves.

Politicians all applaud and support public education as democracy's great monument and cornerstone, but does the politician, the agent and spokesman of democracy, have no responsibility for public education? Government by the consent of the governed is the most difficult system of all because it depends for its success and viability on the good judgments and wise decisions of so many of us. But judgment and decision depend on information and understanding. In matters of public policy, candidates then have the greatest responsibility of all to inform truthfully, so that the people will understand and will have the tools of good judgment and wise decision.

One can argue, indeed, that all candidates claiming the people's confidence have even a higher mission: honestly to help man to know, as St. Thomas Aquinas said, what he ought to believe; to know what he ought to desire; to know what he ought to do.

To many professional politicians Stevenson, in executing his campaign in his own way, seemed to commit the cardinal crime of talking over the heads of the voters. But it was clear that he had not, else he would not have won the devotion of so many, especially the new and college-educated middle class emerging from World War II. He was called an egghead, and he tossed back a Latinism of his own devising: *"Via ovum cranium difficilis est"* ("The way of the egghead is hard").

If Stevenson appealed to the voters' powers of cerebration, he also did not neglect their risibilities. "If the Republicans will stop telling lies about us, we will stop telling the truth about them," he said, and even the Republicans were obliged to laugh, as they did when he told a Fort Dodge, Iowa, audience: "The Republicans have a 'me too' candidate running on a 'yes but' platform, advised by a 'has been' staff."

Cracking jokes violated another canon, one venerated

equally with the rule about not appearing to be too smart. Richard Lee Strout, writing in *The Times Magazine,* put Stevenson the humorist's position this way:

Did Washington crack jokes? Certainly not. Lincoln did—and they caused him no end of trouble.

The difficulty was put pithily about a century ago by Senator Thomas Corwin, a onetime Governor of Ohio and Secretary of the Treasury under Millard Fillmore. Corwin felt that he might well have become President himself if his enemies had not given him the reputation of being funny. "Never make people laugh," Corwin glumly told General James Garfield on one occasion. "If you would succeed in life you must be solemn—solemn as an ass. All the great monuments are built over solemn asses."

General Garfield, incidentally, became President.

But beyond the literateness, apart from the humor and beneath the gameness of Stevenson in the campaign, voters sensed a man of profound democratic convictions, a man totally lacking in pettifoggery and smallness; a man of abundant humanity; a man of wryness about himself; a man who in defeat (and it could not have been a sweet one) could tell his Lincoln story without an ounce of pomposity or self-pity.

These were some of the qualities for which he gained admiration in defeat both in 1952 and in 1956, when he was an even worse loser. And it was an admiration that, perversely, made him greater in defeat than he might have been in victory; and that ultimately made him the spokesman for the whole American people in the United Nations; for Stevenson may have lost two elections and botched a chance for a third nomination, but to the peoples and statesmen of the world he was an authentic voice of the United States. That is not the least of the many paradoxes of his life.

When Stevenson left the Leland Hotel in the provincial

city of Springfield that November morning in 1952 he could have been departing for that political limbo to which the American people frequently consign Presidential also-rans. Our history is littered with men who have put up a good fight for the White House and who could scarcely be remembered ten years afterward.

Even in this century the only exception that comes readily to mind is William Jennings Bryan. But he is somewhat remarkable for having run three times and lost three times; moreover, the once Boy Orator of the Platte is recalled mostly nowadays as a crumpled old man fluttering a palm fan and expostulating against evolution in a hot Tennessee courtroom. Alton B. Parker, Charles Evans Hughes, James A. Cox, John W. Davis, Alfred E. Smith, Alf M. Landon, Thomas E. Dewey—distinguished though they may have been as national candidates—were not taken up by the public after defeat.

One has to go back more than a hundred years to Henry Clay to find a parallel to the popular fondness for Stevenson. The voters, of course, did not love him so much in November, but his was an enduring place in public affection for all that. Indeed, after his defeat in 1952 he got more than the customary letters from avowed fans telling him the writers had been with him all the way; he received thousands of letters from voters half-apologizing and half-explaining why they had not voted for him. Many of the writers said they felt a compulsion to write; and that, on such a scale, was a new sort of political testimony in this country. It demonstrated that Stevenson the man had got under the skin of a very large number of people.

Many defeated national candidates have passed days in trying to explain what happened to them. Many of these observations have been ponderous. Stevenson had no stomach for that. "Come in, gentlemen, I'm offering post-mortems on toast," he greeted members of the press when they arrived at the Executive Mansion in midmorning on that November 5 in 1952. He looked refreshed, and his sea-blue eyes were as merry as ever.

If at the very moment of defeat he "hurt too much to laugh," he got over it, at least to the extent of making others laugh, by the time of the Gridiron Club dinner in Washington on December 13. The club, an organization of newspapermen, leaves its collective pencils home so that its speakers may talk frankly. Stevenson took advantage of this forum to deliver an uninhibited yet subtle post-mortem in a speech that revealed as much of him as it did of the campaign. His remarks were too full of pungency to be suppressed, and a copy of them got out.

"A funny thing happened to me on the way to the White House. Let me tell you about it," he began. And this is what he told:

While I did not carry many states, I seem to have run way ahead in the Fourth Estate, excluding, of course, you publishers. I can think of no state I would rather have carried, and perhaps I should begin by apologizing to those of you who work for a living and who thought I was out in front, somewhere between Mississippi, Britain and France. The fact was, of course, that the General was so far ahead we never saw him. I was happy to hear that I had even placed second.

It is apparent that I was not the first choice of a great many. But no one will say, I trust, that I snatched defeat from the jaws of victory. . . .

At the Gridiron dinner just four years ago . . . I was happy and carefree and had nothing to worry about, nothing except the organization of a new administration to clean up the state of Illinois after the long years of the usual Republican misrule. And now I don't even have that to worry about. I, a Democrat, had just been elected Governor by the largest majority ever received in Republican Illinois. And here I am, four years later, and just defeated by the largest majority ever received in Democratic America. Wasn't it Jim Watson who said that he entered the Senate with almost no opposition from the people of Indiana, and that he left the Senate with none?

I feel a little the same way. But I wonder if I'm not entitled to some kind of a record. Did anyone starting from scratch ever enter our public life with such widespread approval, and then leave with such widespread approval—all in the space of four years? Frankly, I think the chroniclers of our times have overlooked the meteoric beauty and brevity of my political career. Well, I had not planned it that way. I had wished to continue as Governor of Illinois, there to erect and fortify a shining temple of administrative purity and political probity. But the gods decreed otherwise—after meeting in the Chicago stockyards. Mindful of the Chinese maiden's philosophical acceptance of unwanted and aggressive attentions, I concluded to accept my fate gallantly and joyfully, with consequences that were reported by most of you publishers—also joyfully.

Now I content myself that is all for the best. After all, didn't Socrates say that the duty of a man of real principle is to stay out of politics? So you see I'm delighted that the sovereign people have put an even higher value on my principles than I did. Yes, I have much to be thankful for, and it would be out of character if I didn't frankly confess my happy state of mind, even here, surrounded by my late executioners. . . .

I am happy that almost 27 million voted for me. . . . That figure still staggers me. But I need a much stronger verb to describe what the still larger number of those who liked Ike does to me! I have not compared notes with the President-elect on how he enjoyed the campaign. Indeed, now that the affair is over, I hope sometime to know him, which recalls many editorials and articles you gentlemen wrote last spring about how I wanted to run against Senator [Robert A.] Taft [of Ohio] but not the General, who was my old friend. . . . I would tell him that for my part I enjoyed the campaign in spots. There were times, I confess, when I was afraid I wouldn't die, times when I felt I wouldn't do it to a dog. Let me add, by the way, that, like every red-blooded American patriot, I own a dog. It was not a campaign contribution. And I think the General would say to me there are times when he wishes he was in my shoes—you see I've had them fixed.

A lot of wonderful things happened to me during the campaign. People shook hands. Have you ever shaken four thousand hands, one after the other, with a bright word for the owner of each hand? . . . In San Francisco a woman in the crowd shook hands with me through the car door and shortly announced she had lost a diamond ring. I traveled tens of thousands of miles, up and down this vast country, on such a sight-seeing tour as few men are privileged to make. . . .

I got several hours' sleep a night; they fed me pretty regularly; I got a little tired of cheese-on-rye sandwiches and coffee in cardboard containers. And I frequently thought, unhappily, of Froude's line in the life of Bunyan: "The excitement of perpetual speech-making is fatal to the exercise of the highest powers." I became very familiar with the sound of my own voice. I hope the Recording Angel will note that I did not say "the sound of my own words." . . .

And now that the tumult and the shouting have died, and Walter Lippmann and Joe Alsop have gone back to writing the next chapter of the *Domesday Book,* how does the vanquished hero feel, and what of the future?

Well, gentlemen, there are certain pleasurable aspects of defeat. Although there seemed little perceptible editorial enthusiasm for me during the campaign except in some of the better papers, I have been stirred by the virtues which so many essayists discovered in me the moment it became clear the outs were in. Much of this comment seemed to suggest that it couldn't have happened to a nicer guy. And, lest you get ahead of me, I say that I couldn't have lost to a nicer guy. . . .

Then there were the letters. We gave up counting before long and began to weigh them. So many of them were from people who voted for the General, and evidently felt they owed me an explanation. Curious why people will go to all that trouble to write a long letter when a little X in the right place would have been so much easier. But I am grateful to them all, and I wish there was some refined way befitting my station to explain to each of them that we spent a lot of money we didn't have. But I suppose if I did they might write again, in a less friendly vein, and say, "Just like a Democrat."

As to my future. There are those . . . who feel that I should devote my classic talents to the welfare of mankind by frequent talking. Then there is another smaller group who insist that God, and/or the electorate, has appointed me the scourge of the Republican Party. And finally there is a much smaller group that feels that it is not wholly unworthy or improper to earn a living. My sons are numbered in the latter group. . . .

To those of us who constitute what I trust will be known as the responsible opposition, these are times of unusual complexity. Mention of Mr. Taft suggests, for example, that for the moment at least we Democrats are intruders in a family quarrel. Indeed, it is difficult to be certain, for the present, whether we Democrats will be disagreeing with the new President or acting as his bodyguard.

But whatever happens to the Republicans, the Republic will survive. I have great faith in the people. As to their wisdom, well, Coca-Cola still outsells champagne. They make mistakes. They do sometimes. But given time they correct their mistakes—at two- and four-year intervals. . . .

As to you, the press, a last word: It is the habit of journalists, as of politicians, to see the world in terms of crisis rather than continuity; the big story is turmoil and disaster, not the quiet spectacle of men working. I trust there will be none among my party who will hope for just a small, dandy little catastrophe to vindicate us. I am aware of the thesis that bad news sells papers. But neither publishers nor politicians have the right in this age to hope for the worst. Every newspaperman has talked at one time or another of how to handle the story of the end of the world; but who will be around to buy the extras?

Every lesson of history is that democracy flourishes best when speech is freest. No issue is more important—and more troublesome —in this time of conflict with massive repression than the preservation of our right even to bore each other. (I was flattered, by the way, by an unsigned letter last week that said, "Please start talking again, Governor, or we'll be bored to death before we're starved to death.")

Never was the responsibility of the majority of the press greater to make clear that it is concerned about the freedom of all Americans, and not merely about its own liberty to agree with itself. Your typewriter is a public trust. Its sound may be the most beautiful noise you know, but it has meaning and justification only if it is part of the gloriously discordant symphony of a free society.

On the final day of the 1952 campaign Stevenson visited a grade school at Half Day, Illinois, not far from his home at Libertyville. As William M. Blair reported the event:

He started his talk with the children, blue jean and lumber jacket clad, by asking them to indicate how many "would like to be the Governor of Illinois, the way I am."

As the hands shot up from the three lines of children he said, "That is almost unanimous," and continued, "Now I would like to ask the Governor if he would like to be one of those kids." With this, he waved his hand and shouted, "Yah, yah, yah!"

Stevenson's perceptive feeling for small children and for the wonderfully complex simplicity of childhood was genuine, for his own childhood was a secure and happy one, a privileged sanctuary.

Adlai Ewing Stevenson 2d was born into a prosperous, sedate and unspectacular aristocratic family that had a history of dignified and substantial public service. His birth occurred in Los Angeles on February 5, 1900, where his father, Lewis Green Stevenson, was at the time assistant business manager of William Randolph Hearst's *Los Angeles Examiner*. His mother was Helen Davis Stevenson. The boy was the couple's second and last child, their first having been Elizabeth who was born in 1898.

The baby was named for his grandfather, a durable, kindly, gregarious Illinois politician, a bit on the patrician side, one of whose distinguishing physical characteristics was a glorious, turn-of-the-century, waterfall mustache. The high point of his public career was four innocuous years as Grover Cleveland's Vice President from 1893 to 1897. Previously, he had served two terms in the House of Representatives, and he was Assistant Postmaster General during Cleveland's first term in the White House. In that post he earned the nickname of "The Headsman" for pruning forty thousand Republican postmasters from the payroll.

He had a gentleman's fondness for office, and the stamina to seek it, for he ran with Bryan in 1900 and for the governorship of Illinois in 1908, when he was seventy-three.

The source of Vice President Stevenson's first name was Adlai Osborn, an uncle of his great-great-grandfather, who was the Clerk of Rowan County, North Carolina, in 1775. Osborn's parents presumably found it in the First Book of Chronicles, the 29th verse of the 27th chapter, which, describing David's officers, reads:

"And over the herds that fed in Sharon was Shitrai the Sharonite: and over the herds that were in the valleys was Shaphat the son of Adlai."

Adlai appears only once in the Bible, from which were plucked so many wondrous and bizarre forenames by God-fearing folk of the eighteenth and nineteenth centuries. Its proper pronunciation is less certain than its source. "Adlay" was used by the Stevenson family, but outsiders, employing it as a form of address, sometimes said "Adlie."

Through his mother Adlai was the great-grandson of Jesse W. Fell, a restless Quaker, who, after wandering for several years about Ohio and Illinois and acquiring a law degree in the process, settled in Bloomington, Illinois. He was the town's first lawyer and its first newspaper publisher, founding *The Bloomington Observer* and *McClean County Advocate.* Fell's claim to a place in history was his friendship with Abraham Lincoln, whom he first met in the winter of 1834-35. He was instrumental, in 1858, in arranging the Lincoln-Douglas debates, and, later, in proposing Lincoln as a Presidential candidate. In the Civil War Fell was paymaster of the Union Army.

Lewis Stevenson, who married Fell's granddaughter, returned to Bloomington to live shortly after Adlai was born, managed the family's considerable farmlands and ventured into politics as Secretary of State of Illinois in 1914.

The town where Adlai grew up was a mellow, self-satisfied community, with red-brick streets. The Stevenson house, at 1316 East Washington Street, was a large, comfortable, three-story, gabled, gingerbread affair in the Victorian manner, with a wide piazza, trellises of rosebushes and a captain's walk on the roof. Flagstones led to the porch, and there was a vegetable garden, an apple tree and a pump in the back yard. The house was furnished with subdued elegance, but a note of somberness was struck by a stained-glass window in the stairway wall—a customary evidence of good taste in the homes of the well-to-do at the turn of the century.

Adlai's own room was not sumptuous, but from it he could look out over an acre of lawn sloping down to the country club. He was reared unaccustomed to vulgar display and to the imperatives of haste. "I have Bloomington to thank for the most important lesson I have learned," he said later, "that in quiet places reason abounds, that in quiet people there is vision and purpose, that many things are revealed to the humble that are hidden from the great."

This, however, was a backward glance, for Adlai's youthful companions were not primarily the quiet, humble people, but a rather closed circle of immediate family and relatives. In the winter he was generally in the South with his mother; the summers were spent at a lake resort in Michigan. Through his parents and grandparents he was introduced to national notables as they passed through Bloomington, or as they came to call at other places where the families were staying.

Adlai, or Laddie as his mother called him, was schooled at home until he was nine. Interlarded with the basics were copious chunks of Scott, Dickens, Thackeray, Bret Harte and the "respectable" poems of Robert Burns, not to mention the Bible. He was, from all accounts, a sensitive and serious boy, with good manners; slips in decorum, or deportment, as it was termed, upset him.

A moment of deep tragedy marred Adlai's childhood, the accidental death of Ruth Mary Merwin, his fifteen-year-old cousin. She was present at a teen-age party in the Stevenson home over the Christmas holidays in 1912, as was a young military academy student. It was suggested that the student go through the manual of arms, and Adlai brought him a .22-caliber rifle for the purpose. The student examined it for bullets in the barrel or magazine, and then executed the manual. Adlai was given the rifle. As he tried to emulate the student, it went off and a bullet mortally wounded Miss Merwin.

Adlai's father, returning home within minutes, asked

which boy had fired the rifle. "I did," Adlai replied, and went upstairs to his room and cried.

An inquest found no blame for the girl's death, but what went on in young Adlai's mind is difficult to guess. The incident lay dormant until 1952, when a correspondent for *Time* magazine read an account of the inquest in a forty-year-old issue of *The Bloomington Pantagraph* and asked Stevenson to recall the episode.

"Stevenson," according to the correspondent's account, "looked away for a moment and then said, 'You are the first person who has talked to me about that since it happened— and this is the first time I have spoken of it to anyone.' I asked the Governor whether he minded telling the story. 'No,' said Stevenson, 'I'll tell you everything I can remember about it.' Then he told me the whole story, in a matter-of-fact way."

Young Stevenson was not a notable student; as a gentleman's son he was not expected to be. He got through grade school all right and was so indifferent a high school student that he was sent East to Choate to be prepared for Princeton, which he had chosen partly because of family reasons and partly because he had been impressed by Woodrow Wilson on meeting the former Princeton president when he was Governor of New Jersey.

Choate enabled Stevenson to get into Princeton, where he joined the Quadrangle eating club and competed for a position on *The Daily Princetonian*, the student newspaper. In this capacity he made his first appearance in the news columns of *The Times*. It was an inconspicuous, one-paragraph article that appeared in the editions of February 2, 1921. Under the headline, "Elected Heads Of Princeton Paper," the article read:

[16]

Thomas Covington McEachin of Jacksonville, Fla., was today elected to the Chairmanship of the Daily Princetonian, the highest undergraduate non-athletic honor that can be awarded at Princeton. Adlai Stevenson, grandson of the former Vice President of the United States, a junior, from Bloomington, Ill., was elected managing editor of the Princetonian at the same time.

At college he also acquired the nickname of "Rabbit" for an enthusiastic, leporine way of eating raw vegetables. His fondness for garden products never left him, and close observers liked to joke that whenever he ate a salad his nose twitched and his ears wiggled.

From Princeton, where his grades were average and his work not marked by originality, he went to Harvard Law School, departing there after two years of indifferent marks. The following two years he spent in various editorial jobs on *The Bloomington Pantagraph*, which had come into the Stevenson family through Adlai's mother and the Fell family. Mrs. Stevenson's father, who had married Fell's daughter, owned the property.

When his interest in becoming a newspaper editor waned, he enrolled in the law school at Northwestern University in Chicago and took his degree in 1926. But before he settled down to practice, he took another swing through Europe, which he had frequently visited before either with his family or with college classmates. This time, though, he included the Soviet Union, a venturesome expedition in those years.

Back in Illinois in 1927 he joined Cutting, Moore & Sidley, Chicago's oldest law firm. As a Democrat through his father and grandfather, Stevenson was an odd man out in a city whose business community was not only strongly Republican but also vigorously self-centered. Robert McCormick's *Chicago Tribune* reflected that condition. The young lawyer's politics, however, were rendered pardonable, if not palatable, by his Republican mother and her historical associations with Lincoln.

At this point in his life Stevenson apparently decided to buckle down. His mind, if not profound, was deft and nimble and his memory was retentive; and he made these the servant of a strong sense of obligation to his family name, which required him to learn to be an acceptable lawyer and a conscientious citizen. He started at forty dollars for a sixty-four-hour week as an inside lawyer, handling corporate and general matters. He was not then, or ever, a courtroom figure; but he acquired a sound, substantial, conservative legal knowledge.

In this period he also expanded socially, meeting and marrying, in 1928, Ellen Borden, the daughter of a Chicago financier. She was nine years her husband's junior and much interested in literature and the arts. The marriage was terminated without rancor by divorce in 1949. Mrs. Stevenson's distaste for public life was the stated reason.

Stevenson's eloquence on the public platform, the syntactical excellence and the clarity of construction of his speeches—which seemed so natural in 1952 as to be a part of him—sprang from prolonged practice, stimulated by his interest in foreign affairs. When he settled in Chicago, Stevenson joined the Chicago Council on Foreign Relations, a citizens' group that invited experts or notables to inform them about events abroad.

In due course Stevenson became president of the Council, and so he was obliged to learn to speak without bumbling. Diligent practice at home and a little cue card held in the palm of one hand at the rostrum got him nicely through the first speeches. And repeated practice added polish and assurance, but it took ten or fifteen years.

Stevenson's activity in the foreign relations group brought him into friendship with powerful and influential leaders in Chicago, such as Frank Knox, the publisher of *The Chicago Daily News*. Moreover, as frequent host to visiting dignitaries from Europe and elsewhere, he got to be on speaking terms with many world statesmen.

Friendship and the Depression brought Stevenson to Washington for his first government post. The friend was George Peek, in the capital in 1933 to organize the New Deal's Agricultural Adjustment Administration on the invitation of his friend, Henry A. Wallace. Stevenson was qualified both as a lawyer and as an amateur farm expert—plus the knowledge gained in salvaging farm mortgages and managing farm properties for his law firm.

He was special counsel with the AAA for less than a year, and in the course of meeting people he became acquainted with Lyndon B. Johnson, then an aide to a Texas Congressman. Stevenson served briefly with the Federal Alcohol Control Commission, then returned to Chicago, where he shortly became a full partner in his law firm with a yearly share of profits. More important, he resumed his work in the Council on Foreign Relations, where he became a recognized spokesman for internationalism. He was thus prepared, on the fall of Paris in 1940, to organize a chapter of the Committee to Defend America by Aiding the Allies, and to bring to Chicago mass meetings such people as Carl Sandburg, Wendell Willkie and Dorothy Thompson.

In the summer of 1941 Stevenson was off to Washington again, this time for almost seven years. This was the real beginning of his career in public service. Friendship was at the start of it, as it was so often in events in Stevenson's life, for he moved, by birth and position, among those at the center of power, where the casual word and the arm over the shoulder count for preferment.

Frank Knox, the Chicago publisher, was the friend. A Republican, he had joined the Cabinet as Secretary of the Navy in 1940 when Franklin D. Roosevelt was striving for a bipartisan foreign policy. Knox brought Stevenson in with a telephone call. "Everyone else around Washington has a lawyer and I guess I ought to have one too," was the way Knox extended the invitation.

Stevenson was given an office outside Knox's, where he performed much of the portly Secretary's legal work, ghosted his speeches, acted as a deputy, briefed him when he had to testify before Congressional committees. Stevenson was an affable, hard-working, well-informed factotum; and he got to know virtually everybody in Washington. They all called him Adlai, and some of them, like Roosevelt, tended to be fatherly toward him.

Stevenson himself liked to tell of his first important meeting with the President. On Knox's orders and carrying a secret message from Admiral Chester Nimitz, Stevenson, after chasing by plane, train and foot, caught up with him at Portland, Maine, and gained admittance to his private railroad car. In Stevenson's version this is what took place:

"Well, Adlai, how are you?" the President asked. He had known my father in the first war and I had met him once or twice years before and very briefly.

I said I was all right but that I had some papers to show him.

"That's fine, Adlai," he said, "let's have a look at them."

I opened up my briefcase and got out the Kearney shipyard papers. I showed him the letter of transmittal and all the rest of it, and pointed out where he was supposed to sign. He looked them over for a moment and then said:

"Well, yes . . . Now, Adlai, you just leave these with me, and I'll read them over. We'll have a meeting at the White House in the morning. You fly back and arrange it. Tell the Secretary I'd like to see Myron Taylor and the Attorney General at 9 o'clock—and you can be there too."

"But, Mr. President," I said, "these are supposed to be signed right now!"

"I think it will work out all right this way," said the President.

"Well," I said, "if you say so, I guess it will be O.K."

It sounds impossible that even I could talk like such a fool but I was so nervous I hardly knew what I was saying—mostly, I suppose, because I hadn't yet said the really important thing I had on my mind. I could see he was waiting for me to leave, and I had to come out with something. The talk went about like this:

"I have something else to tell you, Mr. President."

"Do you, Adlai? What is it?"

"Well, Mr. President, it's from Admiral Nimitz. He said to tell you . . . alone."

"Oh, I think you can tell me here, Adlai."

"Can I write it down for you to read?"

"Why certainly, Adlai."

He gave me a menu and I wrote on the back of it, "Admiral Nimitz has heard from a heretofore reliable source that Stalin today started negotiations with Hitler."

Then I gave him back the menu. He read it carefully and then looked up at me.

"Adlai," he said, "do you believe this?"

Now that was one thought that had never crossed my mind. I said, "Why . . . I don't know, Mr. President."

"I don't believe it," said FDR. "I'm not worried at all. Are you worried, Adlai?"

I said I guessed I wasn't. Then I got up to go. On the way out, in my embarrassed confusion, I walked right into a closed door, thus bending my crooked nose some more. I flew back to Washington, woke Secretary Knox to tell him about the meeting at the White

House and we all went over there at 9 o'clock. The crowning humiliation to me was that the President hadn't even opened my precious Kearney shipyard papers. He pulled them out and settled the whole business in 10 minutes. As for the negotiations between Stalin and Hitler, the President was, of course, right again.

Stevenson, never one to let a good story go unembellished, told the substantial truth about his meeting with Roosevelt, but the fact is that Roosevelt took a greater liking to Stevenson than Stevenson let on. Later, indeed, Roosevelt assigned Stevenson to head a politico-economic mission to Italy. Meanwhile, however, Stevenson was functioning as Knox's one-man everything, and his circle of friendships and acquaintances in the Navy and in civilian Washington expanded even more, and they came to include Senator Harry S. Truman of Missouri, chairman of the so-called Truman Committee that was investigating war production.

As Knox's troubleshooter, Stevenson toured all the major war zones in the Pacific and in Europe. And everywhere Stevenson went, he ran into old friends and made new ones. On Knox's death in 1944 Stevenson resigned his Navy post and then was attached, briefly, to the Army Air Force.

At this juncture another friend, Archibald MacLeish, got on the telephone to Stevenson with a request to take a minor job in the State Department in connection with the upcoming United Nations Conference at San Francisco in April, 1945. Stevenson was not at first assigned to the United States delegation, which was headed by Edward Stettinius, the Secretary of State. The delegation's press relations were deplorable, so terrible in fact that one publisher traded punches with Stettinius in a corridor in the Fairmount Hotel.

Arthur Krock, *The Times* correspondent on the scene, offered a solution. "Send for Adlai," he said, and someone did. Stevenson turned out to be an excellent and imperturbable press relations man for the delegation; and, of course, he made more friends.

When the Preparatory Commission for the United Nations met in London the following August, Stevenson went along as a deputy to Stettinius, who had by then resigned as Secretary of State but who headed the delegation with the rank of ambassador. Stevenson, by a stroke of fortune, was put in charge of the delegation after Stettinius returned to the United States with gall bladder trouble.

In London, Stevenson was on intimate terms, of course, with the Americans on the delegation—James Byrnes, Ben Cohen, Charles Bohlen and John Foster Dulles. And even though Stevenson held only the rank of minister, he established friendships with Gladwyn Jebb and Philip Noel-Baker of Great Britain, Wellington Koo of China and René Massigili of France, as well as with diplomats from Eastern Europe and Central and South America. Even the dour Andrei Gromyko of the Soviet Union was charmed by Stevenson.

At the first meeting of the United Nations General Assembly at Lake Success, New York, Stevenson, still chiefly a backstage diplomat, was senior adviser to the United States delegation. At its conclusion he was offered an undersecretaryship in the State Department or an embassy in Argentina or Brazil, but turned them down for a return to law in Chicago, where he stayed until Truman named him alternate delegate to the General Assembly's second session, which concluded in the fall of 1947.

Having tasted public life, Stevenson had discovered that even in his minor and supernumerary role he had developed a fondness for it. He liked the bustle of big affairs, the decision-making, the friendships, the feeling of being where power was. At the same time, Stevenson felt that, beyond the trivia (which certainly pleased him), he had an obligation to public service. In one of his war tours of Europe he had run across an item in *Stars and Stripes*, the service newspaper, reporting an opinion poll in which seven out of every ten American parents had said they didn't want their sons to enter public life.

"Think of it!" Stevenson used to say. "Boys could suffer and die in their cold, muddy, bloody campaign for the things we believe in but parents didn't want their children to work for those same things. I decided then that if I ever had a chance I'd go into public life."

Just what form this would take in 1947 was not clear. Diplomacy? He didn't think he could afford foreign posts. Domestic politics? He was a man of cultivation and experience, but virtually unknown to the voting public. He had, however, a truly impressive roster of friends of national importance, including Secretary of State Byrnes. It was he who mentioned Stevenson's name to Jacob M. Arvey, the cagey Democratic power in Illinois. The mention was casual, and it took place at an informal luncheon in July, 1947, that Senate Secretary Leslie Biffle gave for some Washington cronies. The mention, moreover, was for a United States Attorneyship in northern Illinois, but it got Arvey started, although his immediate reaction to Byrnes's praise of Stevenson as "a gold nugget" was: "Adlai Stevenson? Who's he?"

Byrnes proceeded to tell him; and when Arvey returned to Chicago he checked into Stevenson, for he was casting about for a candidate for Governor or Senator in 1948. One of those he telephoned first was his friend Judge Harry M.

Fisher, who was also a Stevenson friend. The result was that Fisher brought Arvey and Stevenson together for luncheon. Arvey came away impressed but not convinced.

Shortly after this Louis Kohn, a young Chicago lawyer, heard Stevenson speak at a meeting of the Chicago Council on Foreign Relations. He liked what he heard, and pressed Stevenson to enter politics. Stevenson was somewhat interested and Kohn, encouraged, called on Hermon Dunlap Smith, an insurance executive and a Stevenson admirer and friend, and Stephen Mitchell, a lawyer who knew Stevenson from a distance and liked him. The three men formed a Stevenson for Senator Committee, and quickly augmented it with a couple of dozen influential names. With this in hand, Kohn, Mitchell and Smith went to see Arvey, a friend of Kohn's from their Army days together in New Guinea. Following further meetings with Stevenson, Arvey agreed to recommend him for a top place on the Democratic ticket. But which one? Stevenson rather wanted the Senatorial spot, but Arvey leaned to Paul Douglas, a University of Chicago economics professor who was just out of the Marine Corps and who was, into the bargain, an impassioned orator. In Arvey's view, Douglas was the man to campaign against Wayland (Curley) Brooks, a Marine Corps man in World War I. Besides, Arvey thought of Stevenson as more of an administrator than a legislator, and administration is one of the principal chores of a governor.

At this juncture, Stevenson wavered. He wanted the Senatorial nomination, but he didn't want to hurt Douglas, another old friend; and he didn't know whether he really wanted to run for Governor. Diffidence and vacillation were among Stevenson's shortcomings; they plagued him all his political life. In this instance he couldn't (or didn't) make up his mind until a few hours before the deadline of December 31, 1947.

Although Arvey's recommendation was the equivalent of nomination, Arvey had some trouble with his precinct leaders. First, the rumor got around that Stevenson had attended Oxford. This, if true, was a revolting and horrible circumstance, sure political death in a city that for years had loved its Mayor, Big Bill Thompson, for his offer to punch King George V of England in the nose if that unwary monarch ever dared set foot in Chicago.

The rumor about Stevenson was, of course, easy to squelch, although Arvey took the precaution of nailing it down directly in a conversation with Stevenson.

The second problem for Arvey and the precinct captains was epitomized by one of them who complained: "Where the hell did you dig up this guy Add-lay? Let alone not knowing him, the voters can't even pronounce his name. He'll get his ears beat back."

Arvey himself liked Stevenson's assets, but he was realistic enough to discern that he had liabilities, too—that, among other things, he was a swell and, worse, an unknown one. Ultimately, Arvey persuaded his precinct men to go along on the dubious argument that no one really expected Stevenson to win in 1948, which figured to be a Republican year anyway. Stevenson, the ward heelers were told, would at least bring cachet and tone to the ticket.

Stevenson was duly nominated. His speeches, which he mostly wrote himself, were clear and direct and sparkling, but not sensational or dazzling. (Stevenson wrote his drafts in longhand on legal-size yellow lined paper. He was a rapid workman, and he could turn out a basic speech in an evening.)

[26]

Stevenson's main campaign theme was the issue of corruption in the administration of Dwight Green, his Republican opponent. Corruption was hardly a fresh or startling issue in Illinois, whose voters generally abided it. Green, who expected to win handily, rarely bothered to reply to Stevenson, and when he did it was to refer to him as "a cookie-pusher" and "a striped-pants diplomat." *The Chicago Daily News* enlivened the campaign at that point by reporting that its files contained no striped-trousers pictures of Stevenson and by publishing an old photograph of Green in full regalia— morning trousers, a claw-hammer coat, a top hat and a white waistcoat.

Things might have gone on like this, save for the murder of an obscure gambler in Peoria, Illinois, about midway through the campaign. *The St. Louis Post-Dispatch* dug into the crime, joined shortly by *The Chicago Daily News*. What they found was corruption of a magnitude singular even for Illinois. The Green administration was heavily compromised.

One result was that the voters began to listen to Stevenson, although his campaign funds were so meager at one point that some of his wealthier friends were avoiding him on the street for fear he would touch them for a contribution.

One of the points that Stevenson made about himself that attracted the voters, especially after the gambling scandals broke, was that he had made no political commitments to anyone, not even to Arvey. Impressed, the voters seemed willing to try probity for a change.

And that is precisely what happened, to a stunning degree. Stevenson not only carried the state, but by a plurality of 572,067 votes, the largest ever received up to that time by a gubernatorial candidate. What made the plurality all the more remarkable was that Harry S. Truman took the state on Stevenson's coattails, for his plurality over Thomas E. Dewey was only 33,612. Paul Douglas's Senatorial plurality was 407,728 votes.

Stevenson was well and truly started in public office.

CHAPTER II

---✦---

GOVERNOR IN SPRINGFIELD

THE ELECTION of Adlai Stevenson as Illinois's thirty-second governor was reported by out-of-state newspapers, but only routinely, for the big story was Harry S. Truman's unexpected defeat of Governor Thomas E. Dewey of New York for the Presidency.

In postelection analyses, Irving Dilliard of *The St. Louis Post-Dispatch* noted that Stevenson and Douglas had carried Illinois for Truman. And Arthur Krock, in his "In the Nation" column in *The Times*, observed that "professional politicians, who work at their trade daily and live by it, are viewing with deep respect the 'new' Democrats in states essential to the national victory who drew so many more voters to the national ticket than the head of it . . . especially Mr. Stevenson. . . .

"Quite naturally," Krock went on, ". . . Mr. Stevenson is being surveyed as a possible Presidential candidate of the Democrats in 1952."

Krock wrote another column that December, reporting on the Gridiron Club dinner, in which he said that Stevenson "was of unusual interest to the assemblage" as a 1952 prospect, not least of all because of his internationalism in foreign policy.

Stevenson's reaction, in a letter to Krock, was succinct: "Is anyone really looking me over? If so, the speculation will end soon."

Whatever scouting was under way, Stevenson was hardly headline material outside his own state. When he took office January 10, 1949, *The Times* recorded the event over the head, "Illinois Swears In Its New Governor," and the writer of a caption under the accompanying photograph thought it necessary to distinguish Stevenson from the State Supreme Court justice who administered the oath by noting that the Governor stood to the right.

"In an inaugural address outlining his administration's program, the Democratic chief executive asked members of the Democratic-controlled House and the Republican-controlled Senate to 'show the world what a government consecrated to plain talk, hard work and prairie horse-sense can do,' " *The Times* dispatch from the state armory in Springfield read. It went on:

Mr. Stevenson asked for a joint resolution of the General Assembly to submit to a referendum the question of a constitutional convention, to revamp the state's present organic law.

In the sphere of social security, he called for consolidation of some services, emergency legislation to increase aid to old-age pensioners and the blind to at least $55 a month, reduction of the population of the state's mental institutions by more home care and preventive means, and a review of the adequacy of workmen's compensation awards in view of increased living costs. He asked a fair employment practice law.

The article and the picture were printed only in the newspaper's first edition.

Both Stevenson's inaugural address and his accomplishments in office reflect his social and economic thinking—subjects on which he was frequently misrepresented.

His principal achievements were these:

He sent state policemen to stamp out commercial gambling in downstate Illinois when local officials failed to act.

He lopped thirteen hundred nonworking politicians from the state payroll.

He set up a merit system in the state police force that ended the custom of politically preferential appointments.

He increased state aid to school districts.

He started a broad road-improvement program that included enforcement of truck-weight limits, a higher gasoline tax and larger truck license fees to pay construction costs.

He overhauled the state's welfare program, placing it on a merit basis and obliging financially able relatives to pay for the care of patients.

He modernized the state government through a series of reform measures.

He converted the political State Commerce Commission, the utility rate-fixing agency, into a nonpartisan body.

This record—a not particularly dazzling one—is that of a moderate reformer, a person of social conscience who is basically conservative in outlook. Stevenson, in his speeches as Governor and in two national campaigns, kept within the framework of social and economic moderateness, so much so, indeed, that Truman once complained that "Stevenson went out and conducted a campaign [for the Presidency] that was not in support of the Democratic program of President Franklin D. Roosevelt and myself."

Stevenson's differences with the New Deal and its Fair

Deal successor centered on the cost of government, taxation and negligence toward official irregularities. He was, after all, by birth, upbringing, education and legal training, as well as by association, a part of the upper economic establishment, albeit an enlightened one by comparison with some of its members who were still stuck in the nineteenth century.

Enlightenment is perhaps the key to Stevenson's attitudes on social questions. He accepted Social Security and the concept that society had an obligation to its less advantaged members, as he did the conclusion that trade unionism had arrived to stay and that industry had civic responsibilities.

"I believe emphatically in what is called for want of a better word 'free enterprise,'" he said. "But free enterprise in our world must result in more than profit for the few. It must be a source of well-being for the many, or it won't be free very long."

His views on the welfare state were temperate. "I don't like doles. I don't like subsidies. I don't like any interferences with free markets, free men and free enterprise," he said. "But I also know that there can be no real freedom without economic justice, social justice, equality of opportunity and a fair chance for every individual to make the most of himself."

Stevenson made no effort to dissemble his attitudes, yet he acquired the reputation of being a liberal evangelist, a Tennysonian Lochinvar and a Wordsworthian "happy Warrior."

Stevenson the liberal was in part a projection of his liberal admirers and his conservative foes, with both groups tending to be simplistic in their evaluations and with each employing "liberal" as if it were a word or an ideology susceptible of precise definition. The fact that the word is so elastic and so subjective helped to make the label stick; and as it did it created illusions about Stevenson.

There is no doubt, however, that there are elements of Stevenson's political views, as distinct from his economic and social ones, that set him apart from most politicians of his time and give him claim to enduring significance in American life. The core of Stevenson's politics was a sturdy and insistent and reasoned support of democracy both as a governing process and as a way of life. His conception of democracy, going far beyond mere head-counting and the orotund rhetoric of faith in the people, called for a Jeffersonian type of self-government adapted to the complexities of a nuclear and cybernetic age by a maximum amount of decentralization.

"I think government should be as small in scope and as local in character as possible," he said. He said this again and again and in a variety of ways to illustrate the point that big government fosters feelings of remoteness and alienation in the citizen, whereas under conditions of small government he acquires a sense of immediacy and identification with the problems and apparatus of his government.

Democracy, Stevenson was convinced, was "perhaps mankind's most audacious experiment," and he went on to offer his definition of it in a notable speech in 1963 to a Fund for the Republic dinner.

And I suppose that most of us, if we were asked to name the most profound issues at stake in the world today, would say the issues of freedom and democracy. We would say that the Western world, for all its errors and shortcomings, has tried for centuries to evolve a society in which the individual has enough legal, social and political elbow room to be not the puppet of the community, but his own autonomous self.

And we would say that the enemies of freedom, whatever the magnificent ends they propose—the brotherhood of man, the kingdom of saints, "from each according to his ability, to each according to his needs"—miss just this essential point: that man is greater than the social purposes to which he can be put. He must not be kicked about even with the most high-minded objectives. He is not a means or an instrument. He is an end in himself.

This, I take it, is the essence of what we mean by democracy— not so much voting systems or parliamentary systems or economic or legal systems (though they all enter in), as an irrevocable and final dedication to the dignity of man.

Further, Stevenson's view of democracy encompassed dissent, and for this he made and endured enemies, especially during that nightmare grotesquerie when Senator Joseph R. McCarthy of Wisconsin and other professional patriots were powers in the country. Stevenson was certain that democracy grew and thrived on dissonance and disagreement, whereas his adversaries wanted conformity and correspondence. He declined time and again to equate criticism with treason.

"Self-criticism is the secret weapon of democracy," he said in welcoming the Democratic National Convention to Chicago in 1952. This was a theme he often returned to.

"Of course, democracy is not self-executing," he remarked almost ten years later. "We have to make it work, and to make it work we have to understand it. Sober thought and fearless criticism are impossible without critical thinkers and thinking critics. Such persons must be given the opportunity to come together, to see new facts in the light of old principles, to evaluate old principles in the light of new facts, and by deliberation, debate and dialogue to hammer out the consensus that makes democracy possible."

Stevenson's belief in the indispensability of dialogue was unwavering, even when it took raucous forms. Shortly before his death he told the alumni of Harvard University:

I don't share the concern of some of my contemporaries about student demonstrations [over United States policy in South Vietnam]. I rather like their involvement in great issues. But if I could offer demonstrators one word of advice I would say that to state goals is easy; to tell us how to get there is not so easy. A moral commitment is hardly meaningful without a practical hope of improving the human condition.

If advocacy of democracy (and its concomitant, dissent) accounts for Stevenson's reputation as a liberal, his attitudes came from John Locke, the Founding Fathers and John Stuart Mill—thinkers with impeccable credentials.

But Stevenson's democracy was no static or sterile system resting on authority and tradition. What stirred so many was his conviction that democratic man was capable of a triumphant future.

"We dare not just look back on great yesterdays," he said in 1952 and many times in later years. "We must look forward to great tomorrows. What counts now is not just what we are *against*, but what we are *for*. *Who* leads us is less important than *what* leads us—what convictions, what courage, what faith."

Stevenson was frequently derided in his public life as a social radical and as a political visionary, but the enemies he made for his internationalism were even more numerous, although the epithets they employed were despairingly uninventive. "One-worlder" and "liberal weeper" were the most common of them. They were bestowed for the most part by rock-ribbed conservatives who regarded the United Nations as a threat to the nation's sovereignty or by those who resented Stevenson's strictures against isolationism.

Actually Stevenson opposed isolationism because it was, in his opinion, no longer a valid posture for the United States. And he was not a "one-worlder" in the sense of advocating world government. What he had in mind was a comity of nations in which the United States should play a role commensurate with its democratic heritage, its wealth and its technological prowess.

One glimpse into his thinking came in 1949 in an article he wrote for *The Times Magazine* entitled "The Challenge of a New Isolationism." This is the gist of what he had to say:

As a resident of a great Midwestern state once known for its supposed isolationist tendencies, I think old-fashioned isolationism is moribund. America has come of age, I believe, in these eight short years of toil and heartache. The misconceptions of adolescence, the carefree self-concerns of our youth vanished with the whirlwind that swept us to the center of the world's stage. And now we in the Midwest, like most of us everywhere, though bedeviled with the indecisions of a maturity that knows what it wants but isn't sure how to get it, have at least discarded some of the illusions which beclouded our earlier thinking.

When I venture the brave conclusion that "isolation" is a thing of the past, I mean the old traditional concept that America can live alone and like it; that we can live secure and prosperous behind our barricades of ocean and within our continent of plenty. . . .

But in less than four years the United States had junked long-cherished concepts of neutral rights and the Senate had ratified the United Nations Charter! The reasons are as plain in the Middle West as elsewhere. Can a pilot who flew the ocean as casually as a mailman makes his route ever again believe that we can isolate ourselves? Do the millions of Americans who traveled to the ends of the earth and back during the war think of Paris or even Moscow as far distant? Like their parents they may wish it were so, but unlike some of their parents they know it isn't. How many people who saved sugar coupons for a birthday cake believe we are a self-sufficient world apart? Ask the Middle Western farmer what he has found out about his markets.

No, the impact of global war on our economy, on the millions of civilian soldiers and sailors who have lived and fought, sweated and shivered, laughed and groused in places they never heard of before, not only destroyed Fascism abroad but a lot of isolationist notions here at home. . . .

But the death of one discredited dogma does not preclude the rise of others. While we've abandoned the old road, we have by no means defined our goals or the means of reaching them. We have not found common ground nor taken the pledge of abstinence from our past vices of wishful thinking and cut-rate security.

While it can hardly be argued that there is much evidence of a resurrection of the body of isolation there is plenty of evidence of a reincarnation of its spirit. There is a conspicuous and growing tendency to be internationally minded in principle but not in practice, to favor international cooperation in the abstract while opposing concrete steps to make it effective. . . .

Another warning signal is the constant and alarming identification of our policy with the containment of Communism. Does public support for the foreign aid program, for example, represent genuine recognition of global economic problems, or is it merely a reflection of the widespread fear of Communist Russia? Do people realize that some such program would have been necessary even if relations with the Soviet Union were the most cordial? Or have we merely created the happy illusion that we fully understand the economic realities?

Policy based on an anti-Russian crusade involves great dangers. Defense and economic aid might be sharply altered at the first sign of a truce in the cold war. If we wobble in accordance with the aggressiveness of their actions and pronouncements, the men in the Kremlin will exercise undue influence upon our policy. One who blindly opposes everything the Soviets favor and supports everything they oppose is just as much a stooge of Moscow as the most abject fellow traveler. If our policy cannot stand on its own feet independent of the whims of the Kremlin, we run the risk of withdrawing into economic isolation the moment the immediate military threat disappears. . . .

While we have learned, I think, the military lesson of two wars in a shrunken world, have we learned the economic lesson? While we have learned that peace is indivisible, have we also learned that prosperity is indivisible?

I doubt it. While there is general agreement that winning wars is too expensive and that we don't want to have to win any more, it is hard for us to understand why winning peace in a world yearning for peace is so expensive, too. The "Economy First" people can't see why we should be scattering money all over the world when taxes are so high at home. "Participation? Cooperation? Sure—but not at the cost of our domestic economy."

Then there are the imperialists, the zealous converts to internationalism, who talk defiantly about taking over the whole world and running it as we see fit, and, incidentally, to our advantage—somehow. Another group says: "War is inevitable, so let's have it now." But this group is small and getting smaller, and includes few if any responsible leaders of our thought.

There are many more voices in the discordant chorus. At one extreme are the pessimists and skeptics who see no hope for peace and security and have already written off the United Nations and "cooperation" as a dismal failure. At the other, more hopeful, extreme are the world-government groups. Exploring uncharted seas, demanding more, not less, international cooperation, they have already enlisted the support of some twenty-nine Senators and over a hundred members of the House for various proposals leading toward the establishment of some form of actual world government.

Illustrations of the variations in our thinking could be multiplied. But from one end of the spectrum to the other no one, or almost no one, is preaching the old-fashioned isolation of eight years ago. Everyone seems to agree to some degree of world participation, some more, some less. Many a sturdy isolationist of yesterday is even in the world-government camp today. But more of them are viewing with alarm the relinquishment of an atom of "our sovereignty." Thus, it was on constitutional grounds that the American Bar Association recently went on record against the Genocide Convention.

Others view with even more alarm the appalling cost and the uncertain dividends from the billions we have invested in foreign aid and rehabilitation which are so badly needed at home. . . .

So while I conclude that there is little indication of any revival of the pre-Pearl Harbor state of mind, it seems to me that there are dangers perhaps as great. . . .

Now my thesis is: There is no resurgence of blind, classical isolation in the Middle West, but there is a rapidly growing tax consciousness, and sooner or later we will have to face some stern issues. Can we, will we, pay the price of peace? Will we weary of the long ordeal? Will the disappointments, failures and frustrations light the fires of reaction? Is a neo-isolation in the making? Can a democracy hold fast to a long-term foreign policy of resistance and assistance? Or will popular short-term domestic policies carry the day? Can we make positive, progressive, forward adjustments as the war recedes in perspective and our war-born economy slows down? Can we steer a middle course between disillusioned pessimism and retreat on the one hand and overextension and fiscal irresponsibility on the other?

We have identified our enemies since the war; we have hammered out by trial and error a policy of tangible cooperation to improve the lot of mankind within limited spheres; we have taken an oath of allegiance to the world; we have abandoned "live alone and like it"; we have embraced "live together or perish." But the going will get harder before it gets better, and the test of political maturity and consistency is still ahead of us. Hardheaded horse sense about the world, as about our business, is a prescription easy to write and hard to fill. The cost of peace insurance is very high in dollars and still higher in determination and applied democracy.

The first essential is leadership. The demagogues who say we can have our cake and eat it too are many and masterful. The hard way is never the popular way, but it is often the best way. One of the first steps is to do a better job here in our own front yard. More than we realize, the future depends on the quality of government and public management right here at home in our cities, counties and states. Political corruption, extravagance, moral lethargy and expediency among our public officials are old but eradicable. If we can do a better and thriftier job of domestic housekeeping, we will have more confidence in ourselves, to say nothing of the confidence of others in our wisdom and purpose.

For all his concern with foreign affairs, Stevenson, from his induction as Governor in 1949 and for the next three years, was immersed in Illinois. He genuinely liked his job. The break-up of his marriage aside, he was a happy, even expansive, public servant.

When Stevenson moved into the white brick and stone Executive Mansion, a building whose ornateness attested its 1856 origin, he was nearing his forty-ninth birthday. He weighed 185 pounds and although he exercised only fitfully (weekend tennis and an occasional walk) he was not flabby. He impressed callers as affable and earnest and, despite an Eastern accent, not at all stuck up. For one thing he was a good listener and for another he worked in an atmosphere of informality. His office attire frequently consisted of a brown tweed sports jacket, odd trousers and a striped shirt. His favorite footgear was a pair of old golf shoes with the spikes removed.

The fact that he appeared so much in this get-up touched off reports that he didn't have many clothes, but the truth was that he had a sizable wardrobe of well-cut suits and Brooks Brothers button-down shirts, and Homburg hats into the bargain. He simply did not choose to wear them, chiefly because he lived in the Executive Mansion and had his offices in its basement.

At the Mansion the Governor occupied a top-floor, high-ceilinged bedroom with white walls and a green carpet on the floor. He maintained a punctual schedule—being on time was a compulsion with him. He arose at 7:30 o'clock; at 8:30 on the dot he sat down to a substantial breakfast (for which he allowed a half-hour, including the reading of the principal state morning newspapers); and was at his desk shortly after 9. He usually worked through the day, for there were a bottomless pile of documents to be gone through and visitors to see. Luncheon was sometimes at his desk and sometimes upstairs in a small dining room in company with William McCormick Blair, Jr., one of his administrative assistants, who also lived in the Mansion, and Carl McGowan, his chief aide. The Governor's office day ended about 6:30, in time for a bourbon toddy (whisky, water, ice and a little sugar) before dinner at 7. More often than not, he worked on state business after dinner.

With the Governor at the Mansion was King Arthur, a gloomy Dalmatian that answered to the name of Artie. Being a country dog, he did not take confinement to the Mansion or its grounds kindly, and in breach of a city ordinance he sometimes ran around the neighborhood at night. The neighbors complained, and Stevenson had an explanation for Artie's errancy.

"Artie is a constant source of embarrassment to the state police and to me, too," he said. "After all, a Governor's dog may not have to be above suspicion but he should at least try to obey the law. Still, I'm afraid Artie really has a miserable life here, so we try to make allowances."

In much the same common-sense manner he refused to approve a solemn bill to restrain the movement of cats, telling the legislature:

This legislation has been introduced in the past several sessions of the Legislature, and it has, over the years, been the source of much comment—not all of which has been in a serious vein. It may be that the General Assembly has now seen fit to refer it to one who can view it with a *fresh outlook*. Whatever the reasons for passage at this session, I cannot believe there is a widespread public demand for this law or that it could be, as a practical matter, enforced.

Furthermore, I cannot agree that it should be the declared public policy of Illinois that a cat visiting a neighbor's yard or crossing the highway is a public nuisance. It is in the nature of cats to do a certain amount of unescorted roaming. Many live with their owners in apartments or other restricted premises, and I doubt if we want to make their every brief foray an opportunity for a small game hunt by zealous citizens—with traps or otherwise.

I am afraid this bill could only create discord, recrimination and enmity. Also consider the owner's dilemma: To escort a cat abroad on a leash is against the nature of the cat, and to permit it to venture forth for exercise unattended into a night of new dangers is against the nature of the owner. . . .

We are all interested in protecting certain varieties of birds. That cats destroy some birds, I well know, but I believe this legislation would further but little the worthy cause to which its proponents give such unselfish effort. The problem of cat versus bird is as old as time. If we attempt to resolve it by legislation, who knows but what we may be called upon to take sides as well in the age-old problem of dog versus cat, bird versus bird, even bird versus worm. In my opinion, the State of Illinois and its local governing bodies already have enough to do without trying to control feline delinquency.

For these reasons, and not because I love birds the less or cats the more, I veto and withhold my approval from Senate Bill No. 93.

More celebrated from a serious point of view, and more telling of the Governor, was his veto, in 1951, of the Broyles bill. This piece of legislation, inspired by the hysteria of the cold war and supported by the powerful Illinois Department of the American Legion, was designed to protect against "subversive activities." The pressure to approve the bill was considerable, given the prevailing climate of opinion. The veto message was thus an act of some courage. It read in part:

The stated purpose of this bill is to combat the menace of world Communism. That the Communist Party—and all it stands for—is a danger to our Republic, as real as it is sinister, is clear to all who have the slightest understanding of our democracy. . . .

Agreed upon ends, our concern is with means. It is in the choice of methods to deal with recognized problems that we Americans, in and out of public life, so often develop differences of opinion. Our freedom to do so is a great source of strength and, if not impaired by mistakes of our own, will contribute greatly to the ultimate confusion of the enemies of freedom.

The issue with respect to means raised by this bill has two aspects. One is the question of the need for it in relation to existing weapons for the control of subversives. The other is whether this addition to our arsenal may not be a two-edged sword, more dangerous to ourselves than to our foes.

Were the latter alone involved, I should hesitate to impose my judgment upon that of the majority of the General Assembly. But it is precisely because the evil at hand has long since been identified and provided against that we here in Illinois need not now do something bad just for the sake of doing something.

[The message then detailed the Federal laws against subversion and those on the Illinois statute book since 1919, and remarked the close parallels between them and the Broyles bill.]

Not only does Senate Bill No. 102 appear wholly unnecessary, but I agree with the Bar Association that if the present sedition laws could be strengthened by expressly prohibiting the commission of acts as well as the advocacy thereof, this could best be accomplished by amending the existing laws rather than enacting new and more laws. Criminal laws, especially on subjects of vital importance, should not be confused by patchwork and duplication.

But it is in the enforcement provisions that I find this bill most objectionable. The Attorney General of Illinois is directed to appoint a Special Assistant Attorney General who must assemble and deliver to the State's Attorney of each county all information relating to subversive acts or activities within such county. The local State's Attorney then must present this matter to the grand jury. The Assistant Attorney General in Springfield must maintain complete records of all such information which may, with the permission of the Attorney General, be made public.

This transmission of such information and the subsequent presentation of it to the grand jury is mandatory under the Act—and covers . . . all information, however inconclusive or insignificant. I know of no precedent of any such interference with the normal discretion accorded to a public prosecutor. One of the most important responsibilities of State's Attorneys and one of the greatest protections of the citizen is the exercise of sound judgment in sifting the many rumors, charges and countercharges which come to State's Attorneys' attention. This is true in the operation of the criminal laws generally, and it must, of necessity, be even more true when we are dealing with criminal laws relating in large degree to the state of men's minds.

I can see nothing but grave peril to the reputation of innocent people in this perpetuation of rumors and hearsay.

[The message then observed that another provision of the bill required a complex loyalty oath of all state employees and all applicants for state jobs, and of all teachers.]

By such provisions as these, irreparable injury to the reputation of innocent persons is more than a possibility, it is a likelihood. If this bill became law, it would be only human for employees to play safe and shirk duties which might bring upon them resentment or criticism.

Public service requires independent and courageous action on matters which affect countless private interests. We cannot afford to make public employees vulnerable to malicious charges of disloyalty. So far as the employers are concerned—heads of departments and of schools and so on—the only safe policy would be timid employment practices which could only result in lowering the level of ability, independence and courage in our public agencies, schools and colleges.

Lastly, the bill provides that candidates for public office, other than offices for which an oath is prescribed by the Constitution, shall file an affidavit that he is not a subversive person. . . .

Does anyone seriously think that a real traitor will hesitate to sign a loyalty oath? Of course not. Really dangerous subversives and saboteurs will be caught by careful, constant professional investigation, not by pieces of paper.

The whole notion of loyalty inquisitions is a natural characteristic of the police state, not of democracy. Knowing his rule rests upon compulsion rather than consent, the dictator must always assume the disloyalty, not of a few but of many, and guard against it by continual inquisition and "liquidation" of the unreliable. . . .

The democratic state, on the other hand, is based on the consent of its members. The vast majority of our people are intensely loyal, as they have amply demonstrated. To question, even by implication, the loyalty and devotion of a large group of citizens is to create an atmosphere of suspicion and distrust which is neither justified, healthy nor consistent with our traditions. . . .

Basically, the effect of this legislation, then, will be less the detection of subversives and more the intimidation of honest citizens. But we cannot suppress thought and expression and preserve the freedoms guaranteed by the Bill of Rights.

Stevenson's veto message won him supporters, but it also gained him critics and led to the accusation that he was "soft" on Communism. Like many such charges in the witchhunting period, it was easy to make; and it was embellished by an affidavit that the Governor made as to what other people thought of Alger Hiss prior to his indictment for perjury in 1948.

Stevenson had known Hiss rather casually since 1933, when both men worked in the Agricultural Adjustment Administration in Washington. They had last met, again casually, at the United Nations General Assembly meeting in 1947. Stevenson was not asked his own opinion of Hiss. What he was asked was to state Hiss's reputation for integrity, loyalty and veracity "from the speech" of persons who knew him. Stevenson answered one word, "Good," to the interrogatory.

This deposition was twisted, notably by *The Chicago Tribune*, to make it seem that Stevenson was a character witness for Hiss; and the Governor was so taken to task that he felt obliged to defend himself.

The affidavit arose, he explained, "because, when I was asked by Hiss's lawyers to testify as to Hiss's reputation, I agreed to answer any questions as best I could but declined to go to New York [for the trial].

"It seems to me," he continued, "that it will be a very sad day for Anglo-Saxon justice when any man, and especially a lawyer, will refuse to give honest evidence in a criminal trial for fear the defendant in an action may eventually be found guilty. What would happen to our whole system of law if such timidity prevailed? ...

"I just can't imagine what people would have expected me to do. Was I supposed to say that I didn't know Hiss, when I most certainly did know him? Was I supposed to say that his reputation was bad? Obviously it was good, or he would not have held the exalted public position he was in."

In the end, the deposition and its consequences receded in importance, although at one time, when it was resurrected briefly in 1952, it did disturb the White House for its possible adverse effect on the Governor as a Presidential possibility.

At the time the affidavit was executed, it was little more than an interruption in a busy Governor's day, for Stevenson's main thrust was efficient Illinois government. He found the task, even with its enormous volume of paper work and its long telephone calls and its endless conversations with petty politicians, fascinating and rewarding. Indeed, his office preoccupied him to such a degree that he never bothered to cash in on Truman's political debt to him, or to speak much outside the state.

Stevenson, in fact, might have remained a good but relatively obscure governor had it not been for a complicated concatenation of events that began late in 1951 when Truman was maturing a decision not to be a candidate for the Presidency in 1952 and was casting about for a likely Democrat to head the ticket. There were a number of appealing possibilities—men who lived in populous states with large Electoral College votes or who were nationally and favorably known, among them W. Averell Harriman in New York, Vice President Alben W. Barkley and Senator Estes Kefauver of Tennessee.

Stevenson's name was one of those that crossed Truman's mind because of his demonstrated vote-getting capability, because he was not involved in any party feuds and because he was a Midwesterner. This geographic consideration weighed heavily because it was then believed that Senator Robert A. Taft of Ohio, a conservative and an isolationist, was a likely Republican candidate. It seemed to Truman, as it did to many Democratic leaders, that a Midwesterner, and especially an eloquent, personable and persuasive one, might offset Taft in his own bailiwick. Kefauver was eager to be that man, but the party hierarchy regarded him as an untamed lone wolf. Barkley was willing but aged. Stevenson was possible, but his national reputation was minuscule.

Truman completed his informal canvass of the field in January, 1952, by deciding to designate Stevenson as his heir. Made in time to permit a publicity build-up for the Governor, it was a canny bit of business that Truman communicated in confidence to Stevenson at Blair House in Washington the evening of January 22. The President was flabbergasted to be turned down. As he recalled it later, this is what happened:

When I decided not to run for re-election to the Presidency, I sent for Governor Adlai E. Stevenson of Illinois. He had won the governorship by more than half a million votes and was making a fine record in office. I had great expectations for him and, during our meeting in Blair House, I offered to support him as a candidate for President in the 1952 elections.

Stevenson told me that he had an obligation to the people of Illinois to run again for Governor so he could complete the program he had initiated. I thought it strange at the time that he would reject a call to party leadership and service to the nation at so critical a moment in our history.

Stevenson's visit to the temporary White House set off a beehive of rumors. These were enhanced by three coincidences: his felicitous speech on rights for Negroes delivered to a National Urban League dinner in New York January 20 and commented on approvingly by *The New York Herald Tribune;* a leading article in *The Atlantic Monthly,* on the stands that week and with his portrait on the cover, dealing with political corruption and crime; and a cover picture and a major article in *Time* magazine, pegged to the Blair House conference and containing a neatly packaged biographical sketch.

There was also a minor coincidence—a fellow passenger on Stevenson's plane from Washington to Chicago after the Truman meeting was John Foster Dulles, a former United Nations colleague and widely regarded as a foreign affairs expert. It created news when the two emerged from the plane together, Stevenson jaunty and Dulles dour as usual.

The situation was summed up by Arthur Krock in *The*

Times of January 25 under the heading, "Governor Stevenson Comes to Washington and——." The column read in part:

Adlai E. Stevenson Week was bound to come and here it is in full spate. It was bound to come about this time in 1952 if President Truman was still silent as to his intentions toward seeking another term because:

1. "He [Stevenson] comes from a great state which it will be almost essential for the next President to carry. And he was elected by the record majority in its history [leading the Democratic Senatorial nominee, Paul Douglas, by 164,339 votes and Mr. Truman by 538,455]"—a quotation from this space under date of December 13, 1948.

2. As Governor he has given Illinois an admirable and clean administration, after succeeding to a mess.

3. His foreign policy is substantially that of President Truman, and, except for the Far East, he helped to formulate it and represent it in the United Nations, of which also he was one of the architects.

4. His differences with the National Administration on domestic policy—on cost of government, taxation, negligence toward official irregularities and corruption—have been implicit in his own record in Illinois, but, not being explicit, have not put him on the President's political blacklist.

5. He is personable, comparatively young and the inheritor of a famous Democratic name from his grandfather, who was Vice President with Cleveland.

So it long has been obvious, and often noted here, that when Mr. Truman and the Democratic Party came to survey the field for possible nominees other than the President in 1952, a long and favorable look would be given to Governor Stevenson. Such an inspection was made Tuesday night by Mr. Truman at Blair House.

If a Cagliostroan aspirant for the Presidency had contrived to put together by necromancy a boomlet for himself, he could not have succeeded so well. Boomlet it was, for Stevenson, despite his disclaimer to Truman and to others, was quickly the subject of news articles, picture stories, interviews and comments on radio and television. In the electronic age it doesn't take long for an accumulation of such news coverage to make even the most obscure governor superficially well known. In Stevenson's case, the result was that three hundred letters a day on the Presidency abruptly came into his office, in contrast to the normal one hundred a week, and those mostly on state business.

There was nothing official, of course, for Truman, playing his politics characteristically close to his vest, would not publicly disclose his decision not to run again until March 31. And Stevenson, of course, was discouraging speculation about himself, not only to Truman's annoyance but also to that of the press corps, many of whom thought he was playing cat and mouse. The conviction arose that he was indecisive, a charge that still rankled in the last year of his life. A journalist who asked him then about the accusation got this response:

I declined [to be a candidate] for two reasons. One, I was already an avowed candidate for re-election as Governor of Illinois. . . . And, two, I didn't *want* to run for President. I had no such ambition. I wanted to finish the job I'd started in Illinois.

For the ensuing six months I was beset right and left by individuals and delegations from all over the United States putting pressure on me to announce that I was a candidate and to enter the primaries and compete for the nomination. When I refused to do so and never wavered and was very decisive, and then was subsequently nominated at the convention and accepted, I was told, "You're indecisive."

Nobody can believe you when you say you're not a candidate. It's a curious thing. The more decisive you are in not seeking an exalted office, the more they say you're indecisive. My very decisiveness was attributed to what they called indecision.*

* From an article by Lillian Ross in *The New Yorker*, © 1965 The New Yorker Magazine, Inc.; reprinted in *Adlai Stevenson*, by Lillian Ross, J. B. Lippincott.

All the available evidence suggests that Stevenson was correct in saying that he did not want to run in 1952 and that he resisted efforts to get him to become an active candidate for the nomination. It is also evident that he was not astute about himself and the political bind he was in.

Truman's recollections, published in 1960, illustrate the situation admirably. After the fruitless conference in January, Truman wrote:

> I asked Stevenson to come to see me a month later, and again I asked him to become a candidate. Again he refused. After another month I tried once more. I sent Frank McKinney, the chairman of the Democratic National Committee, to see him and to urge him to reconsider. But Governor Stevenson told McKinney he would not run under any circumstances.
>
> Stevenson was the best prospect in sight among the rising young Democrats, and I was hoping he would supply the new leadership the party needed. At the same time, we had no idea that the Republicans would nominate a soldier who was a war hero. We thought they would choose Senator Robert A. Taft or some other conservative, and that it would not be difficult to elect a Democrat. Therefore, I was very disheartened by Stevenson's reluctant attitude.

Meantime, with Truman's formal announcement that he would not seek re-election, heightened pressure began to be applied to Stevenson. "I've been asked more questions than the Quiz Kids and Mr. Anthony put together," he complained at one time, but on another occasion he remarked: "I seem to spend a lot of time reading about myself in papers and magazines these days. The awful thing is, I can't say that I mind it much either."

On April 16, however, Stevenson appeared to take himself definitely and positively out of the running in an announcement from his office that said:

I have repeatedly said that I was a candidate for Governor of Illinois and had no other ambition. To this I must now add that in view of my prior commitment to run for Governor and my desire and the desire of many who have given me their help and confidence in our unfinished work in Illinois, I could not accept the nomination for any other office this summer.

"Stevenson's Doubts Exceeded His Ambitions as Politician," read the past-tense headline over James Reston's analysis the following day in *The Times*. This is how Reston saw the Governor's situation and the predicament of the Democratic Party:

A complex set of motives led to the withdrawal of Governor Adlai E. Stevenson of Illinois from the Presidential campaign.

From the very first night, at Blair House last January, when President Truman asked him to consider running for the Democratic nomination, Mr. Stevenson's doubts ran ahead of his ambition.

He did not feel ready for the responsibility. He did not share the regular politician's sense of obligation to the party. Unlike most politicians he had no sense of his own capacity to do the job better than other men. He was almost elaborately nonpartisan in his approach to the question. . . .

Governor Stevenson has been accused privately during the past couple of months of conniving to get the Democratic nomination, of waiting until he was safely renominated for Governor before giving the word that he would accept the nomination if he were selected by the party convention at Chicago in July.

This, however, was nothing more than the usual assumption of a political community that never quite believes that every politician is not secretly trying to win the Presidency. Mr. Stevenson is the one politician to hit this town in a long time whose private confidences and public statements have been the same thing.

Shortly after President Truman announced he would not seek reelection, a friend of Mr. Stevenson [it was Arthur Krock] wrote the Governor this letter:

"I'm in the process of collecting several bets I won on the President's decision not to run again. Flushed with this success, I send you this prediction:

"Soon after the Illinois primary on April 8, you will be an actively receptive candidate for the Democratic nomination for President. Want to bet?"

Mr. Stevenson replied on April 3:

"Don't bet—with me or anybody else—a word to the wise. A.E.S."

Mr. Stevenson found the thought of a national campaign distasteful. He did not want to involve his three sons in it. His former wife was bitterly opposed to any action on his part that involved even the remotest possibility that the Stevenson children should get caught up in the goldfish-bowl life of the National Capital, and, like Mrs. Truman and Mrs. Fred M. Vinson, wife of the Chief Justice, her strong opposition was apparently an important factor in his decision to get out.

Moreover, Mr. Stevenson felt strongly that he had an obligation to try to continue his administration in Illinois—an obligation not only to the extraordinary group of young men in his own official family there but to himself.

Though he has been widely praised for the job he has done in Springfield, he himself is not satisfied with it. He felt that he had learned a lot in his first term. He felt that some of the work of that term would not be completed unless he ran again, and unless he developed a toughness of mind that he felt he did not have in the early days of his governorship.

Specifically, he wished to see the Illinois Constitution amended and improved and eventually to arrange for an Illinois constitutional convention, if politically possible. Also, he had—and has—plans for an improved state highway system and for a program of welfare care and research which, he hoped, would be a model in the nation.

It is interesting that Mr. Stevenson did not always have such hopes for his administration. Originally, he lived a very lonely life in the big Victorian Executive Mansion in Springfield. Moreover, he found the constant battle against the Republican-dominated Illinois Legislature and the equally constant fight against the pork-barrel Democratic politicians in Chicago arduous and distasteful.

His confidence in some of his own officials, too, was betrayed during his first term, and as a result of all these things he seriously considered giving up his political career altogether after the first term.

Curiously, the increasing mention of his name for the Presidential nomination seems to have added more to his interest in the Illinois job than anything else. If some people thought he could be the party's nominee, he seemed to be saying, at least he should have enough confidence in himself to go on in the rough and tumble of Illinois political life.

Thus he made up his mind late last year to seek renomination. He confided this decision to his associates in Springfield, many of whom were staying with him at considerable personal sacrifice because they believed in the job they were trying to do. Accordingly, he was loath to change his decision when the party leaders finally got around to their campaign to make him run for the Presidency.

If President Truman, who says he made up his mind not to seek re-election over a year ago, had approached Mr. Stevenson earlier than last January, the Illinois Governor's decision might have been different. The President did not confide in him, however, and did not even talk politics to him until after Mr. Stevenson's decisions in Illinois had been made this year.

Finally, it would be surprising if the Governor did not take into consideration the possibility that he would be beaten in 1952, if nominated, whereas he might win in 1956. But this does not seem to have been a decisive factor. The Stevenson story is not the usual story of a politician who overestimates his abilities and calculates his every move. Indeed, it is the contrary, which is why it is an interesting and somewhat unusual American political event.

If Stevenson hoped that his statement of April 16 would take him out of the race or lower the heat on him, he was mistaken, for a movement to draft him got under way the following day. And the day after that, when he spoke in New

York at a dinner for Averell Harriman, he received a heartier
ovation than the four avowed candidates present—Senator
Robert S. Kerr of Oklahoma, Senator Brien McMahon of
Connecticut, Senator Kefauver and Vice President Barkley
—and Harriman put together.

Again the Governor sought to underscore his unwilling-
ness to be a candidate by being humorous.

"I think I have the answer to all of our perplexities here
tonight," he told the 2,500 diners at the Commodore Hotel.
"I found this letter on my desk just before I left Springfield,
Illinois, this afternoon:

HONORABLE GOVERNOR STEVENSON,
SIR,
    You should marry Mrs. Franklin D. Roosevelt and you
    should run for the Presidential nomination and put Mrs.
    Roosevelt on the ticket for Vice President and you will go
    over big.

"Now I propose to send this message to Mrs. Roosevelt
with the respectful comment that I think it an excellent idea,
but after all this is leap year.

"I believe I am here at the head table this evening by
misrepresentation and fraud; that you invited a candidate
for the Presidency and you got a candidate for Governor."

Then, significantly, Stevenson became serious: "The burdens of the Presidency dwarf the imagination. And the next
President will have something more to face than most any of
his predecessors. He will require guidance toward coexistence in this world with a ruthless, inscrutable and equal
power in the world. This is a new and fearsome position for
the United States, and its President will be sorely tried."

Oddly, although Stevenson's humorous reference to Mrs.
Roosevelt was intended to turn the key in the door against

himself, so eager were his partisans to read portents where none existed that many of them, according to *The Times*, interpreted the remark "as indicating that he might be subject to a draft if the Democratic National Convention should propose it."

So the draft movement persisted, and indeed gathered force as Kefauver won primary votes and moved, technically at least, into a leading position for the nomination. His coonskin cap and his homespun handshaking seemed omnipresent. The press corps build-up, meanwhile, continued at the Illinois Executive Mansion; and in the face of the Governor's adamancy its members took to interviewing one another. The result was more speculation, with Stevenson still good-humored and still attempting to make his disavowals stick.

"I ran out of words trying to be witty," he said afterward, and he took to denigrating himself, as when he replied to one interviewer who said he intended to write the Governor's biography: "I don't see how you're going to do it. My life has been hopelessly undramatic. I wasn't born in a log cabin. I didn't work my way through school nor did I rise from rags to riches, and there's no use trying to pretend I did.

"I'm not a Willkie and I don't claim to be a simple, barefoot La Salle Street [Chicago] lawyer. You might be able to write about some of my ancestors. They accomplished quite a lot at one time or another, but you can't do anything much about me. At least, I'd hate to have to try it."

Nonetheless, while Stevenson was nay-saying in April, May and June, his thinking on virtually every public question of moment was being diligently circulated through a most carefully written interview that he had granted earlier to *U.S. News & World Report*.

Added to this were remarks that the Governor tossed off to newspaper and magazine interviewers either in defense of a bipartisan foreign policy in Korea or on national questions.

The cumulative effect of his formal interview and his subsequent remarks was, to a very large degree, to draw attention to himself and to multiply the exertions of those who wanted him to run; for while Stevenson was saying nay he also seemed to be saying a great deal about his views on public matters that could lay the groundwork for a candidacy.

And now time was inexorably closing in on the Governor, for it was June and the nominating convention was only a month off. Cabell Phillips, in a dispatch that *The Times* printed in its Sunday edition of June 29, told the story under the headline, "Leaders Turn On Heat For Stevenson's Assent":

Democratic leaders here and in Illinois are anxiously telling Governor Adlai E. Stevenson that the hour is a lot later than he seems to think, and that if he has any intention of trying to get the Presidential nomination, or even of being in a position of receptivity to its offer, he had better do something about it. . . .

Whether Governor Stevenson's prolonged refusal to say that he is or is not receptive to the Democratic nomination is a matter of deliberate strategy on his part to secure it—and most believe that it is not a part of any such strategy—his continued silence is beginning to have an adverse effect on his prospects.

This is becoming manifest in several ways.

Political leaders in many important Democratic strongholds are having trouble holding their followers in line for a promised Stevenson candidacy.

The prospects of Senator Estes Kefauver continue to mount in the absence of a Stevenson alternative.

The word is getting about that the Governor wants to pick his opponent—that he would be willing to run against Senator Robert A. Taft on the Republican ticket, but not against General of the Army Dwight D. Eisenhower. This is bad for his prestige.

A sample of this restless state of affairs was afforded this week when New York's Democratic State Chairman, Paul E. Fitzpatrick, publicly declared his certainty that the Illinoisan was *not* a candidate. Since Mr. Fitzpatrick is not known to have any special pipeline to the Governor's mansion at Springfield, nor to be privy to facts withheld from more intimate Stevenson associates, political observers put these possible interpretations upon his remark:

a. It was a step to forestall a premature breakaway of the ninety-four-man New York State delegation. While this group is officially committed to Averell Harriman, Director for Mutual Security, it is reported to be available for Mr. Stevenson or another Administration-approved candidate after the first ballot. But meanwhile it has to be held in line.

b. The Fitzpatrick remark was an around-the-corner prod to the Governor saying, in effect: "Look, sir, it's time to fish or cut bait. Please make up your mind."

Whatever the motive behind Mr. Fitzpatrick's surprising declaration—and his belief that the Governor has eliminated himself irrevocably from the race is not shared by others in the know—it did serve to highlight the chaotic state of affairs in Democratic circles over the problem of finding a candidate of wide acceptability.

It is ironic that Governor Stevenson should so nearly fulfill the exacting specifications for that candidate and be so hard to get. The effort to overcome his reluctance is occupying the time and ingenuity of a number of quite highly placed folk.

It is accepted as a fact here that the chief of the "we want Stevenson" forces is none other than President Truman himself. While the President denies any interference in the choice of the candidate, highly competent reports have described him as offering the chance to the Governor and of continuing to hold it open in spite of the latter's polite turndown last spring.

Certain it is that others working more openly in behalf of Governor Stevenson would not be so engaged without a green light from the party's boss.

These include Interior Secretary Oscar L. Chapman and the Secretary of the Senate, Leslie Biffle. Both are close intimates of the President and are rated as among his ablest political lieutenants. Both have been in touch in recent weeks not only with Governor Stevenson but with other influential party leaders who have a direct concern in his candidacy.

But perhaps the most direct liaison between Washington and Springfield is maintained by "the third Senator from Illinois," Scott Lucas, who was Senate majority leader when he was defeated by Republican Everett Dirksen in 1950.

Mr. Lucas has not found a flourishing Washington law practice any barrier to the continuance of an active political life. He, too, is in frequent communication with the Governor and other political figures in Illinois.

Closer to home, the brunt of the pro-Stevenson movement is being borne by Colonel Jacob M. Arvey, Democratic chairman for Cook County (Chicago). One of the most powerful figures in the party, he is the transmission belt along which much of the pleading from other quarters is passed along to the Governor's office in Springfield.

Pressure on the Governor to make himself available has been maintained at a pretty high voltage ever since Mr. Truman removed himself from the race in April. He has been told and retold that he is: (a) the one man who can weld the Democrats into a unified fighting force in 1952, and (b) the only one who has a chance to beat anyone the Republicans put up, including General Eisenhower.

This persuasion has been applied orally at occasional meetings here in Washington, in Chicago, and in long, earnest evenings over dinner and highballs in the Governor's residence in Springfield. It has been applied by long-distance telephone calls, by letters and by inundations of laudatory newspaper and magazine clippings from every section.

Apparently, the first round of the battle has been won. It is the consensus of the most prominent missionaries that the Governor has been persuaded that he must make the race if called.

Stevenson's position as the focus of a pincers movement became all the more hopeless as the desperation of Truman and the top power brokers of the Democratic Party escalated when Barkley blew the gaff. In his hunt for someone— anyone but Kefauver—Truman had thought seriously of Barkley.

"I called in Vice President Alben W. Barkley to discuss the situation," Truman wrote in 1960.

The Vice President had been with me the second time I had proposed to Stevenson that he run for the nomination. Barkley had also heard me instruct Chairman McKinney to make one final effort with the Illinois Governor. But now, after three refusals by Stevenson, and with time running short before the Democratic convention assembled in Chicago, it was essential to settle upon another prospective candidate. I turned to Barkley himself—the best-known and most beloved Democratic figure—and asked him if he would run. . . . He agreed to have his name submitted to the convention.

But Barkley's candidacy ran into trouble right from the start. His personal advisers and representatives mishandled the situation. . . . Their negotiations with representatives of organized labor were conducted in a manner that led to misunderstanding. Barkley was a friend of labor, and his failure to get labor's full endorsement hurt him deeply. It prompted him to announce his withdrawal for the nomination on the day the convention opened.

That day was also Stevenson's most agonizing. He had been appealed to by professional politicians and amateurs alike, by close friends and distant ones, by clangorous advisers and quiet ones. The gravamen of all their appeals was that most solemn and awesome responsibility of a politician —his duty and obligation to his party. And the still reluctant Stevenson threshed and flipped about like a fish in a net. But he was caught, and there was no way to jump out.

From his own standpoint, he realized that he was most

likely to lose. "I had limited political acquaintance, no manager, no staff, little money in the till, little press support," he
said. "And I was running against General Eisenhower, a
national hero for ten years, and also the inevitable accumulation of irritations and anxieties of twenty years of government in a time of profound changes—irritations and anxieties
which had been vigorously, if not objectively, cultivated for
a long time by Republican orators and most of the press. The
best confidential polls indicated that we had no more than
35 per cent of the popular vote."

Thus, even on the day before the convention opened and
the ineluctable was clearly evident, Stevenson, as a district
delegate to the convention, pleaded with the Illinois caucus
not to nominate him and not to vote for him if nominated.

Describing the climactic first day of the convention,
Stevenson later wrote:

At the opening of the convention, I made a welcoming speech as
Governor of the host state, along with Martin Kennelly, the Democratic Mayor of Chicago. Something of a demonstration followed;
so, after one more appearance in the hall, I stayed away on the other
side of the city. Hearing that Archibald Alexander, candidate for
Senator in New Jersey, or Governor Shricker of Indiana might
nominate me, I called them both by phone and asked them not to.
Alexander agreed, but my esteemed friend, Governor Shricker,
rebelled.

At this moment, Stevenson yielded to duty. He could do
nothing else. He decided to call Truman at the White
House.

"Then, out of the clear . . . Governor Stevenson telephoned me," Truman remembered in 1960.

He said that his friends wanted to nominate him for President.
"Would you object if I agreed to run?" Stevenson asked me.

Well, I blew up. I talked to him in language I think he had never heard before. I told him that for months I had been trying to get him to be the candidate. Now, at the last possible moment, he had changed his mind. But he was still the best prospect we had, and I said I would support him.

But even with Truman's backing, Stevenson was not a shoo-in.

"If I had not flown to Chicago from Washington," Truman said later, "Stevenson would not have been nominated. I got the leaders of the convention to confer with me immediately on my arrival, and told them that I regarded Stevenson as the logical candidate. As a result, he received the nomination. . . . It required the intervention of the President to get Stevenson through."

The deed was done early in the morning of July 26, and it was three o'clock, Central Daylight Time, when a weary and drawn Stevenson advanced to the rostrum amid a fearful din of cheers and music for his acceptance speech, one of the strangest ever uttered in American politics.

"I accept your nomination—and your program," he began and then went on:

I should have preferred to hear those words uttered by a stronger, a wiser, a better man than myself. But, after listening to the President's speech, I feel better about myself.

None of you, my friends, can wholly appreciate what is in my heart. I can only hope that you will understand my words. They will be few.

I have not sought the honor you have done me. I *could* not seek it because I aspired to another office, which was the full measure of my ambition. One does not treat the highest office within the gift of the people of Illinois as an alternative or as a consolation prize.

I *would* not seek your nomination for the Presidency because the burdens of that office stagger the imagination. Its potential for good or evil now and in the years of our lives smothers exultation and converts vanity to prayer.

I have asked the Merciful Father—the Father of us all—to let this cup pass from me. But from such dread responsibility one does not shrink in fear, in self-interest or in false humility.

So, "If this cup may not pass from me, except I drink it, Thy will be done."

That my heart has been troubled, that I have not sought this nomination, that I could not seek it in good conscience, that I would not seek it in honest self-appraisal, is not to say that I value it less. Rather it is that I revere the office of the Presidency of the United States.

And now, my friends, that you have made your decision, I will fight to win that office with all my heart and soul. . . .

The ordeal of the twentieth century—the bloodiest, most turbulent era of the Christian age—is far from over. Sacrifice, patience, understanding and implacable purpose may be our lot for years to come. Let's face it. Let's talk sense to the American people. Let's tell them the truth, that there are no gains without pains, that we are now on the eve of great decisions, not easy decisions, like resistance when you're attacked, but a long, patient, costly struggle which alone can assure triumph over the great enemies of mankind, poverty and tyranny—and the assaults upon human dignity which are the most grievous consequences of each. . . .

I ask of you all that you have; I will give you all I have. . . .

And finally, my friends, in the staggering task you have assigned me, I shall always try "to do justly and to love mercy and to walk humbly with my God."

By the weekend, following the nomination of Senator John J. Sparkman of Alabama for the Vice Presidency, Stevenson was back in the Executive Mansion at Springfield, "there to contemplate the wreckage of my hopes to run for Governor and the problems of a highly inexperienced candidate for the Presidency."

CHAPTER III

---∞---

TALKING SENSE TO THE
AMERICAN PEOPLE

A FEW DAYS before Stevenson's selection by the Democratic National Convention he had told the Illinois delegation that he was "mentally, temperamentally and physically unfit" to be President; but now that the nomination had been thrust upon him he prepared to campaign with energy, originality and independence.

Largely because Truman's hand in the convention was so evident, Republicans began immediately to speak of Stevenson as a "captive candidate," the implication being that the White House would pull the strings for his campaign. Realizing the difficulties that even the appearance of such a role would pose for him and sensing also that he had to invest the campaign with the flair of his own individuality, Stevenson marshaled a staff composed largely of political amateurs and established his headquarters at Springfield rather than in a big city.

In justification of his decision, Stevenson wrote later:

I concluded to organize and run my part of the campaign my own way. As I was still Governor, I established my headquarters in Springfield instead of New York, as in the past. I enlisted an old Chicago friend, Stephen Mitchell, as Chairman of the National Committee in Washington and induced Wilson Wyatt of Louisville to come to Springfield to organize and manage my headquarters. And I finally persuaded Dwight R. G. Palmer of New York along with Beardsley Ruml to undertake the thankless and indispensable job of raising the money to finance the campaign. For myself, I set about the business of what I was going to say and left to the others the decisions as to where and when I would say it.

In addition to the formal staff that centered on Springfield, hundreds of informal groups were either set up or sprang up. They were composed of people new to politics—young people for the most part, newly graduated from college and full of fervor and enthusiasm. It was they who manned the store-front campaign offices, who fashioned posters, passed out handbills, drummed up the crowds, stood on soapboxes.

To them Stevenson was a fresh voice that enunciated ideals for which they were prepared to work; for this element in politics was also hostile to bossism and to the malarkey of the clubhouse. They were interested in principles and conceptions; and they harkened to Stevenson because what he said was principled and what he stood for was not shopworn. Twenty years before they would have flocked to Franklin D. Roosevelt or, earlier, to Woodrow Wilson. Now, in 1952, Stevenson was passionately their man.

Stevenson then prepared for his first major address outside Illinois—an event with unusual overtones. The occasion was the national convention of the American Legion in New York. The appearance of Presidential candidates at a Legion convention was a political ritual, and their speeches could be counted upon not to strike a too controversial note. The Republican candidate, Dwight D. Eisenhower, who spoke on the convention's opening day, followed tradition. The fact that he was a general and a World War II leader assured him an ovation from the delegates, and of course he got it.

Stevenson's task—that of following a headliner—was all the more difficult because his military service had consisted of a brief and undistinguished hitch as a Navy seaman apprentice in World War I. He was, moreover, committed to talking "sense to the American people" and had determined to make a start with the American Legion.

The Legion was meeting in the concrete and steel cavern that is Madison Square Garden. For Stevenson's debut, August 27, the triple-tiered arena on the city's dingy West Side was two-thirds full. Twelve thousand Legionnaires, three thousand fewer than had turned out for Eisenhower two days earlier, were on hand when Stevenson entered the hall. He wore a Legion cap that denoted membership in the Advertising Men's Post No. 38 in Chicago, and he was flanked by the Mayor of New York, Vincent Impellitteri, and the Legion's national commander, Donald R. Wilson.

Stevenson began, blandly enough, with a touch of humor. "I have attended too many conventions not to know how you are all beginning to feel here on the afternoon of the third day," he remarked. "I know you work hard at Legion business most of the day, and then devote the balance of your time to the museums, the art galleries, the concerts and other cultural monuments in New York. And, of course, you also, incidentally, have to listen to speeches. I console myself with the thought that this punishment, while cruel, is not unusual."

The subject of his speech was patriotism and, abandoning drolleries, he proceeded to give this as his definition of it:

What do we mean by patriotism in the context of our times? I venture to suggest that what we mean is a sense of national responsibility which will enable America to remain master of her power—to walk with it in serenity and wisdom, with self-respect and with the respect of all mankind; a patriotism that puts country ahead of self; a patriotism which is not short, frenzied outbursts of emotion, but the tranquil and steady dedication of a lifetime.

I said the dedication of a lifetime. These words are easy to utter, but this is a mighty assignment. For it is often easier to fight for principles than it is to live up to them.

Then came a confrontation with the Legion and other special-interest groups that might pay lip service to patriotism but that wanted particular treatment all the same.

Patriotism, I have said, means putting country before self. This is no abstract phrase and, unhappily, we find some things in American life today of which we cannot be proud.

Consider the groups who seek to identify their special interests with the general welfare. I find it sobering to think that their pressures may one day be focused on me. I have resisted them before and I hope the Almighty will give me the strength to do so again and again. And I should tell you, my fellow Legionnaires, as I would tell all other organized groups, that I intend to resist pressures from veterans also. I intend to resist them if I think their demands are excessive or in conflict with the public interest, which must always be the paramount interest.

And let me suggest, incidentally, that we are rapidly becoming a nation of veterans. If we were all to claim a special reward for our service beyond that to which specific disability or sacrifice has created a just claim, who would be left to pay the bill? After all, we are Americans first and veterans second, and I think the best maxim for any administration is still Jefferson's: "Equal rights for all, and special priviliges for none."

This passage, in a capsule, was one of Stevenson's benchmarks, and it illustrates at once one of his strengths and one of his shortcomings. The strength was simple adherence to principle, which drew to him the devoted admiration of those who were tired of hypocrisy in politics. The shortcoming was that the secret of political power is flexibility, which is sometimes called accommodation of interests.

A small incident very shortly after his nomination illustrated this. A powerful Texas Democrat came to Springfield to seek the Governor's support for private ownership of offshore oil rights, support that would help him in a key Southern state.

Stevenson and his visitor were closeted for two hours as his aides fretted in an anteroom. When the conference broke up, the Texan walked unsmiling to his car and drove off. Stevenson emerged, serene and grinning.

"It must have been pretty tough in there," an aide said. "What did you work out?"

"Oh, it wasn't so tough," Stevenson replied. "I didn't have to work out anything."

"What happened?" he was asked.

"I just tried to make him see that a man doesn't try to be President just to give away the resources of the American people. I don't know whether I convinced him. Anyway, I may have given him something to think about."

Stevenson, moreover, was not a man to keep his tongue stilled when silence might have been prudent. And it was considered prudent in 1952 not to tangle with Senator Joseph R. McCarthy, Republican of Wisconsin. The Senator was then in the heyday of his malign power as a scourge of suspected "security risks," "traitors" and others he suspected of remote or tenuous associations with Communism or

Communists. The Senator was a master of innuendo who put witnesses before his investigating committee in the position of the guilty who must prove their innocence. McCarthy, whose name with an "ism" attached to it was later used to denote a dark age in our recent history, was a product of the early days of the cold war when the nation's nerves were frayed by Soviet successes in Eastern Europe and American setbacks in Korea. He propounded a cabalistic theory to account for such events—that conspirators in high places, Communists themselves or having Communist associations or thoughts, had betrayed the United States. It was an attractive theory because it was so simple, and thousands believed that McCarthy was a savior of the Republic for having exposed its "enemies." He became himself something of a totem, and those who disagreed with him could easily find themselves under heinous suspicion.

Stevenson, of course, was no Communist, nor did he have Communist sympathies; but he was too aware of the true processes of history to accept the notion that its great events are the work of conspirators. At the same time he was affronted by the crudities of McCarthy and the easiness with which he and his committee asperged the actions and motives of honorable men. A man less deeply committed than Stevenson might have disliked McCarthyism in private but, like Eisenhower, might have been silent or cagey in public. But it is to Stevenson's great credit that he said in public what he thought in private and that, moreover, he took the American Legionnaires, to whom McCarthy was a folk hero, as an audience.

And this is what Stevenson told them:

Now it seems to me that true patriotism is based on tolerance and a large measure of humility.

There are men among us who use "patriotism" as a club for attacking other Americans. What can we say for the self-styled patriot who thinks that a Negro, a Jew, a Catholic or a Japanese-American is less an American than he? That betrays the deepest article of our faith—that, I say, betrays the deepest article of our faith, the belief in individual liberty and equality which has always been the heart and the soul of the American idea.

Now what can we say, too, for the man who proclaims himself a patriot—and then for political or for personal reasons attacks the patriotism of faithful public servants? I give you as a shocking example the attacks which have been made upon the loyalty and the motives of our great wartime Chief of Staff, General Marshall. To me this is the type of "patriotism" which is, in Dr. Johnson's phrase, the last refuge of scoundrels.

I say to you that the anatomy of patriotism is complex. But surely intolerance and public irresponsibility cannot be cloaked in the shining armor of rectitude and of righteousness. Nor can the denial of the right to hold ideas that are different—the freedom of man to think as he pleases. To strike freedom of the mind with the fist of patriotism is an old and an ugly subtlety.

And the freedom of the mind, my friends, has served America well. The vigor of our political life, our capacity for change, our cultural, scientific and industrial achievements, all derive from free inquiry, from the free mind—from the imagination, the resourcefulness and the daring of men who are not afraid of new ideas.

Most all of us favor free enterprise for business. Let us also favor free enterprise for the mind. For in the last analysis, there isn't a man in this room who wouldn't fight to the death to protect the freedom of inquiry and the freedom of the mind. Why is it, then, that we are sometimes slow to detect, or are indifferent to, the dangers that beset it?

Many of the threats to our cherished freedoms in these anxious and troubled times arise, it seems to me, from a healthy apprehension about the Communist menace within our country. Communism is abhorrent. Communism is strangulation for the individual and death for the soul. Americans who have surrendered to this misbegotten idol have surrendered their right to our trust. And there can be no secure place for them in our public life. Yet, as I have said before, we must take care not to burn down the barn to kill the rats. All of us, and especially patriotic organizations of enormous influence like the American Legion, must be vigilant in protecting our birthright from its too-zealous friends while protecting it from its evil enemies.

The tragedy of our day is the climate of fear in which we live, and fear always breeds repression. Too often sinister threats to the Bill of Rights, to the freedom of the mind, are concealed under the patriotic cloak of anti-Communism.

I could add, incidentially, from my own experience that it is never necessary to call a man a Communist to make political capital. Those of us who have undertaken to practice the ancient but imperfect art of government will always make enough mistakes to keep our critics well supplied with ammunition. There's never any need for poison gas.

Now another feature of our current scene that I think invites a similar restraint is the recurrent attacks in some communities upon our public schools.

To my way of thinking, there is no justification for indiscriminate attacks on our schools and on the sincere, devoted, and by no means overpaid teachers who labor within them. If there are Communist teachers, of course they should be excluded. But the task is not one for self-appointed thought police or for ill-informed censors. Even as a very practical matter we do not stop Communist activity or education in this way. What we do is give the Communists material with which to defame us. And we also stifle the initiative of teachers and depreciate the prestige of the teaching profession, which should be as honorable and esteemed as any among us.

[Stevenson then turned to his vision of a patriotic America, a remarkable and almost poetic evocation of national greatness.]

It was always accounted a virtue in a man to love his country. With us it is now something more than a virtue. It is a necessity, a condition, if you please, of survival. When an American says he loves his country, he means not only that he loves the New England hills, the prairies glistening in the sun, or the wide rising plains, the mountains and the seas. He means that he loves an inner air, an inner

[71]

light in which freedom lives and in which a man can draw the breath of self-respect.

Men, like many of you, who have offered their lives for their country know that patriotism is not the fear of something; it is the love of something. And I say that patriotism with us is not hatred of Russia; it is love of this Republic. It is love of the ideal of liberty of man and of mind in which this Republic was born and to which it is dedicated.

With this patriotism—patriotism, in its large and wholesome meaning—America can master its power and turn it to the noble cause of peace. We can maintain military power without militarism; political power without oppression; and moral power without compulsion or complacency.

Now the road we must travel is long, but at the end lies the grail of peace. And in the valley of peace we see the faint outlines of a new world, fertile and strong. It's odd that one of the keys to abundance should have been handed to civilization on a platter of destruction. But the power of the atom to work evil gives only the merest hint of its power to do good.

I believe that man stands on the eve of his greatest day. I know, too, that that day is not a gift, but a prize; that we shall not reach it until we have won it.

Legionnaires are united by memories of wars, and therefore no group is more devoted to peace. I say to you now that there is work to be done, that the difficulties and the dangers that beset our path at home and abroad are incalculable. There is sweat and there is sacrifice; and there is still more of patience and of quiet persistence in our horoscope. Perhaps the goal is not even for us to see in our lifetime.

But we are embarked on a great adventure. And I say let us proclaim our faith in the future of man. Of good heart and of good cheer, faithful to ourselves and our traditions, we can lift the cause of free men so high no power on earth can tear it down. We can pluck—we can pluck, if you please, this flower, safety, from this nettle, danger. Living, speaking like men—like Americans—we can lead the way to our rendezvous in a happy and peaceful world.

Stevenson's approach was bold as well as cerebral in this speech, as it was throughout the campaign, and in retrospect he can be seen as preparing the way for John F. Kennedy in 1960. In its day, of course, it was a "wrong" tactic, or at least one for which the electorate was unprepared.

But the overriding fact was that Stevenson was pitted against Eisenhower. The Illinois Governor's name was not a household word, as was Eisenhower's. The General, into the bargain, was the beneficiary of traditional American political generosity to military heroes that included Washington, Jackson, Taylor and Grant. Moreover, Eisenhower's public personality was benign, and "I Like Ike," Irving Berlin's song from the Broadway musical *Call Me Madam*, was a natural appellation.

People did like Ike: he had an engaging grin, a fatherly manner and a pleasant way to him; and in the mood of the day he benefited from lack of previous involvement in politics. He had been Supreme Commander of Allied Forces in Europe, president of Columbia University and then head of the North Atlantic Treaty Organization, and his precise political affiliation had been so uncertain that Truman had once offered to back him as a Democrat.

Three Republican slogans were reasonable facsimiles of the public mood in 1952: "the mess in Washington," "time for a change" and "bring the boys home from Korea." Inflation, the high cost of living, charges of favoritism and dishonesty in the government and the unhappy deadlock in Korea all militated against a party that had been in power since 1933 and augured for a new, prestigious and unentangled figure in politics—and that was Eisenhower. He had a reputation for getting things done. He was the man for the nation's mood of disappointment in the present and uneasiness about the future.

With all this, Eisenhower was not a simple choice for the Republicans. Their convention, which met in Chicago two weeks before the Democrats', was acrimonious in a division between the party's liberal and conservative wings. The latter backed Senator Taft of Ohio, whereas the former, with strong Eastern support, was for the newcomer. To assuage the losers and the party professionals, Senator Richard M. Nixon of California, a known quantity, was picked to run with Eisenhower.

Eisenhower, appearing before the convention to accept the nomination, pledged a "Great Crusade" for "total victory"over the Democrats. It was a crusade that had already enlisted a large segment of the nation's publishers, whose editorial pages called for Eisenhower. This was a sore point with Stevenson, who complained in the campaign and afterward that he was treated with hostility by the press.

At the time Stevenson and Eisenhower were nominated the character of neither man was intimately known to a large public. Taking note of this, James Reston assessed both men in a postconvention article in *The Times Magazine*. This was his appraisal:

In some ways the two men are similar. Both have not so much the elements of greatness as the elements of goodness—to use that old-fashioned and much-neglected word.

Both start out with an awareness of the responsibilities of the job and the limitations of human character.

Both have a sense of duty—Eisenhower's coming from a lifetime of service to his country, and Stevenson's from a family tradition of political service that goes back to the middle of the nineteenth century.

Both have an inspirational quality which flows in Stevenson's case from an idealistic nature and a rare facility in the use of words, and in Eisenhower's case from simple faiths, extraordinary self-confidence and a kind of personal magic.

Both appeal to the noblest qualities in the American character and both speak a great deal about things of the spirit, though neither really seems to be sustained in his present trials by profound religious conviction.

Both are essentially pragmatic in their approach to problems, suspicious of extremes or ideological solutions, good at bringing diverse elements together—as Eisenhower proved in Europe and Stevenson here in Illinois. In short, they are middle-of-the-roaders, Eisenhower to the left of his party, and Stevenson to the right of the New Deal, further to the right than most people realize.

Both have had their greatest character development in middle age. Neither showed extraordinary promise in college, nor in his twenties, thirties or early forties. But after getting new responsibilities—partly by accident and against their own will—both had an unusual spurt in their late forties and early fifties. Indeed, this is one of the things that make any estimate of Stevenson somewhat hazardous—at fifty-two he is still growing in powers of decision, self-discipline and in his judgment of people.

The differences between these two men, however, are equally as striking if not more so than their similarities. All human beings are complicated—too complicated to fit in a magazine—but Stevenson is a far more complicated human being than Eisenhower.

He is a worrier. He has that most attractive personal quality of human sympathy. He can see not two but at least four sides to every question and, being a sensitive man, it is not easy for him to decide for one side and against the other three—and then put the decision behind him.

At the end of the Democratic convention I wrote an article in which I said the General was decisive and the Governor indecisive. This may be true in the realm of things that affect the Governor's personal life, but after watching him in Springfield for a few weeks, and talking with men here who have been working for and against him since he became Governor, the truth seems more complex.

He can make policy decisions. In the three weeks after the convention he moved the center of his party from Washington to Springfield, stood out against the pressures of the bosses and appointed his own men to run his own campaign—against the Democratic Party's tradition and against some of its most powerful figures, including at times the President himself.

Whether he can stop worrying about the decision after he makes it, however, is another question. He seems to me to have trouble on this score. The old arguments still stick in his mind.

Stevenson worried a whole lot before he ditched the political pros and turned his campaign over to the amateurs—and he's still worrying a little about it—but most everybody seems to think he came up with the right idea.

Eisenhower, on the other hand, may have worried about the pros and the isolationists in the Republican back room; but he enlisted them in his crusade, and this is still one of the most controversial decisions of the precampaign period.

Another striking difference between the two candidates is Eisenhower's outward self-confidence and Stevenson's outward self-doubt. Either by nature or by training, Eisenhower always manages to look as if he is complete master of the situation. Stevenson, on the other hand, is forever belittling everything he does. He is constantly telling stories on himself which purport to demonstrate that he is a complete boob. The sum of most of these stories seems to be that there he was on the edge of an easy triumph and kicked the ball all over the field. . . .

Eisenhower's attitude is:

"We'll murder 'em."

Stevenson's:

"They'll murder me."

There is, I think, this basic difference between the General and the Governor which may be revelant: The General is a remarkably optimistic human being, Stevenson a congenital skeptic. Eisenhower really believes in his heart that somehow we will find a way not only to avoid war but to have some kind of an honorable peace. He doesn't quite know how or why, but he believes it anyway. In a way, he actually seems to distrust the intellectual approach. By all the laws of reason and intelligence, he says, the British should have lost the war and the Germans should have won before we ever got into it, but they didn't. This is part of his nature which you see even in the way he plays golf. He's a bad putter, for example, but when he addresses the ball, even if he's fifty feet away from the cup, the thing that is in his mind is that ball curving boldly and triumphantly into the hole.

Not Stevenson. He can always see himself missing the eighteen-inchers, and he frankly cannot believe in that happy world of tolerable coexistence with the Russians. The late Ernest Bevin, former British Foreign Secretary, used to say: "The fascinating thing to me about the Americans and the Europeans is that if you throw an idea or a proposal on the table, the Americans always seem to see the possibilities in it and the Europeans the difficulties." As a broad definition of approach, this seems to me to apply respectively to Eisenhower and Stevenson. . . .

The campaign will undoubtedly exaggerate the difference between these two men, since the Republicans are pulling Eisenhower to the right and the Democrats are pulling Stevenson to the left, but despite their party differences and their different personalities, they seem to me to be remarkably close together in what they believe as human beings.

There have been two groups of men in our national life in the last generation or so, one group in one party and the other in the other, which have been very close together—the liberal New England Republicans, such as Senators Henry Cabot Lodge and Leverett Saltonstall of Massachusetts, and the border-state Jeffersonian Democrats such as Woodrow Wilson and John W. Davis.

It is popular for the moment to say that Eisenhower is extremely conservative and Stevenson quite liberal, but both of them seem to me to be as close together as the modern New England liberals and the progressive border-state Democrats.

Eisenhower may not fit this exactly. His background is so different that the comparison may seem ridiculous, but in terms of the policies he naturally approves, he is not far away.

When you hear Eisenhower talk in private of his early days of poverty in Abilene, of his eighty-four-hour work week in the Abilene dairy, of the recurring economic crises on the Kansas prairies, of the necessity of maintaining the advances of the last twenty years, of the necessity of trading abroad and of organizing the nations of the world, of the importance of planning in the Army and the necessity of "organization" in a democratic society, it is not at all difficult to understand why Harry Truman wanted him to seek the Presidency on the Democratic ticket or why there was doubt for a long time about whether he was a Republican or a Democrat.

Equally, if you have watched Stevenson over the past few weeks, studied his background, observed his friends, looked into his education and his career in the formative years of his life, it is not difficult to understand why he wants to emphasize that he is a change from the New and Fair Dealers.

This is not just a tactic in the campaign. There is no group of men in American public life today that Mr. Stevenson resembles more than the intelligent, urbane, well-heeled New England liberals who did so much to win the Republican nomination for General Eisenhower: Governor Sherman Adams of New Hampshire, Senators Lodge and Saltonstall of Massachusetts, Representative Christian Herter of Massachusetts.

No matter how much the rivals had in common, it was Stevenson's task to roll up votes for himself, and that involved putting himself and his program before the public in as engaging a manner as possible. Thus he turned to television, then still an electronic youngster new to politics, and to the airplane, which permitted him to cover a great deal of territory at a fast clip. Only on the last of his five major swings about the country—through the Eastern industrial states with their big bloc of electoral votes—did the Governor campaign by train.

The platform on which Stevenson campaigned pledged to continue the domestic policies of Truman's Fair Deal, to seek repeal of the Taft-Hartley Labor Law, to encourage equal rights and fair employment practices, to prosecute corruption, to economize in government (but not in defense), to continue bipartisanship in foreign policy and to conclude the Korean conflict with honor. It also praised the United Nations as one of the cornerstones of United States policy. Stevenson, of course, elaborated on these planks in his own way in more than two hundred speeches.

Extensive use of air travel added a dimension of urgency to the campaign and at the same time it made for hectic days. A typical day would find the candidate visiting three or four cities, the routine in each consisting of a brief airport rally and news conference, a motorcade tour with the area's leading Democrats and a speech in the downtown area. In these circumstances a fresh speech for each city was not feasible, but it is remarkable how many variations Stevenson was able to introduce to keep his talks from becoming tired.

As a television personality, Stevenson was excellent. Speaking in the privacy of a studio, he appeared relaxed and informal and homey. His voice was good and his avoidance of histrionics created a favorable impression, although to some he seemed more like a lecturer than a campaigner.

In one such television speech he defined four of the major campaign issues: corruption in government, maintaining prosperity, Communism and Korea. As to corruption, he reminded the nation:

"No approach to the problem of corruption in government is good enough if it ignores the deeper problem of corruption in men. We do not think that a bank is corrupt because the cashier embezzles. The problem of corruption, of graft in its simplest form, is a problem of individual morals, public and private. Behind every crooked tax collector is a crooked taxpayer."

Stevenson's plan to keep production and employment high and to arrest inflation was to rely on a pay-as-you-go tax policy, strict control of government expenditures, restraints on excessive private borrowing and, if necessary, further wage and price controls.

Turning to Communism, one of the most sensitive issues of 1952, Stevenson was forthright if unsensational. This is what he said:

These mortal enemies cannot be permitted to get close to the bloodstream of America, particularly its government. I don't believe oaths and affidavits are much good, for a real Communist never hesitates to lie. Nor is catching and punishing Communists after their treachery enough to end the hazard.

I think generally that postscreening of government employes and the quiet, effective, professional work of the FBI is the best way to turn over every stone in this country and see what lies beneath it.

This is a job for professionals, and I think it can be done without slandering innocent people. I distrust those who have made political capital out of broadside charges discrediting hundreds of loyal government employees.

I do not believe that we can jettison our processes of justice without endangering freedom for every American.

Beyond this I say to you that the battle against Communism in America is an infinitely tough one, a harder battle than most of the Republican leaders have ever admitted, or evidently even understand.

Why is it if these politicians who scream loudest about Communists in America have fought hardest against every Democratic program to fight Communism itself.

They criticized our efforts to block the Communist invasion of Korea; they have opposed our efforts to make the people of Europe and of Asia secure in order to reject the false gospel; they have opposed making the people of America secure enough so that they will never turn again, as some did, in the 1930's to the false prophets.

The FBI figures show that we have in this country now only a fraction of the Communists that we had twenty years ago.

The point is that we've got to fight Communism, not just Communists.

We've got to see to it that the soil is so healthy that Communism just can't grow or survive in it. And that means the creative construction work of assuring good jobs, decent homes, good education and free political institutions.

In tackling the issue of Korea, where the war was going badly, Stevenson was again pedagogical in offering an explanation of American presence.

Every one of us knows in his heart why we had to stand up and to fight in Korea.

We all know that when the Communists attacked across the Thirty-eighth Parallel that was the testing point for freedom throughout the world.

The men in the Kremlin thought that they would be unopposed, and if they were the whole question of the future could be settled in one blow. If they had been allowed to conquer free people in Korea, they could have picked away at the free world and engulfed more millions piece by piece, one by one.

Sooner or later we would have had to fight, and the later we made our stand, the bigger and the harder the war would have been.

Stopping the enemy in Korea before Japan was threatened and before East Asia, with all of its resources of manpower—rubber, tin, oil and so forth—fell to the Communists was received with enthusiastic shouts of approval by the overwhelming majority of the American people, and even by the Republican leadership.

Now, however, they attempt to make you believe that it was almost an act of treason. But what do you think they would be saying now if we had not stopped the enemy in Korea, if Japan was threatened and if East Asia was falling bit by bit to the enemy. Would they not be saying now that Harry Truman and Joseph Stalin were boyhood friends in Outer Mongolia?

And another thing—the Republican leadership is now telling us that the danger to this nation is from within, not from without, that danger lies not in Moscow but in Washington; your enemy is not

Joseph Stalin but Harry Truman or even possibly Adlai Stevenson.

A campaign addressed not to men's minds and to their best instincts but to their passions, emotions and prejudices is unworthy at best. Now, with the fate of the nation at stake it is unbearable.

With the darkest evil and the mightiest force ever gathered on earth arrayed against us and our friends this is no time for such talk.

It is not for me to stand in judgment upon the men who pervert the truth and say such things, but for your sake and for mine, for the sake of my sons and your children and the future of millions of our friends overseas, and the future of our nation and for those who languish in prison behind the Iron Curtain, we must know the truth and come to grips with the facts of life, look them in the face and stare them down—and so doing triumph over them.

We are not, I take it, a race of whimpering weaklings who can't face the truth, but a race of men and women proud, courageous and unafraid.

This speech, like so many others in 1952, reflected Stevenson at his best and, from the professional politicians' standpoint, at his worst. His appeal was to thought and reason and to the perspectives of history, but it lacked specifics and earthiness. In American politics, blaming somebody rather than something has always been attractive because somebody is tangible, whereas something is not. Truman was renowned as a man who "gave them hell," meaning his opponents, and this approach was easily understood. Issues without the personal component were not so easy to grasp. Thus Stevenson's insistence upon sticking to issues earned him the reputation of talking over the head of the man in the street.

Nonetheless, Stevenson strove valiantly to identify with his audiences and to make an asset out of the handicaps under which he labored—that he was bound to uphold and

defend the totality of the New and Fair Deals. In opening
his campaign formally in Detroit on Labor Day he adverted
to the charge that he was a "captive candidate." Talking to
twenty thousand automobile union workers in Cadillac
Square that hot September 1, he called for repeal of the Taft-
Hartley Law, one of organized labor's particular aims, and
then accented his own independence of labor and other political blocs.

"Contrary to the impressions fostered by some of the
press," he said, "you are not my captives, and I am not your
captive. On the contrary, I might as well make it clear right
now that I intend to do exactly what I think is right and best
for all, for all of us—business, labor, agriculture—alike."

(A couple of weeks earlier, in an informal talk in Springfield, he had resorted to ridicule to dispose of the "captive"
charge. "They say I am a 'captive' of the city bosses, and then
the 'captive' of the CIO [Congress of Industrial Organiza-
tions], and then the 'captive' of the Dixiecrats, and the
'captive' of President Truman, and then the 'captive' of Wall
Street, and finally I have been called the 'captive' of an organization called the ADA [Americans for Democratic Ac-
tion].")

After the Detroit rally, whose cheers heartened him, Stevenson went on to Flint, Michigan, another labor strong-
hold. Sitting on the platform there with his legs crossed, he
was photographed with a sizable hole in the outer surface of
the sole of his right shoe. Published across the country the
following day, the photograph caused a great deal of amusement, and a shoe with a hole became a trade-mark of sorts of
Stevenson's campaign, symbolizing as it did the paucity of
Democratic funds. Stevenson himself laughed about the incident and later wore other shoes, at least one pair of which

was contributed by shoe workers from Brockton, Massachusetts. It was a light touch, that episode, and it probably made Stevenson more human.

A component of the "captive" accusation was the Republican cry that it was "time for a change." It placed Stevenson on the defensive and he thought he had to respond, which he did in a nationally televised speech in Denver September 5.

"Which party," he asked, "best understands the meaning of change in the modern world? Which party has ignored it? Which has anticipated the need for change and done something about it? Which party has resisted about every important change for the last twenty-five years? Which party is most likely to cope effectively with the vast changes already in the making?"

The argument was lawyerlike and not nearly so pungent as the way Stevenson had phrased it informally in Springfield a month earlier. "Now, I had always thought that Americans liked change for the better and disliked change for the worse," he said then. "But a new doctrine is abroad in the land—a doctrine of change for the sake of change. Whether that change is for the better or for the worse is apparently something we are to find out after the election. So it is like buying a surprise package at a novelty store. Maybe the cigar is a good one, or maybe it will explode in your face."

Associated with the call for change was what Republicans termed "the mess in Washington." It wasn't, in all truth, much of a "mess," although there were some suspicious irregularities that, presented in inflated form, bothered the public. Government grain had disappeared in mysterious circumstances from a private warehouse in the Southwest;

Assistant Attorney General T. Lamar Caudle had been dismissed after his extraofficial activities were questioned; "5 percenters"—agents who helped private concerns to obtain government contracts—were exposed as active in Washington; and there were charges of shakedown and bribery in the Internal Revenue Service. Outside Washington, but linked to the easygoingness of the capital, was a cheating scandal at West Point in 1951 in which ninety cadets were booted out of the Military Academy.

Eisenhower and the Republicans were making a major issue out of corruption. Stevenson was also aware of the laxities in the Federal establishment, and these, along with other differences with the White House, placed him in a complex predicament.

He could not (and did not) wholly endorse all the Democratic Administration's record, yet he could not be selective and critical, except in a roundabout manner. Once, in Baltimore, he implied a mild criticism of Truman's handling of a steel wage dispute; and in a Springfield, Massachusetts, speech he deleted from his prepared text an encomium to Truman's "vision and courage" in foreign policy. Stevenson's solution was to generalize and to link himself with Roosevelt as much as with Truman.

"You know," he told a party gathering in New York, "the Republicans have been talking of late as if I were ashamed of the [Democratic] accomplishments in war and peace of the past twenty years which they, by some miraculous agility, both embrace and condemn at the same time. I've been tempted to say that I was proud to stand on that record, if the General would move over and make room for me."

Stevenson's sally at Eisenhower was one of many that were

calculated to personalize the campaign and to disclose that Stevenson's tongue could be sardonic and ungentle. Early in the campaign Stevenson began larding his speeches on issues with personal barbs. James Reston noticed this September 6. "Fasten your seat belts, mates," he wrote. "The political weather is getting rough." Then he went on to report from Kasson, Minnesota, where Stevenson was campaigning:

Last week, the script called for what was invariably defined as a high-level campaign. The formal campaign is six days old and the two candidates are now trading high-level punches in the nose.

When General Eisenhower came home, he said peace was the great issue of the election; now he says it's the "mess" in Washington.

When he attended that now famous luncheon with the reporters in Denver before the conventions, he resented suggestions that he was making overtures to the Republican Old Guard. Now he is composing whole symphonies for their benefit.

When the delegates visited him in Denver's Brown Palace Hotel last June, he used to give them a little lecture on avoiding half-truths and slogans. Now it looks from here as if he is concentrating on that oldest chestnut of them all: "Kick the rascals out."

Governor Adlai E. Stevenson of Illinois has also changed his tactics a little.

He hesitated to run for the Democratic nomination partly because the prospect of General Eisenhower in the White House did not fill him with mortal terror. Now he sees the General as a captive of the Old Guard and the Old Guard as a menace to every soul in Christendom.

Before the great draft in Chicago he seemed to be impressed with the argument that the defeat of General Eisenhower would deliver the Republican Party once more into the hands of the conservatives, perpetuate the acrimonious debates over unreal issues of foreign and domestic policy, and jeopardize the two-party system in America.

Yesterday he raised this argument himself and dismissed it with a wisecrack. "I believe," he said, "that this is the first time it has been contended that now is the time for all good Democrats to come to the aid of the Republican Party."

Finally, Mr. Stevenson has modified his public comments about his opponent. If he mentioned him at all right after the Democratic convention, he was almost deferential.

This is now out. He still praises him, but usually just before he decapitates him with a phrase. Also, he has taken to feeling sorry for him in public, a stance which will not appeal to the General's sense of humor.

The Democratic strategy has been not to attack General Eisenhower, but to concentrate on the McCarthys, the Jenners and the Republican voting record. By Monday evening in Michigan, however, Governor Stevenson was ridiculing the General for not knowing the difference between the closed shop, the open shop and the union shop; and by last night's big rally here, he was going out of his way to poke fun at him.

"I'm afraid," said the Governor, "that he's like a fly in the fly-paper: the more he struggles to free himself, the more he gets gummed up."

At another point, he remarked: "It would be a sad thing indeed, it seems to me, if a great soldier, to whom we owe undying affection and gratitude, ended up politically between the two Republican parties like that mule I heard about one time that starved to death standing between two stacks of hay, trying to make up his mind which one to eat."

There is a difference, however, between the Stevenson change and the Eisenhower change. Stevenson's is tactical, Eisenhower's seems to be a major strategic decision to go over to the offensive on all fronts. The Governor is combining his quips and cracks with a series of speeches on the major domestic and foreign policy issues and, so far, the General isn't.

The next day Reston gave a detailed explanation of Stevenson's tactics and with it a behind-the-scenes look at his campaign thinking. In an article filed from Lewiston, Idaho, Reston wrote:

There is no doubt that Governor Stevenson has been stung by General Eisenhower's emphasis in the South on the corruption issue, and especially by the suggestions by the General and other Republican speakers that if Mr. Stevenson were elected in November he would be helpless to do anything about corruption in Washington.

To the Illinois Governor, who prides himself on his record of rooting out the corruption in the state government of Illinois, these assertions are regarded as unfair and dishonorable. He resents them and he makes no attempt to conceal his bitterness about them.

Secondly, the Governor has been extremely annoyed in the last few days by what he regards as the attempt of Senator Joseph R. McCarthy of Wisconsin to falsify in the matter of the Governor's deposition on behalf of the convicted perjurer, Alger Hiss, at the time of the former State Department official's trial.

Senator McCarthy, in a speech in Milwaukee last Wednesday, asked Governor Stevenson if he "could be disturbed because I am checking your record since the day you entered government service at about the same time and in the same department as the Hiss, Abt, Witt and Pressman group."

Hiss, John J. Abt, Nathan Witt and Lee Pressman, who have been named as Communists in various Congressional inquiries, were employed by the Department of Agriculture in 1934, as was Mr. Stevenson.

For a couple of days Mr. Stevenson contemplated making a major political statement about the Hiss case in order to repudiate the implications of Senator McCarthy's public statement. But now he apparently has decided not to go through with it, at least for the time being.

Nevertheless, Mr. Stevenson is aware of the political effect of the sort of hard-hitting campaign on corruption that General Eisenhower has been developing, especially since the Democratic nominee gained greatly by emphasizing the corruption issue in his own campaign for the Illinois governorship against the Republican incumbent, Dwight Green, in 1948.

Accordingly, the Democratic nominee has consciously put more bite into his attacks on the Republicans, and there is every indication that he intends to continue doing so in his speeches on the West Coast during the next few days.

There has been some talk within the Governor's own official family on whether it is wise for him to indulge in as much satirical humor in his speeches as he has. He has done this, however, all during his three and a half years as Governor of Illinois; it is his natural way of speaking and of "politicking," and he has rejected suggestions that he should change his natural manner of political attack at this time.

Moreover, the Stevenson strategists are impressed with the following line of reasoning:

General Eisenhower, they observed, was a vivid personality in the minds of the American people when he returned from his command over the North Atlantic Treaty forces near Paris at the beginning of June. The feeling here is that it was essential that Governor Stevenson, who was little known, especially in the West, should establish in the American mind some clear picture of his personality and his approaches to various questions, such as special pressure groups, corruption, foreign policy, farm and conservation policies, etc.

It was felt that the Governor's sense of humor and his sharp satirical quality not only could be used effectively in attacking what Mr. Stevenson called "the two Republican parties" but also that the use of humor and the striking phrase would do as much as anything else to establish his personality in the minds of the voters.

This decision has been heightened by the Republican tactics of the last few days, for the more General Eisenhower attacks Mr. Stevenson as a possible captive of dishonorable public servants, the angrier the Governor becomes. And his natural expression of anger in a political campaign is through sharp satire.

Governor Stevenson, in ridiculing the conservative candidates in the Republican Party and trying to drive a wedge between them and General Eisenhower, is determined, however, that these things should be secondary to the task of laying down between now and November 4 a series of statements defining his policy on all the major questions before the electorate.

[89]

To lighten the burdens of the campaign there were some less serious happenings. In one the five-year-old daughter of a local party leader ignored Stevenson's proffered handshake and jumped up and kissed him on the cheek. Reporters applauded, for Stevenson had vowed to them that he would avoid baby-kissing. "Well, she asked for it," he told the press corps, "and also she is not a baby."

On another occasion he took time out to preside at a birthday party for Mrs. Margaret Munn, one of his secretaries. He carried a birthday cake for her down the airplane aisle and led his aides in singing "Happy Birthday to You."

At a rodeo he permitted himself to be lassoed and held briefly in the rope loop. Then laughing he clapped on a ten-gallon hat and told the cowboys, "This is the first fun I've had since I got into this thing."

Stevenson's gibes at Eisenhower as a captive of the Old Guard in the Republican Party were lent some substance in mid-September when Senator Taft, who had lost the nomination two months earlier, paid a visit to the General in New York. Afterward, Taft announced that he and Eisenhower were in full accord on the campaign issues and that their differences on foreign policy were a matter of degree, not of purpose. Taft's pledge to campaign for Eisenhower, hailed by Republicans as evidence of party unity, was derided by Democrats as an Eisenhower surrender. Moreover, the Republican move gave Stevenson the opportunity, which he found irresistible, to talk about "the two-headed Republican elephant."

At this point, indeed, Stevenson seemed to be having the better of the campaign, and a week later his stock was pushed upward by the Nixon affair. Following an article in *The New York Post*, Eisenhower's Vice-Presidential running mate confessed that he had accepted $18,235 from California businessmen to defray political expenses while serving in the Senate. It seemed for a moment that Nixon might be obliged to resign from the ticket; but instead, in a television speech, he defended his acceptance of the money and denied that he had profited from it or that it had influenced his official conduct in the Senate. Eisenhower was persuaded of Nixon's probity, and he remained on the ticket.

Stevenson's opportunity to capitalize on the Nixon revelations was short-lived, however, for he almost immediately found himself defending an $18,150 fund he had established as Governor of Illinois. This fund, he explained (and perhaps not as promptly as he should have), represented virtually all the surplus of his own gubernatorial campaign fund plus $2,900 donated by Chicago businessmen. The money was used for Christmas gifts to eight state officials who, Stevenson said, had made financial sacrifices to enter public service.

The net effect of this disclosure was to divert attention from Nixon and to lessen whatever advantage Nixon's troubles might have given Stevenson. Stevenson sought, however, to score a point by releasing his income tax returns for ten years and challenging (unsuccessfully, it turned out) Eisenhower and Nixon to do the same. The Governor's statement showed a total income over the ten years of $500,046, mostly from investments, and $211,980 paid in taxes.

In late September W. H. Lawrence, traveling through the country, summed up the campaign for *The Times* in this fashion:

The campaign methods of Governor Adlai E. Stevenson of Illinois and those of General Dwight D. Eisenhower present a study in contrasts, but the two candidates appear to agree definitely on one thing: Each would rather run against some other person than his present opponent.

That was the explanation of why Governor Stevenson moved up and down the Atlantic seaboard, running against Senator Robert A. Taft of Ohio to whom he contended General Eisenhower had surrendered his Chicago victory. That was the reason that General Eisenhower stormed through the Midwest campaigning against President Truman and all the alleged misdeeds of his Administration.

The idea is that Governor Stevenson regards Senator Taft as a much more vulnerable target than General Eisenhower and by implanting in the public mind that the Ohioan would be the "dominant" figure of any Eisenhower Administration he hopes to rally more independent voters and anti-Taft Republicans to the support of the Democratic ticket.

General Eisenhower believes that an anti-Truman and anti-corruption crusade will produce more votes than a positive discussion of his own program or any attack upon Governor Stevenson himself.

Governor Stevenson's weapon is the rapier. His keen and cutting wit coins quip after quip at Republican expense. He talks about "unconditional surrender" on Morningside Heights (a reference to the site of the Taft-Eisenhower unity conference) and says New York henceforth probably will be known as "Munich." He wonders aloud whether Senator Taft now is a six-star general since he has dictated surrender terms to a former five-star Army officer. A friend had telegraphed, he said, that he supposed the postelection scene in Washington, in the event of a Republican victory, would have Eisenhower in the White House, "Taft in Blair House and Dewey in the doghouse."

General Eisenhower's weapon is more like a blunderbuss. He is on the attack constantly, with little reference to his own positive program and he is deadly serious about it all. In fact, he complained to his Midwestern crowds that Governor Stevenson was not taking the issues seriously enough and that he didn't see anything funny about corruption, our casualties in Korea or the high cost of living. His speeches lack the spontaneity of the Governor's.

The General's phrases are old and homely and simple—from the rear platform at any rate—whereas Governor Stevenson's quips are new and bright and shining.

There is no doubt that General Eisenhower draws the larger and more responsive crowds. He was, after all, one of the more famous and glamorous figures of the American scene by virtue of his military career even before he became a candidate for President.

General Eisenhower has made much of the fact that Governor Stevenson's sense of humor is irrepressible, but the fact is that a considerable portion of what the Illinois Governor has to say is so deadly serious that the crowd's response is much more restrained when he talks than it is when General Eisenhower lets fly with another round of heavy artillery aimed at the "Truman gang."

One gets the impression that quite frequently Governor Stevenson is talking over the heads of his audience, that he is, in brief, too literate and too learned for the average crowd that turns out for a political meeting in the town square at midday.

So far as this reporter has been able to observe, General Eisenhower has been doing fine among Republicans and among some disgruntled Democrats, but has hardly made any effort at all to capture the vote of the independents with the exception of his emphasis on the need for a change.

Governor Stevenson appears to have held together most of the elements of the Roosevelt coalition, especially in its reliance upon organized labor and minority groups, and he is now pitching most of his appeal to the independent voter.

The independent voter, Stevenson was convinced, would rally to him if he would but listen to and read Stevenson speeches. He was convinced that literateness was smart politics, no matter what the professionals asserted; so he staked his drive on appeals to the intellect in speeches that were carefully, even painfully, assembled.

Jane Krieger, writing in October in *The Times Magazine*, told how this was accomplished:

One of the most striking characteristics of his campaign is the amount of time he puts in on speech-writing and speech-making. The Governor is staking his whole election on his speeches.

The first thing he does on arriving in Springfield between road shows is to meet with his half-dozen or so writers—or researchers, as they call themselves. These men, most of them under forty, many of them from universities, are concerned with content rather than slick writing. For several hours they sit around the big table in the Governor's office, tossing ideas around for the next batch of scripts. Generally Stevenson says little—too little, the staff members sometimes complain. He asks frequent questions and is an adept brain picker.

After the preliminary meeting the grind starts. The writers work —twelve to fourteen hours a day—in the Springfield Elks Club on drafts of speeches or "position papers," as they call them. The atmosphere is totally unlike Sam Rosenman's description of the frenetic White House room in which Roosevelt's speech-writers worked. No whisky bottles, no sandwiches, not even a Coke. Except for the typewriters, the Elks Club office looks like a postgraduate seminar room.

Until very recently Stevenson never accepted a major speech without giving it a major rewrite. Even now, with the campaign going into its final stretch, the Governor usually finds time to work on the important speeches. What he does is to take several drafts of the same script and get them in shape—which means using material he likes from each draft, writing new paragraphs, shifting old ones around, writing transitions and putting in his own words with the end purpose of bringing "thought to bear on politics," as Matthew Arnold said.

His tools are a pencil (he always writes in longhand), scissors, pastepot and a medium-sized black loose-leaf notebook he keeps in his left-hand desk drawer. In it for years he has been jotting down phrases he made up and wanted to remember, quotes that caught his interest, funny stories people told him.

The results of these efforts were speeches that Stevenson liked and defended against all comers. His attitude and that of his critics was summed up this way in Miss Krieger's article:

Stevenson told an audience recently, "What I have to say . . . is intended for your heads and not your hands. . . . If I were more comforted by your cheers than your thoughts, I would hardly merit the confidence of responsible men." At another time when he was asked if he didn't think he was being too highbrow, he replied, "Not one bit. I believe you should talk up to people, not down. I don't want to sound dewy and romantic about this—dewy-minded, you understand—but if a candidate can't make voters understand what he's talking about, that's his fault, not theirs." His aides add that while reaction to Stevenson's approach may not be a whoop or a bucket of tears, it is often a catch in the throat—and the catch in the throat, they maintain, is likely to be more effective in the long run.

There are those who say he is not spending enough time with the professional politicians or with the representatives of important voting groups. Stevenson can be as unconventional as he likes about his speeches, it is said, but his failure to establish warm, personal relationships with the men whose job it is to get out the vote may be a fatal mistake. One example his critics give is that in a number of areas the Stevenson for President groups still are disorganized and amateurish.

The Governor, for his part, thinks it is more important to reach the voters directly (which he believes his speeches are doing) than to shake hands with the pros. Moreover he seems determined to disassociate himself in the public mind from the pros and he still wants to avoid being too closely identified with the Administraton in Washington.

In line with the above, there are those who say Stevenson is failing to get the wholehearted support of the groups which have kept the Democrats in power for twenty years. Labor leaders, especially, have confessed that Stevenson is not making enough impact on the rank and file. They are uneasy about his occasional criticisms of the New Deal–Fair Deal record—on which, after all, he is running. The other day, after one of the Governor's nonpartisan-sounding speeches, a Stevenson aide told a labor leader jubilantly, "This man is going to get a lot of Republican votes." "Right," said the labor leader, "but how about the Democratic votes?"

Stevenson's answer is that he waged the same kind of campaign in

1948, got the Democratic votes and the Republican votes, too—to roll up the biggest majority in the history of Illinois.

Finally there are those who say Stevenson is overplaying the humor. There has been a good deal of argument over whether the Republicans were smart to publicize Stevenson's sense of humor by attacking it. But some nonpartisan observers still feel that the Governor's wit may be distracting, even that it may boomerang, because "the people expect their statesmen to be solemn asses."

Stevenson doesn't believe his humor will conceal his essential seriousness. His aides feel that he uses humor as Sandburg said Lincoln did—"as a laugh cure for his own melancholy, yet also to clinch an argument, to lay bare a fallacy, to disarm an antagonist."

On one issue, however, Stevenson did not deal in humor —and that was the issue of McCarthy. He had opened his campaign with criticism of him to the American Legion, and there were frequent other thrusts. He was distressed when Eisenhower remained silent about McCarthy in the opening stages of the campaign; he was dismayed when Eisenhower deleted a defense of General George C. Marshall from a speech at McCarthy's request; and he was appalled when Eisenhower endorsed McCarthy for re-election to the Senate from Wisconsin.

All this fused into one of Stevenson's most courageous moments—an appearance in Wisconsin in which he denounced the state's junior Senator and Eisenhower, too. "My opponent," he said of Eisenhower, "has been worrying about my funnybone. I'm worrying about his backbone."

And as for McCarthy, he said, "Because we believe in the free mind we are also fighting those who, in the name of anti-Communism, would assail the community of freedom itself."

From this point to the end of October, Stevenson dealt less gently with Eisenhower, referring to him at one point as

"the honorary Republican candidate for President." There
was, according to James Reston, a "Trumanesque fervor" to
some of Stevenson's utterances. He assailed Eisenhower in
particular for campaigning with McCarthy, "the defamer of
his friend and benefactor, General Marshall"; and he used a
limerick to scoff at the Eisenhower-Taft relationship:

> There was a young lady from Niger,
> Who smiled as she rode on a tiger.
> They came back from the ride
> With the lady inside
> And the smile on the face of the tiger.

Stevenson's new approach, Reston wrote, consisted of
two points: "first, in attacking General Eisenhower personally and trying to demonstrate that the General is not
only incompetent to hold the office of the Presidency, but is
not even his own master in the campaign, and, second, to
emphasize the misery of the American people during the
economic Depression of the early nineteen thirties and to
compare it with the prosperity that has accompanied the
New and Fair Deals."

This offensive seemed to draw the crowds. Earlier the
turnouts to see and hear Stevenson tended to be thin. The
Volunteers for Stevenson were always on hand, along with
those they had managed to arouse by phone calls and door-
bell ringing. The crowds were gay and vocal. The multi-
colored posters, though, were clustered. Now, however,
there were more posters—"Switched to Stevenson" was a
popular one; and the cheers were louder, the applause more
sustained, the sense of mission more assured. One of the
poster signs—"All the Way with Adlai"—seemed now an
augury as well as a jingle, for it appeared at rallies where
other campaigners only spoke about Stevenson.

Democratic hopes rose. Perhaps it could be 1948 all over again. Writing a month before Election Day, Reston took note of the portents:

The latest word from the hound's tooth and clay feet circuit is that rough tactics are paying off in the Presidential campaign.

The Democrats do not admire General Eisenhower's speeches either as examples of oratory or as gems of moral philosophy, but they're afraid that the combination of Ike + Korea + Communism + corruption + $$$ + more $$$ = victory so far. Accordingly, the Democratic tactics are being changed, owing at least partly to the tactics of the other camp (which are not being assessed in this article). Without trying to estimate which side is responsible for the decline, the fact is that the Democrats are now using blunter weapons and aiming lower.

The reports coming in here from the Democratic Party's experts and private poll takers suggest these things:

1. Stevenson is gaining but he is still running behind.

2. Eisenhower's Communism and corruption arguments have cut into the Democratic vote in the big cities.

3. The Korean war is hurting Stevenson, particularly among the farmers.

4. The General has lost the Shakespeare vote, but there is still a powerful "let papa worry about it" feeling working for him among the large mass of voters who pay little attention to politics.

Accordingly the Democratic high command has now set out to "kill papa," to destroy the Eisenhower symbol, or, as it is called here, the Eisenhower "myth." And to do it particularly in California, New York and Pennsylvania, which will be the main targets during the last three weeks of the campaign.

The task of "cutting Eisenhower down to size" is not being left entirely to President Truman. For the first month of the campaign Governor Stevenson directed his remarks to the intellectual carriage trade. The idea in mid-September was—as the Democratic leaders here put it themselves—that the Governor would take the high road and the President would take the low road and they'd meet in the White House in January.

Now, however, while not forgetting the double-domes and the mugwumps, both the President and the Governor are trying to stir up the mass vote. The change in the tactics is best illustrated by comparing what the Governor said at the start of the campaign and what he is saying now.

He started by saying that the one thing he wasn't going to do in the campaign was to "run against Herbert Hoover." Now that vulnerable gentleman seems to be all over the place, and the major theme running through the Governor's speeches now is that if the Republicans get in, it will be 1932 and the Depression all over again.

The Governor began his campaign by saying that nothing should be said on either side which would mislead our friends or our enemies overseas and thus jeopardize the continuity of our foreign policy. But for the past ten days he has been saying in effect that a vote for Eisenhower is a vote for American isolationists. He has implied that Eisenhower in the White House would be another Warren Harding—and this raises the most terrifying ghost in the whole of the free world.

Similarly the Governor started out in his acceptance speech in Chicago by saying, "Let's talk sense to the American people," and by condemning the Republicans for trying to scare the voters into marking their ballots against the Democrats. But anyone who cares to devote Sunday morning to reading a file of the speeches delivered by the Governor in the past ten days will see that underneath the fine rhetoric, the basic appeal is that a vote for Stevenson is a vote for peace and prosperity and that a vote for Eisenhower is not only a vote for Senator Taft but for Depression and maybe even for war.

Now, finally, the Governor began his campaign with the intention of not attacking General Eisenhower personally, and even until about ten days ago he kept referring to Eisenhower as "my distinguished and honored opponent." But now Eisenhower is invariably "the General of the Army" and Governor Stevenson compares him with almost everybody from Joe McCarthy to Charlie McCarthy.

In short, the basic strategy of this campaign now differs little from the strategy of the past four or five campaigns. Mr. Stevenson may not have submitted to the views of the party organization with as much gusto as General Eisenhower, but he has not escaped the power and pressure of his party and its prejudices. As it is now the Governor promises to do everything his liberal predecessors have done, to extend their good works, and to rout corruption, Communism and waste in the process. Similarly his picture of a Republican victory is one of despair for the people at home and terror for the free world overseas.

He does all this more adroitly than Mr. Truman; he does most of his hatchet work on the General in his minor speeches and continues to make high-level talks whenever he goes on nationwide radio and television broadcasts; his speeches are better when he has time to write—which is seldom now—than Franklin Roosevelt's ever were. But the underlying appeal and purpose are almost identical.

One obvious result of this approach is that the Governor's crowds are increasing in size as he steps up the tempo. After an unexciting visit to Michigan, where the crowds were small, the people really began turning out this week. Starting at Milwaukee on Wednesday there was increasing evidence not only of more work by the local Democratic organizations but personal enthusiasm for Stevenson.

This, of course, was what the party's political experts told the Governor would happen if—they put it—he "started gabbing a little harder." But the Governor doesn't look particularly happy about it all. He would have preferred a different strategy; there seems little doubt about that. He does not relish his detours onto the "low road."

But he is appalled at the General's tactics and companions in this campaign. He has lost much of the respect he had for the Republican nominee, and—a point that was in some doubt even after the nomination—he now really wants to win the election and wants to win it very badly.

Every now and then, however, he grows a little wistful and seems to lose some of the confidence which is written into his prepared speeches. On Wednesday in Madison, Wisconsin, he delivered a poignant little talk to a group of party workers in which he said that he was told it was dangerous to try to run a completely honest political campaign and he added that maybe it was.

Then he said this:

"My job in this campaign has been to try, in a very brief period of time, to offset a national hero who has been a household word in every family in America for ten years, and to do this without any preconvention campaign, without any opportunity to travel about the country, and with limited resources. . . . One way we have sought to do this was the simple and obvious way, it was to go about the country stating precisely what we thought about things. . . . This has been my objective and if I have departed from it here and there—shall we say under force of political necessity or some other course, perhaps exhaustion—I hope you can forgive me."

The argument against this altered approach is that it takes the public's mind off large issues, where the Democratic Party is strong, and focuses attention on personalities, where Eisenhower has a tremendous advantage.

The argument for it is that the public's mind wasn't on large issues in the first place, and that Mr. Stevenson had to make them pay attention. Moreover, the element of time is regarded as one of great importance. As the Democratic reports indicate, the Governor is making progress, but as officials here put it, "There may not be enough time for General Eisenhower to lose the election."

Stevenson's newly acquired momentum was not lost on Eisenhower and the Republicans, who were now on the defensive for the first time since the conventions in July. Nevertheless, there was one campaign issue that neither side had done much about, but that weighed heavily with the electorate: the fighting in far-off Korea that had been going on for more than two years.

The Korean conflict had begun in June, 1950, with a North Korean push across the Thirty-eighth Parallel. American troops, under nominal United Nations command, had halted that offensive and had driven north on the peninsula toward the Yalu River and the Chinese border. Then, in late October, 1950, Chinese "volunteers" had joined the fighting and edged General Douglas MacArthur's troops back to the vicinity of the Thirty-eighth Parallel, where the front remained fairly static after July, 1951. MacArthur had been relieved of his command by Truman because he wanted to carry the conflict into China against the President's wishes. Thus by 1952 the fighting had reached the point where both sides were willing to enter into a truce, but an acceptable formula was lacking.

In the United States, still weary and disoriented by World War II, the Korean conflict was not popular. The casualty lists were long; taxes were higher; the draft was taking thousands a month; there were no conclusive victories to cheer about; and the ideals of freedom that the conflict involved seemed remote.

At least one leading Republican sought to personalize Korea by calling it "Harry Truman's war," but neither Eisenhower nor Stevenson was willing to campaign on that level of partisanship. Indeed, both favored an honorable end to the conflict, as they both upheld the necessity for United States intervention in Korea in the first place. Some Republicans wanted Eisenhower to declare for bombing war bases in China, but he rejected this. Nonetheless, he did attack what he called Truman's foreign policy "mistakes" and took Dean Acheson, the Secretary of State, to task as inept and bumbling.

Stevenson, for his part, defended the Korean conflict. "You have heard it said," he told the men and women of the armed forces overseas, "that the Korean is a 'useless' war. Nothing seems to me more mischievous than this idea which has been so extensively used for political purposes in this country. Had we not resisted aggression in Korea, then we would not only have lost Korea but we would have invited the Soviet Union to pursue aggression elsewhere."

From July through most of October neither candidate

offered specific ideas for ending the conflict other than to rely on the likelihood that truce talks would eventually work out.

But the mood of the country, which was one of frustration, wanted a speedy end to the conflict. An honorable truce, of course, but a quick one and a swift return of the GI's.

Stevenson, of course, sensed this mood, yet he called for "persevering in this difficult and sometimes exasperating path [so] we can win our way to a peaceful world. It is a goal worth the price," he went on, "heavy as it is. At any rate there are no safe alternatives. To plunge the world into a greater war or to capitulate in hopelessness is no solution."

Eisenhower himself held similar ideas—at least up until late October. At this point a member of his entourage, realizing that Eisenhower required a dramatic coup to regain the campaign initiative and shrewdly comprehending that the Korean stalemate might provide it, suggested to Eisenhower that he offer, if elected, to go to Korea. The idea appealed to the General and a speech was written embodying that pledge. Eisenhower delivered it in Detroit October 24; and it caught exactly the electorate's feelings of the moment. There was a bit of melodrama, also, to the words, "I shall go to Korea," and a promise, by implication, that Eisenhower would not return empty-handed.

Eisenhower's announcement caught Stevenson off guard. He himself had once considered making a similar promise, but he had rejected the idea as pointless on the ground that he could do nothing in Korea that he couldn't do as well in the United States. He did not consider that Eisenhower would not take the same attitude.

Stevenson's reaction to his rival's pledge was a speech that declared that the root of the Korean problem lay not in Korea but in Moscow. But clearly this was not an answer that the electorate would harken to; Eisenhower had executed a *coup de théâtre*, and possible Stevenson voters slipped away to his rival.

There is, of course, no telling what would have happened if Eisenhower had not made his Korea declaration. In later years Stevenson thought he might have won if it had not been for what he called "that Korea business." In any event, Stevenson lost the initiative after October 24; and when the country went to the polls a little more than a week later it was to vote for Eisenhower.

The General's plurality was about 6.5 million votes— 33,936,252 to Stevenson's 27,314,992. Even so, the loser's percentage of the popular vote was 44.6—at least seven percentage points better than a private poll at the start of the campaign had awarded him. In the Electoral College, however, the spread was greater, for Eisenhower took 39 states with a total of 442 votes, while Stevenson carried 9—Alabama, Arkansas, Georgia, Kentucky, Louisiana, Mississippi, North Carolina, South Carolina and West Virginia—with a total of 89 votes.

Stevenson, in his gallant try, traveled 30,000 miles, visited 32 states and made 200 speeches. The night before the election he told a party rally in Illinois, "I am content. I have said what I meant and meant what I have said. No man can do more and you are entitled to no less."

It was, like so many of his appraisals, candid. The "best" was his speeches. The not-so-good was his inability to be free and easy with the voters, for he had a feeling that glad-handing was a species of hokum. He expressed this feeling to an old friend after a day of arduous handshaking.

"Perhaps the saddest part of all this," he remarked, "is that a candidate must reach into a sea of hands, grasp one, not knowing whose it is, and say, 'I'm glad to meet you,' realizing that he hasn't and probably never will meet that man."

CHAPTER IV

DEFEAT BUT NOT OBLIVION

THE CAMPAIGN MADNESS had passed, the rhetoric had
spent itself, the People had spoken. For the first time in
twenty years the fine old homes in Georgetown and Chevy
Chase would be filled with Republican, not Democratic,
bureaucrats. Harry Truman would slip out of Washington
and drive to Independence, Missouri. Stridently, Joseph R.
McCarthy would proclaim new dangers to the nation, while
Eisenhower would find that it was one thing to lead a Great
Crusade and quite another to lead a political party.

And the defeated candidate? Would he leave politics? "I
couldn't if I wanted to, and I most certainly don't want to,"
he said. After all, Adlai Stevenson was titular leader of his
party. ("About as titular as you can get," he remarked.)

In that first year Stevenson was faced with a number of
quite specific problems, some of which he never resolved.
How, for instance, should he earn a living? As a lawyer, he
said confidently, as he prepared to surrender the governorship of Illinois to William G. Stratton, a Republican. But
could a celebrated public man turn his talents to wills and
estates?

Or should he write a book? All the major publishers wanted him to; his campaign speeches, put between hard covers, stayed on the best-seller lists some eighteen weeks. But what kind of book? Books can embarrass a politician in later years; a position once taken in print is hard to erase. He could write an evasive book, but what good would that be?

And how much should he criticize the Eisenhower Administration? Few problems were to vex him quite so much as this one. It was a fiction to think he was a private citizen; his words were listened to abroad, and he knew it. (After a global tour that first year he said of his fame: "It's really astonishing. I'm several lengths behind McCarthy, but right up close to Eisenhower.")

On January 8, 1953, in Springfield, Stevenson delivered his farewell report as Governor to the people of Illinois. He laid down "ten major future goals for the state" and touched briefly on his own past hopes, but not at all on those for his future. However, toward the end he said:

"Government—local, state and Federal—is not something separate and apart; if it is to be good it must share the attitudes and the competence of the best in our society as a whole. Both business and government are gainers when the best among us from private life will make sacrifices, if need be, to fill vital positions."

Then the former Governor was off to Barbados for a long vacation. When he returned he chose a Jefferson-Jackson Day dinner of eleven Eastern states to berate the month-old Eisenhower Administration. The audience of seventeen hundred in the Grand Ballroom of the Waldorf-Astoria Hotel included most of the celebrated names of the Democratic Party, and Stevenson offered them candidly partisan rhetoric.

He recalled the statement of Secretary of Defense Charles
E. Wilson before a committee of Congress that "what is
good for General Motors is good for the country," and he
noted the "possibility that the successor of the New Deal
will be the Big Deal, while the New Dealers have all left
Washington to make way for the car dealers." "I hasten to
say," he added, "that I do not believe that the general welfare has become a subsidiary of General Motors."

The two parties, he said, were again divided by the old
principles that separated Jefferson and Hamilton. Again, he
said, the doctrine that only men of wealth and business can
govern was in the ascendancy. Again, he said, the Democratic Party must reaffirm its faith in all the people.

Of the Republican President and Congress he said: "Our
prayers go with them in the dark, the evil-haunted night we
all must traverse, confronting an enemy whose massive
power is matched only by its malevolent purpose."

A few days later Stevenson was in Washington, where he
had an amicable luncheon with the President. He also had
an unexpected bipartisan triumph at the Capitol when a
large number of House Republicans attended a reception
given for him by Senate Democrats.

And what of Stevenson as titular head of the opposition?
Arthur Krock wrote:

The Democratic politicians have no other leader at this time with
a popular following comparable to Stevenson's and none with his
personal gifts. Defeat in November, and their unfamiliar role as the
opposition, have drawn together many Democrats who long have
been factionally embroiled. Moreover, though the policies of the
party will be shaped in the committee rooms and on the floors of
Congress, their late Presidential candidate realizes and welcomes
this. . . . If he will serve before live audiences and on television as
the national enunciator of those policies on which he and nearly all

Democrats agree—a fairly good-sized list—they will rate him an indispensable asset. And they got the impression Stevenson will be glad to do this.

The Governor's problem, of course, which is also that of the Democrats who want to keep his leadership strong and fresh, is how politically to survive on a national scale during the term of President Eisenhower.

But Stevenson's prominence for the rest of the year was virtually guaranteed. For the next six months—until late August—he would travel tens of thousands of miles through thirty countries, from Britain to Japan, speaking to everyone, as he later said, "from cobblers to kings." One such experience came in an episode in India, as related by William Manchester, who was present:

"When we reached Trivandrum in southern India, the local cutcherry had prepared a festive outdoor dinner in Stevenson's honor. After the meal, however, an Indian rose and launched—without warning—into a spirited attack on America's foreign policy. The Governor had grave reservations about Foster Dulles. Nevertheless, as an American in public life he felt that he could not remain silent, and during his spontaneous rebuttal—I had been with him constantly for three weeks, and I know he hadn't had time to set down a note—he delivered such an eloquent address that the audience, including those who had crowded the rooftops surrounding the little maidan, cheered him with remarkable gusto. Indeed, their applause continued during our drive back to the local guest house. Someone shouted, 'Turn on the light!' and the Governor obediently reached up and switched on the overhead bulb so they could see him.

" 'That's what they said last fall,' he said. ' "Turn on the light, Adlai, or we won't vote for you." ' He chuckled. 'I did—and they didn't.' "

When he returned August 20, with his seventeen-year-old son, John, and William Blair, his administrative assistant, Stevenson was greeted at a news conference by a roomful of 250 reporters and photographers.

He told them that the danger of world war had diminished and that the Western world was winning the cold war step by step. But "the bright image of America," he said, has been tarnished by "book burning, purges and invasions of executive responsibility." "While abroad," he said, "I have never criticized the Administration's handling of our foreign affairs; rather I have sought to explain American attitudes and positions when I had to and as best I could."

Then, after saying there was "no truth" to the report that the ambassadorship of Sweden had been offered to him, and declaring that he did not know if he would run for President in 1956, he left for Libertyville, Illinois.

A few weeks later, while Stevenson was preparing a report to the nation on his tour, an article in *The Times Magazine* described him this way:

Sitting, as likely as not in a tieless Brooks shirt, dungarees by Sweet-Orr, and loafers, on the screened terrace of a most agreeable country home—guardedly modern, with borrowings from ranch-style—on the banks of the Des Plaines River near Libertyville, Illinois, a few miles west of Lake Forest and twenty-odd north of Chicago, rising now and then to make himself a sandwich or chase the sheep out of the shrubbery, the man who failed to win the last Presidential election but handsomely succeeded in winning respect and admiration everywhere is sorting out his impressions of America and the world and turning over and over in his mind the question of what, precisely, a man in his unique and not altogether enviable position ought to do.

Before he left on his trip, Stevenson had written to a journalist who had praised him in a column, saying:

I can hardly believe I have the formidable destiny you assign me, and I must say that the future is a little bewildering to me. But "sufficient unto the day is the evil thereof," and I am not tempted to cross any bridges for the present, until I finish my appalling journey and have an opportunity to reappraise—that useful bureaucratic word—the situation.

So in Libertyville that month Stevenson sifted and weighed the experiences of the last thirteen months—and reappraised the situation. Even though his own prospects were uncertain, some tasks still presented themselves.

For one thing, he knew that liberalism had to seek out and define new issues. Some of his campaign advisers, most notably Arthur Schlesinger, Jr., had insisted that it was a mistake to have posed the election issues in terms of the early New Deal. Stevenson sought to remedy this. The new issues, he knew, were there; it was a problem of defining them.

On all sides in those days, Stevenson was besieged with advice, with invitations and with the importunings of those who saw him as the salvation of the Republic. These last bothered him; he trembled at the thought of becoming the involuntary leader of a cult. But to a reporter he said he thought that this would all come to an end before too long. "Give me a little time and I'll be sure to pierce my own armor."

In the two weeks after his return from abroad, Carole Evans, a trusted assistant, passed along 460 requests for speeches. These represented only the more fruitful possibilities; others already had been rejected.

Stevenson's aides in Chicago were adept, but not infallibly so, at blocking those who would visit Libertyville. For instance, a group of Yale students, on their way from the West Coast to New Haven, arrived in Libertyville and asked for an evening. The request was granted and both Stevenson and the students enjoyed the confrontation. Peace and quiet, Stevenson found, were relative.

Stevenson leaped back into partisan politics at a hundred-dollar-a-plate Democratic fund-raising dinner in Chicago on September 14. There, before fifteen hundred Democrats, he was again the titular leader, withering the Republicans with a barrage of quips and serious accusations.

He said the Administration had not confronted any major problems—labor, farm or foreign trade, for example—and that its attitude seemed to be "when in doubt appoint a commisssion" and take it up at the next session of Congress. "And the areas of doubt are very wide," he said. "I guess you might call it government by postponement."

Turning to foreign policy, he said he was surprised that the Republicans had not taken credit for scaring Stalin to death. But more seriously he deplored the fact that cuts in the armed forces had been followed by "threatening words in Asia." The Administration, Stevenson said, seemed to be saying to the Communists: "One false move by you guys and we'll cut the national defense budget by another billion dollars."

He went on:

"Our hour is too solemn for such partisan satisfaction. The structure of alliance is at issue. Moscow is using more seductive tactics. The world is weary, and we're on the threshold of momentous negotiations in Asia and Europe, Korea, China, Indochina, Germany. . . .

"The Administration, and it is our government as well as the Republicans', must make fateful decisions that affect us all. The job of the Democrats is to help in every way we can."

The next night, still in Chicago, but now under nonpartisan auspices, Stevenson presented a broadcast and televised report on his trip abroad. Much of it was a plea to the American people to awaken to the face of life overseas. He spoke of the "millions of refugees huddled in squalid camps and hovels stretching from Korea all the way across Asia—remnants, if you please, of many more victims of the wars, the revolutions, the intolerance and the savagery that have cursed our time on earth."

Then he said:

I wish I had an hour or more for Asia, for, if I may risk a prophecy, the hostile world is going to pay more and more attention to Asia, especially huge, uncommitted India.

And I suspect that as Europe's Eastern empires shrink, there will be left to us more of the burden of defense and of helping to guide the great forces which great changes have unleashed in Asia.

And again prophetically:

If I am not mistaken, holding our allies together is going to be an even harder job, which will tax mightily our patience, our resolve and our statesmanship. For we can't 'go it alone.' Unilateralism is but the new face of isolation and it spells disaster.

Looking to the future, it seems to me clearer than ever that the economic, the military and the political integration of Europe is the best hope for balancing Soviet power and for enabling the states of Europe to exercise a powerful, a positive and a peaceful influence in this modern world.

On the whole, Stevenson seemed to question the foreign policy of Secretary of State Dulles, though he never mentioned him. But he challenged directly Dulles' assertion that the time was not ripe for conferences with the Soviet Union at the highest level, and he pleaded for an attempt, at least, to negotiate.

[113]

He said:

If the Soviet Union rejects assurances of nonaggression, if the Red Army will not withdraw behind its borders, if an Austrian peace treaty and German unification are impossible except on Soviet terms, then we will at least have cleared the air. We will have resolved the uncertainties of many about Soviet sincerity and intentions. . . .

And at this moment a new fact confers a grim and pressing urgency on the international situation—the hydrogen bomb. For some years efforts toward the limitation and control of armaments have been stalemated.

Once more, I think, we should fix our sights high as we did in 1947, and resume the initiative in re-exploring the possibility of disarmament. The alternative to safety through an effective plan of arms limitation is safety through more massive spending and more frightening weapons development. . . .

In these circumstances it seems to me we should press forward— not under any foolish illusion that one grand conference would yield security, but rather with realistic recognition that the foundations of stability must be laid, stone by stone, with patient persistence. . . .

The quest for peace and tranquillity isn't a day's work; it is everlasting. We will have to learn to think of the responsibility of leadership not as a passing annoyance but as a status in an independent world that we Americans, Democrats and Republicans alike, must live in, trade in, work in, pray for and pray for in the accents of mercy, justice and faith in a power greater than ours or any man's.

It is difficult to assess the impact of the speech. Stevenson, some professional politicans said, was not a good "communicator." Truman, for one, later recalled that in a long discussion he had with Stevenson in the Blackstone Hotel in Chicago in the summer of 1956, Stevenson had plaintively asked: "What is it I am doing wrong?"

"I walked over to the window," Truman wrote.

Looking down, I saw a man standing at the hotel entrance. I beckoned to Stevenson and then, pointing down, said, "The thing you have got to do is to learn how to reach that man."

I was trying, as gently as I could, to tell this man—so gifted in speech and intellect, and yet apparently so uncertain of himself and remote from people—that he had to learn to communicate with the man in the street.

Perhaps Truman was right. Stevenson's style, which captivated the sophisticated minority, did not allow him to reach out and grab his audience or to leave it with a clear and unmistakable conviction. But he was one of the few persons in public life who could recognize and articulate the delicate shades and nuances of a complex problem.

Out of power, Stevenson did not suffer from having to make command decisions; he was free to express a viewpoint. No one can tell with assurance if that viewpoint ever swayed the Eisenhower Administration; indeed, sometimes the gap between the defeated candidate and the General was more superficial than deep, more style than substance.

But two of the threads that Stevenson the internationalist wove through his speech that night in Chicago were to appear and reappear throughout his public career: the first, the need to seek accommodation between the Western and Communist world; the second, the need to narrow the gap between the affluent and the impoverished nations. Certainly by making these questions subject to public debate Stevenson helped show the way toward a more enlightened, a less bellicose foreign policy other men could follow.

Another theme appeared in Stevenson's speech, too. "Everywhere," he said, "people think they recognize the dominant mood of America in what is called McCarthyism." Stevenson had been urged by a great many thoughtful people to assail McCarthy publicly, but he had been hesitant. By late 1953 there were signs that McCarthy's star was beginning to wane. The Senator still displayed a certain agility, still showered vituperation and innuendo on his chosen targets. But under a Republican Administration there were fewer targets.

Furthermore, many Republican politicians, if not overtly critical of McCarthy, were obviously cool to him. Stevenson knew that a public duel with the Senator would command headlines, perhaps enough of them to revivify McCarthy and rally other Republicans behind him. Accordingly, in the months ahead Stevenson concentrated his attack not on McCarthy but on what he construed as McCarthyism.

That fall, Republicans, led by Attorney General Herbert Brownell, Jr., criticized Truman's nomination of Harry Dexter White in 1946 to a high post in the International Monetary Fund after a report by the Federal Bureau of Investigation had identified him as an alleged espionage agent for the Soviet Union. The accusations offended Stevenson, and he chose to reply to them in Atlanta. A story by W. H. Lawrence began:

Adlai E. Stevenson declared today that the Eisenhower Administration could not long govern the nation and guide the world by "promise, postponement and slander."

Speaking in the heart of the South, to a joint session of the Georgia Legislature, Stevenson asserted that present-day Republicans were trying to hold power by employing the "identical tactics" of "Reconstruction days," by which they retained power for a generation after the Civil War.

Then they had waved "the bloody shirt," he said, and now they are waving "the red shirt," trying to "smear the Democratic Party

Adlai Ewing Stevenson, law student, 1926. (*The New York Times*)

Governor Stevenson of Illinois, 1952. (*Associated Press*)

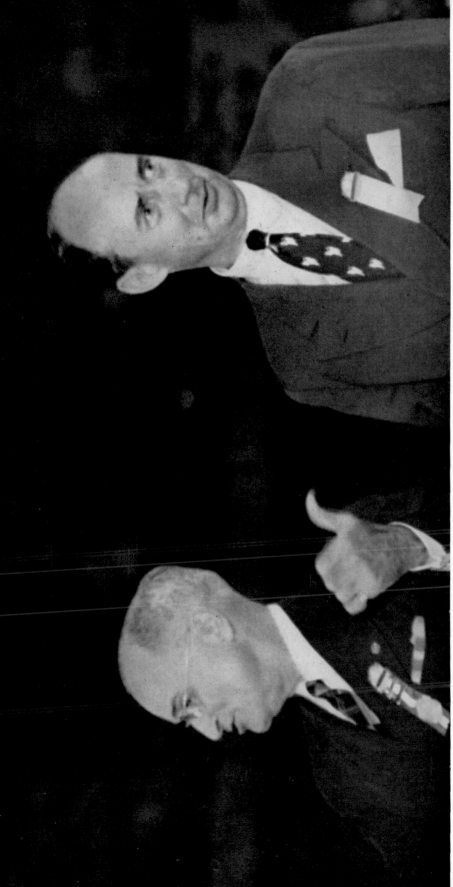

The President and the candidate. Truman presented Stevenson to the Democratic Party convention in 1952. (*Associated Press*)

Stevenson at a quiet moment on the Des Plaines River, Illinois, with his Dalmatian dog "Artie." (*John Fell Stevenson*)

The candidate addressed the American Legion convention in New York. (*The New York Times*)

He demonstrated his tennis form for photographers. (*Associated Press*)

On a campaign trip in Virginia, Stevenson handed his son Adlai 3d his commission as second lieutenant in the Marine Corps Reserve. (*Associated Press*)

He introduced sons Borden and John Fell to an audience in San Francisco. (*Associated Press*)

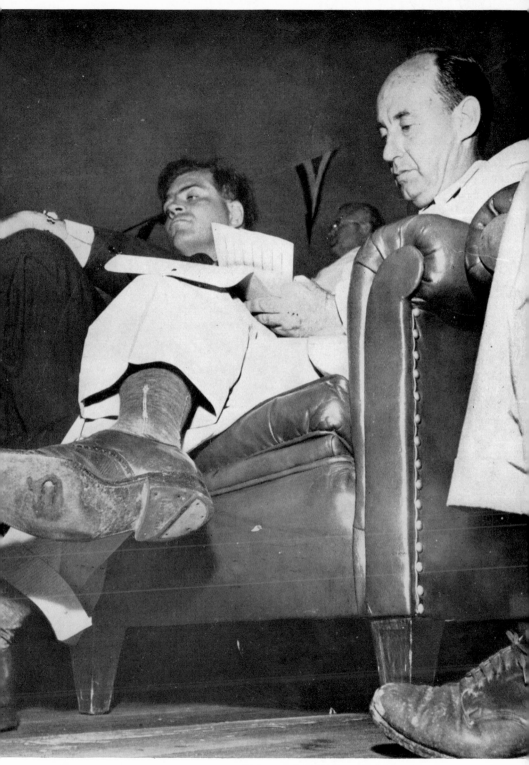

With Governor G. Mennen Williams of Michigan. The hole in Stevenson's shoe became a campaign symbol. (*Associated Press*)

On a world tour after his defeat in 1952, Stevenson was serenaded in a north Indian village. (*Associated Press*)

The defeated candidate obliged a photographer in Portland, Oregon, in 1954. (*Associated Press*)

DON'T BLAME ME!
I VOTED DEMOCRATIC

Hat in the ring. Stevenson announced late in 1955 that he wanted
to be his party's nominee again. (*Associated Press*)

Riding up Broadway in midtown Manhattan, Stevenson was accompanied by Governor W. Averell Harriman and Mayor Robert F. Wagner, the Democratic Senatorial nominee. (*The New York Times*)

During the 1956 campaign enthusiastic crowds surrounded the candidate in the West. (*The New York Times*)

And welcoming hands greeted him in Silver Springs, Maryland. (*Associated Press*)

On a motel patio in Winter Haven, Florida, Stevenson worked on a speech. (*The New York Times*)

He checked over his text before addressing an audience in New York. (*The New York Times*)

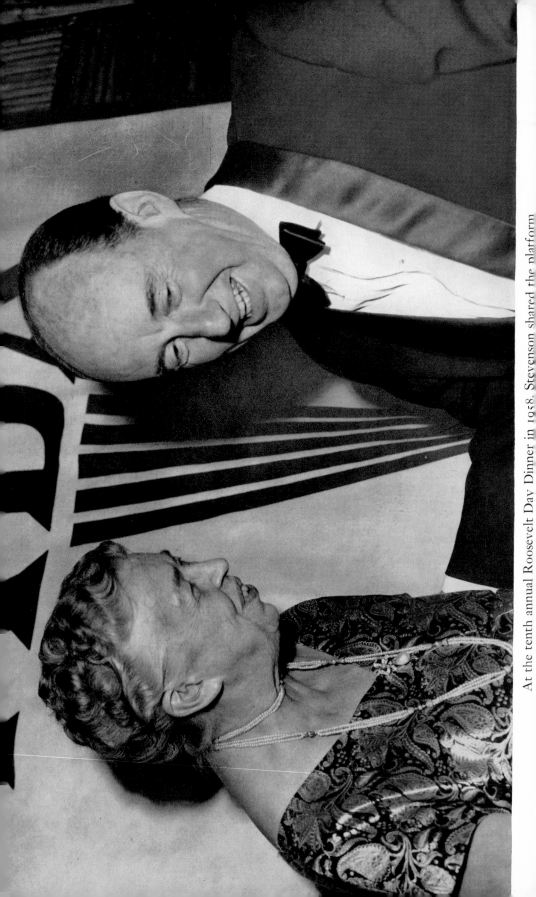

At the tenth annual Roosevelt Day Dinner in 1958, Stevenson shared the platform

Stevenson and Nikita Khrushchev were luncheon partners at the Roswell Garst farm, Coon Rapids, Iowa, in 1959. (*Associated Press*)

Khrushchev and friends: Stevenson, U.N. Ambassador Henry Cabot Lodge (behind Khrushchev), and Roswell Garst. (*Associated Press*)

Stevenson, shown here at a press conference, said that he was not a candidate for the Presidential nomination in 1960. (*The New York Times*)

President-elect Kennedy announced he had offered Stevenson the post of Ambassador to the U.N. (*Associated Press*)

U.N. Secretary General Dag Hammarskjöld and the new U.S. Ambassador in 1961. (*Associated Press*)

A busy day as Ambassador.
Left to right: Collecting
papers as he left home at
8:45. Catching up on mail
en route to his office.
Greeting Dr. V. K. Kya-
ruzi of Tanganyika. (*The
New York Times*)

Leaving at 7:00 for home,
where he dressed for a reception. (*The New York
Times*)

Still in dinner jacket, addressing the General Assembly's Political Committee at 9:05. (*The New York Times*)

At a committee meeting on disarmament with Andrei Gromyko of the U.S.S.R. (*George Rowen*)

Greeting delegates. Jaja A. Wachuku, chairman of the Nigerian delegation, is at right. (*The New York Times*)

In the Security Council. Secretary General U Thant, Stevenson aide Charles Yost, and Stevenson. (*The New York Times*)

In the General Assembly. Stevenson conferring with Dr. J. G. de Beus of The Netherlands. (*The New York Times*)

With President Kennedy at the first annual Joseph P. Kennedy Foundation Awards Dinner. (*The New York Times*)

Conferring with Carlos Sosa-Rodriguez of Venezuela. (*The New York Times*)

Addressing the Security Council during the Cuban missile crisis in 1962. (*The New York Times*)

Stevenson with President Johnson at the United Nations' twentieth-anniversary ceremonies in San Francisco, June 25, 1965. (*Associated Press*)

as the party of disloyalty" and make political capital of the case of
the late Harry Dexter White. . . .

He made a spirited defense of Truman as one "who has done
more than any living man to check the forward thrust of Communism and preserve the blessings of liberty for mankind. . . .

"General Eisenhower promised the people a new morality," he
said. "But his lieutenants have chosen their weapons without regard
for their effect on America's position in the world, or on the level of
political debate in our own halls, or on the level of political responsibility in our own hearts and consciences.

"They have taken McCarthyism away from McCarthy. What an
end to the great crusade!"

A few weeks later, in Philadelphia, he signaled out the
Attorney General for imputing "disloyalty or Communist
sympathy" to Truman in the White case. "The Bill of Rights
is besieged," he said, "ancient liberties infringed, reckless
words uttered, vigilante groups are formed, suspicion, mistrust and fear stalk the land, and political partisanship raises
strange and ugly heads, the security of secret files is violated, and the specter of a political police emerges."

Stevenson said, too, that since the advent of the Eisenhower Administration "four fears"—of depression, of Communism, of ourselves and of freedom itself—had replaced
the Four Freedoms once enunciated by President Roosevelt.
Despite this, Stevenson began the speech by commending
Eisenhower for advocating an international pool of atomic
energy and for reaffirming the desire of the United States for
peaceful, friendly relations with the Russian people. He also
applauded Secretary of State Dulles for rejecting Mc-
Carthy's demand that the United States cut off aid to all
nations still conducting trade with Red China.

The speech illustrated the persistence of the standard that

Stevenson had raised for himself after the election. In truth, there was very little that Eisenhower did of which he could approve unreservedly. But he was determined never to tarnish America's reputation or to debase the currency of political debate with gratuitous criticism. In a letter to a friend earlier in the year he had said: "I hope I can be constructive, but I also propose to be critical when I disagree. Indeed, I have been rather flattering myself about my temperance to date."

But by the spring of 1955 his public utterances about Eisenhower began to lose their temperance. The President, he was convinced, was failing in his appointed role. In a speech at Miami Beach, Stevenson said that a "group of political plungers" had persuaded Eisenhower that McCarthyism represented the Republican Party's "best formula for political success."

Stevenson spoke that night with great earnestness, but his alarm—and anger—were evident when he said: "Our State Department has been assailed and demoralized; the American voice abroad has been enfeebled; our educational system has been attacked; our press threatened; our servants of God maligned; the Executive departments invaded; our foreign policy confused; the President himself patronized, and now the integrity, loyalty and morale of the United States Army have been assailed."

It was not surprising, of course, that Stevenson would attack McCarthyism; that pattern of political behavior represented the antithesis of virtually everything he believed. But Stevenson had chosen the politically unpopular course of associating Eisenhower with the Senator, and this threatened to divide further the Democratic Party.

Three days before, Stephen A. Mitchell, Stevenson's per-

sonal choice as Democratic National Chairman, had announced on the eve of a party rally: "It is now time to make
President Eisenhower our target and charge him with full
responsibility for the actions of all Republicans."

This, however, did not please the Democratic patriarchs
in Congress. Senator Richard B. Russell of Georgia said simply: "That's Mr. Mitchell's opinion and he is entitled to
it."

Further, some Democrats, notably those in the South,
wanted to base the Congressional campaign that year and
the Presidential campaign two years later on issues other
than McCarthyism. Here, too, Stevenson took a contrary
view. He had chosen not to let the issue die.

A few weeks later Stevenson delivered the Godkin Lectures at Harvard University. The lectures, established in
1903 in memory of Edwin L. Godkin, editor of *The Nation*
and of *The New York Evening Post*, annually challenge an
outstanding man in public life to offer the best of his thinking.

On the first night that Stevenson spoke, students lined up
six hours for tickets. McCarthy had made Harvard a principal target of his allegations, but Stevenson dismissed the
Senator and concentrated on the broad theme of his three
lectures—"A Troubled World." The lectures were studded
with aphorisms that suggest his message:

> Only with self-mastery can we hope to master history. . . .
> It is a sign of strength, not of weakness, to be able to keep war
> limited. To generalize hostilities to a world scale would imperil the
> very institutions we seek to save by war. . . .
> In the foreground is the mortal struggle with world Communism.
> But in the background are the opaque, moving forms and shadows
> of a world revolution of which Communism is more the scavenger
> than the inspiration. . . .

Diplomacy is not the art of asserting ever more emphatically that attitudes [of other nations] should not be what they clearly are. It is not the repudiation of actuality but the recognition of actuality and the use of actuality to advance our national interests. . . .

I sometimes think that what America needs more than anything else is a hearing aid. . . .

Foreign policy is concerned with problems which lie beyond our jurisdiction and about which we cannot legislate. There are only two means available for influencing the actions of other states: persuasion and coercion. As a free society, we must rely primarily on persuasion. We can use coercion only rarely and usually only as a defensive measure.

In the lectures Stevenson was a little bolder than most politicians in discussing the Communist world, advancing the politically unpopular notion that relations could not always exist in frozen hostility.

"The United States," he said,

will soon have to formulate a reasoned policy with respect to China. We will shortly have to evolve the minimum conditions on which we are willing to live and let live with the Chinese Communists, with the possibility that, as in Europe, the ideological contest will go on for a long time. . . .

The point is not necessarily that we should support the admission to the United Nations of China or grant recognition or something else in exchange for a settlement. . . . The point is that we must not be imprisoned by our own passions, propaganda or pronouncements.

In a sense, the genius of Stevenson was aided and abetted by the time in which he lived. Reflective politicians were not prominent in the United States of the mid-fifties; the former Governor of Illinois nearly pre-empted the field. Furthermore, the entire West, at a time when it was most challenged and most needed the gift of eloquence, lacked leaders with the energy and ability to speak and write memorable English.

Churchill, for instance, had the ability, but in his later years not the energy; Eisenhower had extraordinary magnetism, but a lamentable tendency to scramble his syntax; Nehru had the gift of expression, and with it a divorcement from the reality of power politics; de Gaulle, who had both the ability and the energy, was at that time living quietly on his French estate.

So to Stevenson fell the task of defining democracy and its challenges. And in a remarkable speech he gave at Columbia University in June, 1954, he spoke of America's greatness—and its "national neurosis." He said, in part:

I am a great believer in national humility, modesty, self-examination and self-criticism, and I have preached these virtues vigorously, although, of course, I haven't practiced them. Of late I have been disturbed, as I am sure many of you have, by what seems to me to be the course at home and abroad of irrational criticism, abuse and mistrust of America, its conduct, its motives and its people.

I don't mean just the voices that have been raised, we thank God, in protest against our current deficiencies, against the attacks on academic freedom, the pressure for conformity, our failures abroad or the present wretched manifestations in Washington of our national neurosis.

Nor do I mean the wholesome and the continuous debate and self-examination that should and must go on among us and among allies; the candid controversy that makes for good neighbors and for good friends. Rather I am talking of the malice, distemper and the new fashion of being cynical, sarcastic, skeptical, deprecating about America or fellow Americans in large groups and therefore about America.

There are rising voices here and abroad that forget that although America occasionally gags on a gnat, it also has some talent for swallowing tigers whole; voices that tell us that our national energy is spent, that our old values have decayed, that it is futile to try to restore them.

There are voices that say that at best we are as Rome; that once our bridges, our skyscrapers, our factories and our weapons fall before the iron law of decay, no trace will be left—no great issues, no great cause to mark our past in universal history.

And there are voices that seem to say that we are as Carthage, that our vital principle is commerce, just commerce; our ethics, our politics, our imaginative faculties, they say, are all bent and twisted to serve our sovereign—commerce.

Other voices cry havoc, fear that America is not equal to the task; that Communism is the way to the future—is irresistible, just as Fascism was for them not so long ago.

Even novelists and poets seem to have been infected. The very excitement in a time of change and testing is suspect.

Now some of this talk may reflect a wholesome attitude abroad and a wholesome attitude here of self-criticism, if in a slightly fevered form. Some of it may even mark the reaction to the easy and the groundless optimism of the nineteenth century.

I don't know, but I do know that if we doubt ourselves we will persuade no one. If we doubt our mission in the world, we will do nothing to advance it. And if we are craven before the slanders that fill our ears we will secede from each other. But to view our present and our future with such sickly anxiety is to ignore the lessons and the achievements of our past.

For the plain truth is that we here in America have written the greatest success story in human history. The plain truth is that on the record of performance we here in America have in a few years made socialism obsolete, shown that Communism is nothing but a noisome, stagnant pool of reaction.

And it wasn't merely in 1776 that America left its footprints on eternity. For in our lifetime, we, the seventh generation of free and independent Americans, have given a tidal force to the forward roll of what was set in motion by the first generation.

If we but lift our heads for a moment above this storm of criticism, of abuse, doubt and "un-American activities," and survey the past fifty years, I think you will say with me "Hooray for America!"

The first and most obvious thing we have to cheer about is our material progress. The miracle of American mass production is commonplace. And under our capitalist system we have increased our wealth to an extent almost unimaginable fifty years ago, at the turn of the century.

Now this increase in our wealth has of course greatly changed our country. The change for the sake of change—as I've tried with a notable lack of success to point out to my countrymen—isn't worthy of applause. What matters is not that we have changed but how we have changed.

[Here Stevenson spoke of the vast increase in national wealth and of the more equitable distribution of national income.]

It is not in terms of money and products that we can see most clearly the change that America has undergone. Rather it is in the attitude of the people and in the role of the government. For we have succeeded not only in making our society prosperous but in keeping it fluid.

And, while this was easy enough in the days of the frontier, it seemed all but an idle dream by 1900. The frontier was closed; the homestead land was gone; women and children labored in dingy sweatshops, and robber barons plundered at will. Miners in company towns and immigrants compressed into filthy tenements were fast becoming a miserable proletariat.

How could the roads of opportunity be kept open? How, short of revolution, could we adjust modern capitalism to democratic ends? To many it seemed hopeless. Yet see what happened: the gap between rich and poor has been greatly narrowed without revolution, without socialism and without robbing A to give to B—although there may be some dissent to that downtown!

Our wealth has been mightily increased and better distributed. The rising tide has lifted all the boats.

How has this transformation been accomplished? By increasing productivity and by putting government to the service of the people. Woodrow Wilson, Theodore Roosevelt, Robert La Follette and so on led a revolt of the American conscience, followed by the reforms under Franklin Roosevelt. They've altered the face of America.

The child labor laws, wage and hour laws, the antitrust acts, banking legislation, rural electrification, soil conservation, Social

Security, unemployment compensation, the graduated income tax, inheritance taxes—it may be too much to say that all this and more amounts to a bloodless revolution, but it certainly amounts to a transformation of our economic and social life.

Now why was all this done? Why did America adopt the concept of man's responsibility for his fellow man? Our decision that the well-being of the least of us is the responsibility of all of us was, of course, not merely an economic and a political decision; it was, at bottom, a moral decision. And it was not, as some are now saying in the nation's capital, all a sinister conspiracy of the great philanthropic foundations.

It rested upon the conviction that it's the duty of the government to keep open to all the people the avenues of opportunity that stretched so broad and so far before us in the days of our frontier. It rested upon the conviction that the government must safeguard the people against catastrophe not of their making.

But this great decision has brought us face to face with vexing problems which have engaged your attention, as I understand it, during this past week—the problems of the conflict between freedom and security, between the individual and his social safeguards.

It seems to me there is something gallant about man's fight to become the master rather than the slave of nature; but there is something rather tragic about his struggle to keep himself free from the impositions of his own social creations.

Now it would be fatuous to claim that we are anywhere near solving this conflict, in my judgment, as it would be fatuous to say that because our material well-being increases year by year all must be well with America. It isn't.

Too many of our people still dwell in wretched slums or on worn-out land. Once again our top soil, our national skin, is blowing away out on the plains. Our schools and hospitals are overcrowded; so are our mental institutions and our prisons. Too many of our cities are wasting away from neglect. And how can we boast of our high estate when more than one of every ten citizens still do not enjoy fully equal opportunities?

Nonetheless our progress has been astonishing—more Americans are living better than ever before. The middle class, whose disappearance Marx so confidently predicted, has expanded as never before in the history of any other nation. And while the Communist conspirators fulminate about the cruel capitalists, the lackeys of Wall Street and the downtrodden masses, we have created a free society that promotes the general welfare of all far better, far more successfully than it has ever been promoted by any other system or social organization.

Briefly, I think America's record is terrific—if I may borrow a word from my junior son. And it is my view that its performance abroad is even more spectacular.

Since the turn of the century we have successively and emphatically renounced, first imperialism, then isolation, and finally our historical neutrality. We have transformed our foreign policy as completely as our domestic policy. Twice America has decisively tipped the scales for freedom in a mighty global exertion.

Instead of isolation, our policy is total involvement; instead of noncooperation, we have been the prime mover in the United Nations; instead of neutrality, we have organized the greatest defensive coalition in history. And in Korea we fought and bled almost alone for the United Nations and for collective security.

But this isn't all. In the process America has fathered three unprecedented ideas: Lend-Lease for Hitler's intended victims in war, the Marshall Plan for Stalin's intended victims in peace, and Point Four to help undeveloped areas. And to pay for it all Americans have borne a tax load, I mean a collected tax load, that is without counterpart save in Britain and that few beyond our borders appreciate.

And what have we asked in return? Why have we done all of this? Some will say self-interest, and there is truth in that because Communism follows the geography of human misery. Some will say magnanimity, and there is truth in that, too. For it would have been easy to go home as we did after the first war, or go it alone as some of our people have proposed.

Call it what you will; the point is to help others help themselves, to help make independence and democracy work, to share the burdens of the less fortunate, to raise the tide a little all around the world, lifting all of the boats with it, just as we have done here at home. It was bold and imaginative. It was wise and responsible; it was good for them and it was good for us. As Edmund Burke said: "Magnanimity is not seldom the truest wisdom."

Now, I have touched lightly, I know, on a vast subject and, while I emphatically approve and loudly cheer America's purposes abroad, past and present, I don't mean to imply for a moment that I approve any more than all of you do all of our foreign policies, past or present—especially present!

My purpose has been just to suggest the main outlines of a success story in which we can all take pride. As we look back to 1900 and look around us today, the infinite evidence of our creative impulses and of our vast achievements ought to be heralded, not mocked.

We have heard the "least of these." We have enlarged our vision, opened our heart, and we have disciplined our strength. We have turned it into a servant of justice—justice not alone for ourselves, but justice for the world-wide commonwealth of free men and of free institutions.

Here, indeed, is a case where mankind has a right to knowledge and to the use thereof—the knowledge of what America has done, how America has spread out the decision-making process, within its many parts.

It is the knowledge of how we have committed 160 million people to vast social projects, not by coercion, but by persuasion and consent, and by a balancing of the rights of the one with the needs of the many.

I say it is a grand and glorious story. On the basis of the record we have outperformed any rival proposals of Communism or of Fascism; and America has nobly accepted her responsibility and proudly met her time for greatness in a troubled age.

Why then all this abuse and criticism? Why then have we of late grown afraid of ourselves? Why have we of late acted as though the whole of this nation is a security risk? Why do you suppose we have given in to the bleatings of those who insist that it is dangerous for a man to have an idea? Why do we talk of saving ourselves by committing suicide—in the land of Jefferson?

So, having said: "Three cheers for America—you've done a great job of work," we have to add: "But look out, America, your work has just begun; though you've nobly grasped the present you could meanly lose the future."

What's the matter with us anyhow? The usual diagnosis is ignorance and fear. Ignorance leads many to confuse ends with means, to act as though material progress were an end in itself rather than a means to great and noble ends. This, I suggest, is the peril of our hardheaded, pragmatic attitude that has helped us so much to achieve our vast social and economic transformation, for if we ever succumb to materialism the meaning will go out of America.

And ignorance begets fear—the most subversive force of all. If America ever loses confidence in herself, she will retain the confidence of no one, and she will lose her chance to be free, because the fearful are never free.

But I wonder if all of these alarming concerns are not America's surface symptoms of something even deeper; of a moral and human crisis in the Western world which might even be compared to the fourth-, fifth- and sixth-century crisis when the Roman Empire was transformed into feudalism and primitive Christianity, early Christianity, into the structure of the Catholic Church, or the crisis a thousand years later when the feudal world exploded and the individual emerged with new relationships to God, to nature, to society.

I sometimes rather wonder if that sentence sounds as wise at Columbia as it did on the farm when I wrote it.

And now in our time in spite of our devotion to the ideas of religious and secular humanism, I wonder if we are in danger of falling into a spirit of materialism in which the aim of life is a never-ending increase of material comfort, and the result a moral and religious vacuum.

Is this leading, as lack of faith always must, to a deep sense of insecurity and a deterioration of reason? And I wonder, too, if today mass manipulation is not a greater danger than economic exploitation; if we are not in greater danger of becoming robots than slaves.

Since man cannot live by bread alone, is not the underlying crisis whether he is going to be inspired and motivated again by the ideas of the humanistic tradition of Western culture, or whether he falls for the new pagan religions, the worship of the state and a leader, as millions of believers in the Fascist and Soviet systems have already done?

That we are not invulnerable, that there is a moral and a human vacuum within us, is, I think, demonstrated by many symptoms, of which McCarthyism—which has succeeded in frightening so many —is only one.

But it is even more certain that there are millions who see or at least who dimly sense the danger, and who want to make life in its truly human meaning the main business of living; who want to express the humanistic tradition of reason and of human solidarity— who want to understand the truth and not be drawn into the mass manipulative influence of sentimentality and rationalization.

I venture to say that there are in the world many with a deep, intense longing for a vision of a better life not in a material but in a spiritual sense; for love, for human solidarity. There is a hunger to hear a word of truth, a longing for an ideal, a readiness for sacrifice. Churchill's famous speech at the beginning of the war is an illustration and so is the totalitarians' appeal to emotional forces rather than to material interests.

But the conventional appeal seems to be so often to the better life in material terms, I wonder if people are not eager to hear about the better life in human terms.

And I think that deep down the ideas of independence, of individuality, of free initiative, represent the strongest appeals to Americans who want to think for themselves, who don't want to be creatures of mass suggestion, who don't want to be automatons.

The question is, I suppose, whether the human and rational emotions can be aroused instead of the animal and irrational to which the totalitarians appeal. But fill the moral vacuum, the rational vacuum, we must; reconvert a population soaked in the spirit of materialism to the spirit of humanism we must, or bit by bit we too will take on the visage of our enemy, the neo-heathens.

I have said to you that in my judgment America has accomplished miracles at home and abroad, but that despite all of this wisdom, this exertion, this goodness, the horror of our time in history is that things are worse than ever before. There is no peace; we are besieged, we are rattled. Perhaps we are even passing through one of the great crises of history when man must make another mighty choice.

Beset by all of these doubts and difficulties, in which direction then do we look?

We look to ourselves—and we are not ashamed. We are proud of what freedom has wrought—the freedom to experiment, to inquire, to change, to invent. And we shall have to look exactly in the same directions to solve our problems now—to individual Americans, to their institutions, to their churches, to their governments, to their multifarious associations—and to all the free participants in the free life of a free people.

And we look, finally, to the free university whose function is the search for truth and its communication to succeeding generations. Only as that function is performed steadfastly, conscientiously and without interference does a university keep faith with the great humanist tradition of which it is a part.

For the university is the archive of the Western mind, it's the keeper of the Western culture, and the foundation of Western culture is freedom. Men may be born free; they cannot be born wise; and it is the duty of the university to make the free wise. The university is the guardian of our heritage, the teacher of our teachers. It's the dwelling place of the free mind.

More than one hundred years ago William Ellery Channing defined the free mind this way:

"I call that mind free which jealously guards its intellectual rights and powers, which calls no man master, which does not content itself with a passive or hereditary faith, which opens itself to light whencesoever it may come, and which receives new truth as an angel from heaven."

I wonder, my friends, how many of us fulfill Channing's definition. And I wonder if that could be part of our trouble today.

In the spring of 1954 Stevenson said that he would soon open a law office in Chicago and resume his private practice. But, of course, he again would neglect the law; the pressures on him in that election year were enormous.

In 1954 he made eighty speeches in states where Senatorial or gubernatorial seats were being contested. From September 18 to Election Day, November 2, he campaigned in thirty-three states and in Alaska. It was an exhausting performance, but for both Stevenson and his party the prizes were high.

The Republicans held a slender margin in the House of Representatives, 221 to 213 seats; a small shift would put the Democrats in the majority again. There were also twenty-four Democratic candidates for the Senate and eleven for governor. In the Senate the balance was even more precarious than in the House. Forty-eight Senators were Republican, forty-seven Democratic, with one independent.

Many political fortunes were entangled in the outcome of the election, but none were more apparent than those of Stevenson, Eisenhower and Nixon. A Republican victory would mean a mandate for the President; a Republican defeat would be a humiliation. Similarly, Nixon had made a personal referendum of the Congressional campaign. Republican victory would add to his stature as tactician and campaigner, and more firmly designate him as heir apparent to Eisenhower.

And Stevenson? He was leading the Democratic campaign and would have the largest part of the credit, or the greatest amount of blame. If successful he would be far ahead of all possible rivals for the Democratic nomination in 1956. Furthermore, in 1948, when he had been elected Governor, his running mate for the Senate was Paul Douglas, then an economics professor. Now, in 1954, Stevenson identified himself with Douglas' campaign for re-election and championed the Senator vigorously. A defeat for Douglas would revive memories of 1952, when Stevenson won only 44.9 percent of the vote in his home state against Eisenhower.

So Stevenson campaigned hard—sometimes with an extravagance of language—harder, perhaps, than he had fought for the Presidency.

In Charlotte, North Carolina, he said the Eisenhower Administration treated the American people as "targets of a sales campaign." In Indianapolis he said that the Democratic tide would end a twenty-month record of Republican failure. In Minneapolis he said that the Republicans had brought the nation to its most "precarious" position since World War II.

In Detroit he said that "while the American economy has been shrinking, the Soviet economy has been growing fast." In Los Angeles he said the real issue was whether Congress should be given the "proved leadership of the Democratic Party" or should continue under "a divided, quarrelsome, squabbling Republican regime." In San Francisco he said that the Administration had placed the "welfare of the right wing of the Republican Party above the welfare of the country."

And in Milwaukee he renewed the attack on an old foe:

"It looks as though the Great Crusade under the leadership of Snow White is going to end up this critical Congressional campaign on the elevated note of subversion, perversion and denunciation of former President Truman.

"I suppose that's what they call McCarthyism in a white collar."

The prepared text of the speech had read "under the leadership of the Vice President of the United States."

On Election Day the Democrats gained two seats in the

Senate, which made Lyndon Baines Johnson the new majority leader. In the House they picked up nineteen seats and
returned Sam Rayburn to the Speaker's chair. They also
added the unexpectedly high total of nine governors to their
party. And, in Illinois, Douglas led a Democratic victory
that included three additional House seats and a host of
state offices.

The next day Truman said gleefully that Stevenson was
his choice for the Presidency in 1956. (He was later to
recant.) Stevenson said he was pleased by this and by the
election results, but that he had no plans for new political
activity. "I have done what I could for the Democratic Party
in the past two years and now I shall have to be less active
and give more attention to my own affairs," he said.

But Stevenson was obviously the front-runner for another
nomination. To friends, neither he nor Eisenhower showed
enthusiasm for another campaign, but neither man emphatically ruled one out. So Democratic politicians, at least, were
convinced that it was Stevenson against the field for the
nomination. In regular public opinion polls and in those
taken privately for politicians, both of which Stevenson
derided, there was not even a close second to the former
Governor.

For a period after the election Stevenson attempted to
repair his law practice. He spoke to a party gathering in
Louisiana in December and then did not emerge for a major
speech until the following April. This was a warning that an
attempt to defend the Quemoy and Matsu islands off China
would probably find the United States standing alone and
facing a disastrous conflict.

He called for a declaration by the United States and its
allies that would condemn the use of force in the Formosa

Strait while pledging to defend the Chinese Nationalist island of Taiwan. The speech, he said, had been prompted by his deep concern over the worsening situation in the Far East and by demands that he express his views on the crisis.

The demands, however, had not come from Democratic Congressional leaders; neither had they come from Administration leaders who sought to enlist his support. Despite his political stature in this time of bipartisan foreign policy, Stevenson had not been consulted by Dulles on a single foreign policy move since the advent of the Eisenhower Administration.

And, even more surprisingly, Stevenson's own Congressional leaders were neither passing on to him the information they received from the State and Defense Departments nor consulting him on party moves in foreign policy. These Democratic leaders and committee chairmen on Capitol Hill, no longer under the discipline of a Democratic President, were enjoying a new freedom, and each was exercising it as he saw fit. Stevenson did not complain about this—his public statements on party affairs were usually conciliatory —but it placed his titular leadership under another handicap and subtly lessened the role he might have played in national affairs.

By the early summer of 1955, it was apparent to all that Stevenson would again be a candidate for the Presidential nomination. He had not committed himself, he had not established an organization, but it was obvious that he was preparing for a long and difficult fight. Again, however, his relations with Congressional Democrats were difficult. Under the heading "Adlai's Not Reluctant but He Sure Is Puzzled," James Reston wrote:

Adlai Stevenson is finding that it is extremely difficult to run for the Presidency without the facilities and trappings of public office.

He is going to run all right, but he is having his troubles. He has no staff to speak of. He has no funds. He has no political organization, and he is almost entirely out of touch with the political leaders of the Democratic Party on Capitol Hill.

This last point puzzles him. He reads in the papers that this prominent Democrat in Washington is for him and that prominent Democrat has just come out for him, but when he sees these same gentlemen, they say nothing to him about the campaign; they do not urge him to run or even inquire about his plans for 1956. . . .

On two occasions recently he has spent several hours with Democratic legislative leaders in Washington. Everybody was very pleasant. There was a lot of talk about the Republican legislative program, and the conversation was dominated by the problems faced by the Democrats on the Hill. But nobody mentioned the campaign of 1956 or indicated that Mr. Stevenson might have some interest in it.

In another conversation with a prominent Democrat in Washington, the subject did come up and the Democratic legislator said he was going to be for Stevenson in 1956. Mr. Stevenson recalled that the same thing had been said in 1952 but that the legislator had not taken part in the campaign.

Stevenson inquired what "being for him" in 1956 would mean. For example, would he campaign for him in Texas? The reply was that the legislator could not commit himself. He might have an awkward situation in his own state, so he couldn't tell.

Stevenson was a seasoned politician, but also an atypical one. He did not like to improvise. He wanted the party's legislative program and its political strategy to be coordinated and, though publicly silent, he was again bothered by the quirks and vagaries of Presidential politics.

Consequently, Stevenson did not announce his candidacy until November 15. Through the summer, however, he cre-

ated his own group of advisers, headed by Thomas K. Finletter, which worked spasmodically as a kind of planning
staff.

By October, Eisenhower, who, in an earlier burst of
Republican rhetoric, had been hailed as the "indispensable
man," was recuperating from a heart attack in Denver. It
was not known if he would be able to run again, or even if
he would choose to finish out his term. Truman now appeared to be leaning toward Governor Averell Harriman for
the nomination, while Estes Kefauver of Tennessee was
exerting his charm on voters in general and Democratic officials in particular.

When Stevenson formally announced his candidacy,
which, he acknowledged, was hardly a surprise, he offered
three main reasons for his decision:

In the first place, I believe it important for the Democratic Party
to resume the executive direction of our national affairs.

Second, I am assured that my candidacy would be welcomed by
representative people in and out of my party throughout the country.

Third, I believe any citizen should make whatever contribution
he can to the search for a safer, saner world.

At a news conference the next day, Stevenson proclaimed
a policy of "no deals" in return for promises of support by
potential Vice Presidential candidates. He said that if Eisenhower were the Republican candidate he would not make
his health a campaign issue, and he said that he would enter
the Minnesota primary in March.

Through it all Stevenson appeared relaxed, pleased with
himself, more at ease than he had been in similar situations
four years before. However, new pressures were arising.

In a story that week, Reston noted:

Almost everybody conceded that Mr. Stevenson was so far ahead that nobody was likely to take the nomination away from him, but the right and left wings of the party were trying to pressure him into running down their side of the road.

Former President Truman, Governor Harriman of New York and Senator Estes Kefauver all were clearly trying to push him into a rougher and more progressive campaign by their speeches at the stockyards Saturday night.

Knowing this, the more moderate and conservative elements in the party, who were not much in evidence here, were talking about running Governor Frank J. Lausche of Ohio or Senator Stuart Symington of Missouri. But the purpose of this was not to defeat Stevenson but to influence him. That is what most of the shouting is about.

Stevenson, however, clung to moderation. "I agree," he said, "that this is a time for catching our breath. I agree that moderation is the spirit of our times." But moderation, which is incapable of a precise definition, was not the spirit of all the people, and by February Stevenson knew it.

In Los Angeles, before a Negro audience, Stevenson was asked if he would use the Army—and Navy, if necessary—to enforce the Supreme Court decision forbidding segregation in public schools. He said: "I think that would be a great mistake. That is exactly what brought on the Civil War. It can't be done by troops or bayonets. We must proceed gradually, not upsetting habits or traditions that are older than the Republic."

There was a murmur of protest in the crowd, and one Negro said: "I think he is a phony."

Later he said he would not favor a suspension of Federal aid from segregated school districts, declaring that the greatest impetus to better race relations would be a strengthened educational system. "You should not cut off your nose to spite your face," he declared.

"Can you imagine that?" a Negro asked his companion.

A few days earlier Stevenson had said that he would try "to fool no one—not with false promises or easy answers to hard problems. . . . I must frankly add to what I've said about myself that it is quite possible that I should not be the best candidate for you, if winning is the first objective of any political race, because I have an allergy for holiday promises."

So Stevenson rejected the easy answers, and perhaps the right ones, too. Shortly after his confrontation with the Negro group he called for removal of the desegregation issue from the campaign, a proposal with which Eisenhower was in obvious agreement.

Nixon, however, pinned a party badge on Earl Warren when he said that "a great Republican Chief Justice, Earl Warren, has ordered an end to racial segregation in the nation's schools," and both Harriman and Kefauver vocally advocated Federal sanctions to achieve equality. Stevenson's eloquence was never able to still the debate. Indeed, at the end of February he strengthened his position on civil rights by saying that the Supreme Court decision on school desegregation did not permit "repudiation or rejection." Then he added:

We are, as a people, at the very dawn of one of our brightest days—the day of full democracy in our public schools. This may well be one of the greatest accomplishments of our generation.

Not as a Democrat but as an American, not as a candidate but as a citizen, I pray to God that this day may not be marred nor this achievement poisoned by the bitterness of any who would assert views, no matter how deeply felt, against the laws of the land and of humanity.

The first real indication of serious trouble for Stevenson came not in a civil rights clash but in the New Hampshire primary in mid-March. Kefauver won all twelve convention delegates with 21,604 votes. Stevenson received only 4,016 votes.

Of course, Stevenson had not campaigned in New Hampshire and had not even formally entered the primary. Friends had entered him in the contest without his overt consent and they campaigned in his behalf. It was a minor victory, but it gave the small Kefauver entourage a psychological boost. The real test was to be in the Minnesota primary, and here Stevenson, with the unstinting support of the state Democratic organization, was heavily favored.

But the day after the primary, *The Times* story by Richard J. H. Johnston began:

> Senator Estes Kefauver of Tennessee scored an upset victory over Adlai E. Stevenson in yesterday's Presidential preference primary in Minnesota.
>
> Not only did he appear to have racked up a majority of 57 percent of the popular vote over his opponent, but the Tennessean also left his adversary with a possible total of only six district delegates as he took all thirty-nine delegates-at-large.
>
> A prediction of the final outcome, based on more than a third of the state's 3,808 voting districts, indicated that Mr. Stevenson would lose by about 68,000 votes in the popular tally.

Many reasons were advanced for Stevenson's loss: Republicans had crossed over and voted for Kefauver because they thought he would be easier to beat in November; Kefauver was a smashing campaigner, Stevenson was not; Stevenson simply could not win an election; there was a ground swell for Kefauver.

After Minnesota, Stevenson said—in a tone of grievance mixed with impatience—that he had hoped the contest between him and Kefauver would have been based on issues. But unfortunately there were few issues that could have differentiated the two. And so Stevenson, battling for political survival, drew the obvious conclusion: the Senator's handshaking campaign was effective; his own style of formal speechmaking was not. There were three remaining primaries—in Florida, in Oregon and in California—and to win he had to adapt his campaign style to the Senator's. Even if Kefauver won all the primaries he probably could not take the nomination: too many party bosses simply did not like him. But he could certainly deny the nomination to Stevenson.

In Florida, in particular, the primary campaign became handshake against handshake, smile against smile. Stevenson made a few formal speeches and so did Kefauver. But most of the speaking was the five- or ten-minute impromptu talk from the courthouse or the bandstand in the square. The press and many politicians began to make much of the "new" Stevenson, who now was campaigning with all smiles, affability, even with cowboy music, but, underneath, the candidate was as sophisticated and witty as ever.

"I'm a Republican from Pennsylvania," one old woman told Stevenson. "Personally," the candidate replied, "I believe in the forgiveness of sin."

On May 19 Stevenson scored a write-in victory over Kefauver in Oregon. The psychological lift was important after the Minnesota defeat. In Florida, meanwhile, the campaign had become oddly bitter. The unpleasantness began when Millard Caldwell, a former Governor and an active campaigner for Stevenson, gave a speech in which he described Kefauver as an "integrationist" and a "sycophant of the Negro vote."

Stevenson, who was seated on the same platform as Caldwell, did not disclaim the remarks, and Kefauver subsequently said he was surprised that Stevenson had stood by and allowed "that kind of scurrilous attack." It was the first of a series of charges that was to grow increasingly bitter.

Stevenson won in Florida, but the turnout was too small to be indicative and the margin of victory was slim. The big test was to be in California on June 5. Sixty-eight votes at the Democratic National Convention were at stake.

Almost from the beginning of the California campaign Stevenson and Kefauver were making speeches that sounded remarkably similar, so thoroughly had they covered the field and so closely did they appear to agree on major issues. Only during the last week did the tactics change. Kefauver began to attack, as he had in Florida, using what Stevenson called "distortions," "abuse" and "misrepresentations."

Stevenson abandoned the style he had used in Florida and again relied more on formal speeches. He said that Nixon, a Californian, was disqualified by his "irresponsibility" to be a spokesman for the United States and had "poisoned four successive election campaigns." He said that he was unsatisfied by the nation's military posture, and he repeated his contention that the United States was losing the cold war.

In a state that was hard pressed to meet the needs of its rapidly growing population he advocated a program of low-interest Federal loans to advance the cause of voluntary prepaid health insurance. He would not be deterred, he said, "by the weary cry of socialism" from doing what had to be done to develop "a people's program for their own health." A few days later he advocated Federal aid to remedy the shortage of teachers and trained scientific talent. He called for an outlay of at least fifty million dollars a year in matching funds to states to improve teachers' salaries and training, a system of government scholarships to students in return for postgraduation terms of teaching, and a Federal research program on such matters as the ability to learn.

On Election Day it was Stevenson by a huge margin. He won both the rural and urban vote, and would enter the convention as the overwhelming favorite.

CHAPTER V

REMATCH WITH EISENHOWER

I N THE SUMMER of 1952 Stevenson wanted most of all to
be Governor of Illinois. Now, in the sweltering August
of 1956, he wanted most of all to be his party's nominee for
President. So when the first Democratic delegates arrived in
Chicago they found him already there, calm, working hard,
exuding confidence and seemingly enjoying himself. He was,
moreover, available to any who wanted to visit him, and he
was full of small talk and pleasantries.

But there was a difference between this convention and
the one four years earlier. Whereas in 1952 the party was
generally united and prepared to yield to President Truman's wishes, now there was restiveness and division, especially among the Southerners, who were perturbed over civil
rights. There was also a feeling among other delegates, particularly those who were professional politicians, that a once-
defeated Stevenson could too easily be twice defeated. The
delegates, too, realized that Eisenhower was a popular President, most difficult to dislodge. A mood of unsureness, even
pettiness, was in the air.

The first breach came almost casually. The convention was to open on Monday, August 13. On the preceding Wednesday Stevenson was interviewed by a roving television crew on La Salle Street. He was asked if he would make a direct approach to the convention's resolutions committee about the platform plank on civil rights. Stevenson said he had already expressed "some views" about it.

"Is your stand as before—one of moderation?"

"I don't know what that means," Stevenson replied. "No one has ever defined it for me."

"That puzzles a lot of us, sir."

"I've had a very strong feeling that the platform should express unequivocal support of the [Supreme] Court's decision [on school desegregation], though it seems odd that you have to express approval of the Constitution and its institutions," Stevenson said.

Then he was reminded that Paul Butler, the new Democratic National Chairman, had said he thought the platform committee would write a stronger proposal on civil rights than it had in 1952.

"I hope so," Stevenson said. "I should hope so."

Almost immediately the chairman of the Georgia delegation said that Stevenson had "committed a stupid blunder." Senator Sam J. Ervin of South Carolina said this "might cost him the election," and Governor James P. Coleman suggested that Mississippi might have to look elsewhere for a candidate.

The next jab came three days later from Truman himself, the man who played a decisive role in obtaining the nomination for Stevenson in '52. The former President announced that "the man best qualified to be the next President of the United States is Governor Harriman of New York."

Harriman supporters were elated. "It's now the Harriman bandwagon rolling to victory," Lloyd Benefield, a Harriman aide, said. "President Truman's statement has much wider meaning than the endorsement of Governor Harriman as a candidate. It means a shift in the dominating spirit of this convention—from one of defeatism concerning the possibility of beating Eisenhower in November to one of conviction that we can and will win." Then he went on to forecast that Harriman might have as many as five hundred votes on the first ballot.

On the day Truman announced his preference, Senator Lyndon B. Johnson of Texas said that he was a "serious candidate," thus inviting Southern leaders to pool their votes behind him. Spokesmen for several Southern delegations that had been counted friendly to Stevenson now said they might switch to Johnson. If these blocs held for as many as three ballots, Stevenson's chance for nomination might vanish, while a compromise candidate, perhaps Senator Stuart Symington of Missouri, might win.

Through it all Stevenson remained confident. The Southern uneasiness and the Johnson candidacy were not threatening, Stevenson's advisers decided. Truman offered a more immediate problem. Stevenson received a steady flow of advisers, supporters and staff members, who agreed that Truman's move would not have a major impact. William M. Blair wrote:

Adlai E. Stevenson displayed to friends and advisers tonight a sense of relief that former President Truman had made a choice.

He was, as his intimates reported, "out from under" Mr. Truman, whose shadow he had dogged for four years. While the welcome relief dominated the Stevenson campaign headquarters, Mr. Stevenson and his followers also showed a keen awareness of the perils ahead in the fight for renomination as the Democratic Presidential candidate.

Four years ago Mr. Stevenson brooded over Mr. Truman's "give 'em hell" role in the 1952 campaign against President Eisenhower. Long after the election he wondered whether Mr. Truman had cost him the election. . . .

When Mr. Truman made his announcement, Mr. Stevenson said:

"President Truman's announcement in no way alters my respect and regard for him, and I am grateful for the many kind things he has said about me in the past. . . .

"I am sure we agree that our party must and will win in November and that only liberal Democratic leadership can restore America's waning influence in the world and take advantage of our great opportunity for social progress at home.

"I expect to be the candidate."

A few years later Truman wrote that long before the 1956 convention opened he saw signs "that Stevenson was still embarrassed by this farmer from Missouri" and therefore he wanted to "make it easier for Stevenson to disassociate himself from me politically."

"As a first move," Truman wrote,

I began to consider endorsing some other candidate. I decided on Governor Averell Harriman of New York. His many years of service to the country in capacities ranging from ambassador to Cabinet officer, and his unflinching loyalty to the New Deal and the Fair Deal, entitled him to be taken seriously as a Presidential candidate. I realized that, in all fairness to Harriman, I had to point out to him that he would have almost insurmountable difficulties in getting the convention to nominate him. The convention was pretty much a cut-and-dried affair for Stevenson. Harriman, deserving as he was, could only be a long shot, even if there were hope of making the convention an open one.

The day after Truman announced his choice Mrs. Franklin D. Roosevelt gently rebuked him. "We must have a candidate who is prepared to go forward," she told a news conference, and she then defended Stevenson against Truman's indirect criticism. She also hinted that Truman might be seeking to cast the convention into a deadlock so that Symington might be the nominee. Then Mrs. Roosevelt, wearing a big button that said "Adlai," whisked across the street to a hotel where she had lunch with Truman.

All this, however, was side show. Under the headline "The Stakes at Chicago," James Reston observed in a column:

> Nothing is certain in a national political convention except total exhaustion, but the question tonight seemed to be not whether Adlai E. Stevenson would win but whether the conservative Southerners or the liberal Northerners would provide the winning margin.
>
> The main fight now is not primarily over the Presidential nomination but over the wording of the civil rights plank in the platform and the identity of the Vice Presidential nominee.
>
> Harry Truman, the Goliath who set out to slay David, has succeeded only in knocking himself out. Or to change the metaphor, he has huffed and puffed and blown down Governor Averell Harriman. And by his angry outburst against Stevenson today he has minimized, if he has not ended, his future campaigning in any Stevenson race.
>
> There remains, however, one even greater paradox in the Truman-Harriman adventure. They joined forces here to drive Stevenson to the left, to make him more liberal and less devoted to the policies and tactics of moderation.
>
> What they have done is to minimize his freedom of action just when he was taking a more liberal line on the civil rights question, and to force him to consider an alliance with the South which would force him to backtrack on his appeal for an unequivocal endorsement of the Supreme Court decision in the platform.

Truman's move against Stevenson, though it was to be ineffectual, did throw the convention into some confusion. Johnson, when he announced himself as a "serious candidate," was urged to join a stop-Stevenson coalition. He was invited to address a number of state delegations and was offered the support of a sizable bloc of votes in twelve states.

Johnson refused. He told Stevenson in private that he would not try to stop him, and he appealed for a civil rights plank in the platform that would be acceptable to both North and South. At the same time, delegations from Michigan, Ohio, Pennsylvania and New Jersey, conscious that the Truman-Harriman tactics had failed and apprehensive over the possibility that the South might provide Stevenson with the margin of victory, began falling into line.

Stevenson himself sought a more meaningful compromise than any that had appeared before between the Northern and Southern sections of the party. The delegates had been parading, shouting and intriguing since their arrival in Chicago, but now in a thousand hotel rooms around the Loop they were settling on compromises that Stevenson could eventually articulate to a nation that clearly was in no mood for daring solutions.

The platform reflected this. The rights plank, for example, pledged the party to "continue its efforts to eliminate illegal discriminations of all kinds, in relation to (1) full rights to vote; (2) full rights to engage in gainful occupations; (3) full rights to enjoy security of the person; and (4) full rights to education in all publicly supported institutions."

However, the key part of the plank said: "We will continue our efforts to eradicate discrimination based on race, religion or national origin. Recent decisions of the Supreme Court . . . have brought consequences of vast importance. . . . We reject all proposals for the use of force to interfere with orderly determination of these matters by the courts."

By latter-day standards the plank seems pallid. Moreover, the cherished hope of offending neither Negroes nor liberal whites would fail.

The platform as a whole, aside from the civil rights section, was vaguely progressive. The most specific plank, in terms of domestic political advantage, dealt with agriculture. Here the Democrats promised to "undertake immediately by appropriate action to regain the full 100 percent of parity the farmers received under Democratic Administrations." As for labor, the Democrats went on record for outright repeal of the Taft-Hartley Act, which Congress scarcely had tampered with in eight years. They also carried forward the traditional Democratic issue of public versus private power by praising public development.

These were standard issues, causing no delegate much discomfort. Foreign policy, however, was something else. Stevenson had spent the last four years preaching accommodation and condemning the Republicans for threatening the Soviet world and freezing relations with Red China. The convention, furthermore, had called together the party's foreign policy experts—including Dean Acheson, Chester Bowles, Paul Nitze, Thomas Finletter and Ben Cohen—and they had advised the platform writers of the virtues of flexibility and moderation.

But these experts did not prevail. The platform writers promised to supply arms to Israel in her struggle with the Arabs, pledged "determined opposition to the admission of Red China to the United Nations" and derided the Republicans for "fraternizing with Communists."

If Stevenson was made uncomfortable by any of this, it was not apparent. He had rejected the advice of those who wanted him to argue publicly with Truman. Now he re-

jected those who wanted him to take issue with the platform. He only suggested mildly that he would have preferred a stronger civil rights plank. The nomination was the
thing, and it proved surprisingly easy.

On the night of August 16 ten candidates were nominated
Two of them dropped out before the balloting began. When
the spokesman for the Pennsylvania delegation announced
that its 67 votes had "put Mr. Stevenson over the top," the
delegates and spectators roared and Chairman Rayburn
stepped forward to command, "No parade now." At the end
of the balloting, Stevenson had won 905½ votes, with only
686½ needed for victory. Harriman was a poor second with
210 votes and Johnson, with only Texas and Mississippi, had
80.

After the inevitable demonstration Governor Raymond
Gary of Oklahoma, who had placed Harriman in nomination, moved to give Stevenson the unanimous support of the
convention. Rayburn put the question as one of choosing the
nominee by acclamation, and there was a massive roar of
"aye." "There are no noes," announced Rayburn without
asking for them.

Stevenson appeared and said:

"I have concluded to depart from precedents of the past. I
have decided the selection of a Vice Presidential candidate
should be made through the free processes of this convention so that the Democratic Party's candidate for this great
office can appear before the nation, not as one man's selection, but as the choice of the party, even as I have been
chosen.

"The choice will be yours. The profit will be the nation's."

The next day Kefauver gained the nomination by the
slimmest of margins. After the second roll call of states had

been completed, but before the result had been announced, Senator John F. Kennedy of Massachusetts had 648 votes—38½ votes short of the required majority, but far ahead of Kefauver. Then the states began to wave their standards to switch their votes. The lead seesawed until Senator Albert Gore of Tennessee, who was running third, withdrew in favor of Kefauver. That settled it.

That night Truman, who earlier had said that Stevenson was "too defeatist to win," and who had been pronouncing Kefauver "cowfever" in private conversations, told the delegates that Stevenson was "a real fighter" and Kefauver "an able and efficient running mate." Kefauver, owl-eyed behind his vast horn-rimmed glasses, said that Stevenson, whom he had bitterly fought in a long primary campaign, "had made unique contributions to the philosophy and tone of politics."

Stevenson, in turn, used the occasion to praise his colleagues and to deliver a plea for the "New America." He said:

> In our hearts we know that the horizons of the New America are as endless, its promise as staggering in its richness as the unfolding miracle of human knowledge. America renews itself with every forward thrust of the human mind.
>
> We live in a second industrial revolution; we live at a time when the powers of the atom are about to be harnessed for ever greater production. We live at a time when even the ancient specter of hunger is vanishing. This is the age of abundance! Never in history has there been such an opportunity to show what we can do to improve the quality of living now that the old terrible, grinding anxieties of daily bread, of shelter and raiment are disappearing. With leadership, Democratic leadership, we can do justice to our children, we can repair the ravages of time and neglect in our schools. We can and we will!
>
> With leadership, Democratic leadership, we can restore the vitality of the American family farm. We can preserve the position of

the small business without injury to the large. We can strengthen labor unions and collective bargaining as vital institutions in a free economy. We can, and our party history proves that we will!

With leadership, Democratic leadership, we can conserve our resources of land and forest and water and develop them for the benefit of all. We can, and the record shows that we will!

All these things we can do and we will. But in the international field the timing is only partially our own. Here the "unrepentant minute," once missed, may be missed forever. Other forces, growing yearly in potency, dispute with us the direction of our times. Here more than anywhere guidance and illumination are needed in the terrifying century of the hydrogen bomb. Here more than anywhere we must move, and rapidly, to repair the ravages of the past four years to America's repute and influence abroad.

We must move with speed and confidence to reverse the spread of Communism. We must strengthen the political and economic fabric of our alliances. We must launch new programs to meet the challenge of the vast social revolution that is sweeping the world and that has liberated more than half the human race in barely a generation. We must turn the violent forces of change to the side of freedom.

We must protect the new nations in the exercise of their full independence; and we must help other peoples out of Communist or colonial servitude along the hard road to freedom.

And we must place our nation where it belongs in the eyes of the world—at the head of the struggle for peace. For in this nuclear age peace is no longer a visionary ideal. It has become an absolute, imperative, practical necessity. Humanity's long struggle against war has to be won and won now. Yes, and I say it can be won!

It is time to listen again to our hearts, to speak again of our ideals, to be again our own selves.

There is a spiritual hunger in the world today and it cannot be satisfied by material things alone—by better cars or longer credit terms. Our forebears came here to worship God. We must not let our aspirations so diminish that our worship becomes rather of material achievement and bigness.

For a century and a half the Democratic Party has been the party of respect for people, of reverence for life, of hope for each child's future, of belief that "the highest revelation is that God is in every man."

Once we were not ashamed in this country to be idealists. Once we were proud to confess that an American is a man who wants peace and believes in a better future and loves his fellow man. We must reclaim these great Christian and humane ideas. We must dare to say again that the American cause is the cause of all mankind.

If we are to make honest citizens of our hearts, we must unite them again to the ideals in which they have always believed and give those ideals the courage of our tongues.

Standing as we do here tonight at this great fork of history, may we never be silenced, may we never lose our faith in freedom and the better destiny of man.

Good-bye—and I hope we can meet again in every town and village of America.

This call for a New America was the start of Stevenson's campaign. It was to be different from that of 1952: Stevenson would attack. Eisenhower and his party were no longer challengers to be beaten off but entrenched rivals to be dislodged. And the issues? Most of Stevenson's advisers believed that the main emphasis should be on domestic policy —underlining the Democratic Party as the one that had led the nation out of the Depression. Too much discussion of foreign policy, they believed, would only remind the voters that the United States had gone to war several times under Democratic administrations.

Stevenson wanted his campaign to center on the program for a New America, but he also believed that foreign policy presented the country with its most important choices. He agreed to minimize foreign affairs, but as the campaign wore on, his emphasis shifted and the military draft and hydrogen bomb testing came to occupy the spotlight.

A week after the Democratic convention, Republicans met

in San Francisco to renominate Eisenhower and Nixon. The two conventions could not have been in greater contrast. At San Francisco the party was dominated by the massive, monolithic Eisenhower wing; the President's wish was the convention's command. Neither Eisenhower's heart attack of the year before nor the fact that he would be sixty-six years old when he began a second term was an issue.

The platform, too, was prepared quietly and without difficulty. For the most part it was simply a reflection of the President's personality and record. The delegates plainly liked Ike, and if they did not like Nixon quite so well it hardly mattered. Harold Stassen made a feeble attempt to force the Vice President into a contest for renomination and succeeded only in casting himself further into political limbo.

By Stevenson's own reckoning, he officially opened his campaign at Santa Fe, New Mexico, on August 27, when he and Kefauver met with party leaders from seven Western states. Democrats said the event marked the start of the "greatest grass-roots campaign in all political history." Certainly the patrician, reflective man from Bloomington, Illinois, had made huge advances in four years as a campaigner, but he still trailed Kefauver in campaign hokum. In Santa Fe that day *The Times* reporter wrote that "the Tennessean was several hundred handshakes ahead and a half-hour behind Mr. Stevenson after they had appeared together in the Old Plaza near the Governor's palace of Spanish and Territorial days."

A week after that trip, Cabell Phillips wrote in *The Times Magazine:*

Quite a lot of moonshine has been uttered of late about this "new Stevenson," leading some to the impression that he has become a sort of Ivy League Frank Skeffington, slapping backs, kissing babies and spouting solemnly in words of not more than two syllables. No such bogus transformation has occurred.

Observing him in action, I was impressed by the fact that he looks to be much the same Adlai that he was four years ago. He is somewhat thicker around the waist—his profile is vaguely ellipsoid, in fact—so that his clothes no longer achieve the sophisticated Princeton drape they once did. But he has not aged in the familiar sense. His complexion is ruddy; his demeanor is relaxed; there is the same lively, alert expression about the eyes, and the same quick and startled smile. He still conveys the impression of a man instantly responsive to the stimuli and the challenges of his surroundings. You would be as likely, in fact, to find Adlai Stevenson in public without his pants as without the protective armor of his calm, urbane self-assurance.

He has taken to mingling much more freely with the crowds who greet him at airports or throng the hotel lobbies where he is staying. I suspect he still does not find actual pleasure or stimulation in this haphazard contact with humanity in the mass; he is still a sensitive and discriminating being. But he goes through the routine of greeting all comers, of shaking their hands, of patting the heads of children, of posing for the cameramen with local dignitaries whose names he has barely caught, of exchanging small talk at countless receptions and cocktail parties with persuasive good grace and poise. This has won him great praises from the "pros," and he has Estes Kefauver to thank for whatever benefits accrue from this "humanizing" touch.

In September Stevenson stayed with domestic issues and chipped away at Eisenhower as a man and as a politician. In Vancouver, Washington, for instance, he accused the President of spending too little time on the job and too much on the golf course. In Sioux City, Iowa, he tried to fan a farm revolt by charging the Administration with fostering a rural depression.

For Stevenson, this was strong stuff, and sometimes it

worked. In San Francisco the delegates to a machinists' union convention shouted, stamped their feet and screamed approval when he denounced Eisenhower for duplicity on labor problems. But in Los Angeles, at a convention of the American Legion, he was booed energetically during a long indictment of the Republican Party.

In this early campaigning it seemed that Stevenson's new pugnacity was something more than the mechanics of Presidential politics, something more than the demand put upon the out-of-power party to dislodge the party in power.

Eisenhower, impressed by the literary quality of the challenger's speeches in 1952, was trying to fashion a committee of artists and writers to help him in 1956. While Stevenson fought, Eisenhower was dealing in lofty generalities. Enclosed in the majesty of the Presidential office, enjoying enormous personal popularity, he was able to put the talents of a vast and well-informed staff to work writing things he wanted to say.

Stevenson could not work so leisurely. He did not consciously choose to lower the tone of his speeches, but he did elect to concentrate on purely partisan audiences several times a week and this inevitably affected the quality of what he had to say. In doing this, Stevenson appeared to be basing his strategy on three suppositions:

There were more Democrats than Republicans in the country, and to win he had to induce the Democrats who supported Eisenhower in 1952 (24 percent of the total Democratic vote in 1948) to come home.

To do this he had to identify himself more firmly with his own party, inspiring the Democratic workers and candidates and thereby creating the strongest possible party organization.

Finally, he had to equate Eisenhower with the Republican Party and picture him not as an American folk hero but as the architect of any Republican failures.

These tactics led to a behind-the-scenes struggle. His principal advisers—James Finnegan, Hy Raskin, Wilson Wyatt and James Rowe—counseled the tactics of expediency. But some writers and intellectuals, who had been attracted to Stevenson in 1952 and who remained in 1956 as members of his brain trust, were unhappy. They included some formidable talents. Among them were Arthur Schlesinger, Jr., John Kenneth Galbraith, John Hersey, John Bartlow Martin and Chester Bowles. They worked under the informal direction of W. Willard Wirtz, then Stevenson's law partner, later a Secretary of Labor. Some in this group believed that in his efforts to stir party enthusiasm Stevenson had lost some of the appeal he had in 1952. Stevenson himself, some friends believed, was bothered by the same question.

The schism between the infighters and the intellectuals was never as wide as was sometimes reported. Finnegan, for instance, was probably as much at home among intellectuals as he was with any precinct leader. But there were honest differences of opinion. "Am I master in my own house?" Stevenson asked his advisers at one point and only partly in jest.

In sketching the issues he believed important, Stevenson was emphatic in rejecting what he called Eisenhower's "reassuring picture of progress and peace in the world today." "I think it unfortunate," he told a rally in Silver Springs, Maryland, "that he [the President] chose again to state only half the facts" about the testing of hydrogen bombs and the draft.

"The President did both of us an injustice by stating these proposals with misleading implications," he said.

When he called the proposal to spare humanity the incalculable effects of unlimited hydrogen bomb testing a "theatrical national gesture," he indicted churchmen and political leaders the world over, including Pope Pius XII, representatives of the Baptist, Unitarian, Quaker and Methodist churches, Commissioner Murray of the Atomic Energy Commission, Sir Anthony Eden and many other sincere and thoughtful persons in the United States and abroad who have made similar proposals.

If the President intends to foreclose debate on these proposals I think he does the nation a disservice, and I must dissent and persist in my efforts to invite public attention to matters of such grave concern as the hydrogen horror and national security.

In Denver Stevenson offered the first of a series of policy declarations in which he would present the blueprint for a "New America." This first policy declaration outlined a program to meet the problems of old people, and it went far beyond anything that had been offered in the Democratic national platform.

He wanted, Stevenson said, retired persons to be able to maintain their accustomed standards of living, facilities and services, so that purpose and significance would not be lost in "the evening of people's lives."

Only one person in eight stops work voluntarily to enjoy leisure, Stevenson said. "For millions, able to work and wanting to do so but denied opportunity," he declared, "age means—more than anything else—frustration."

Then he offered a variety of measures to implement his objectives. Among them were:

No discrimination on the ground of age in employing persons between forty-five and sixty-five.

Encouragement of job opportunities for older persons.

Training programs for older persons and the establishment of an office of older persons' welfare.

Revision of retirement programs and policies to take into account the increasing span of the work life of individuals.

A revision upward of the $1,200 limit on the earnings of older citizens without the loss of Social Security benefits.

A sharp improvement of health, hospitalization and medical research programs affecting the aged and the diseases from which they suffer.

Better housing for the aged and facilities to enable them to make a greater contribution to community life.

The same week that Stevenson presented his plan for the aged he delivered a toughly worded attack on Republican farm policies in Newton, Iowa, at the National Plowing Contest, a traditional convocation for politicians.

There, in the heart of a great corn and hog area, a *Times* reporter who had heard Eisenhower speak the day before noted that, while the President had drawn a larger crowd, Stevenson received far more applause. Farmers in the area were sorely beset by hog prices that were lower than they had been four years before, and Stevenson set out to exploit this.

He called the Republican farm record one of "brazen political expediency," recalled "Candidate" Eisenhower's promises of maintaining at least 90 percent parity and said that Secretary of Agriculture Ezra Taft Benson had once condemned price supports as "modern socialism."

Stevenson continued this, his first big swing of the campaign, into Oklahoma City, where he spoke to a mass rally after an afternoon-long motorcade from Tulsa to Oklahoma City. In the farm, ranch and oil country he evoked the memory of William Jennings Bryan, with whom his grandfather campaigned as a Vice Presidential candidate, and then decried the "big corporations in alliance with big government" that threatened the little man.

This was good Populist oratory, and Stevenson and his listeners seemed to enjoy it. He attacked the "leap year liberalism of the G.O.P." and asserted that Washington threatened the small businessman, the farmer and the worker.

"They are," he declared, "in danger of being swallowed up by big corporations in alliance with big government in a world which has become dangerously indifferent to the fate of the little man." But he cautioned, "We are not against big business. We just do not want to be ruled by it and smothered by it.

"In modern times big business has become more responsible. It has a respected place in our national community. But big business does not own the United States Government—and it is not entitled to run that government to the neglect of the farmers, the workingman, the small businessman and the other plain people of the land."

Sometimes the crowds' enthusiasm seemed to bear no relationship to the tenor of his speeches. In the Minneapolis Municipal Auditorium Stevenson gave an earnest, quiet plea for disarmament, "the first order of business in the world today." The atmosphere, however, was similar to that of an old-fashioned torchlight parade. Supporters arrived from hundreds of miles away. Pretty girls waved placards that said: "The Most Horrible Thought of the Year—President Nixon," "Vikings for Adlai," "Minnehaha Falls for Adlai" and "Swedes Like Adlai." The crowd cheered Stevenson to the echo.

At the end of September James Reston, in Milwaukee, summed up the campaign this way:

The paradox of the election campaign so far is that both candidates are doing better with their weak arguments than with their strong.

The President is winning votes with his foreign and defense policy arguments, though his claims in these fields are more dubious than in any other part of his record.

At the same time, he is losing votes on his farm policy, which was probably the most necessary and courageous innovation of his entire Administration.

Adlai E. Stevenson, likewise, has been wowing the voters with an essentially phony argument that Eisenhower is a captive of big business, while the Democratic candidate's solid and justifiable thrusts against the Administration's Middle East record, its education record, and its government personnel record seem to have made very little impact.

The conversation of the voters after the big political rallies is very interesting. They are clearly taken by the President's personality. They like his looks, his obvious sincerity, and his smile.

Many of them are clearly impressed by a kind of growing religiosity that is creeping into his speeches. Women, in particular, refer to him as "a good man" . . . "a religious man" who will always "try to do the right thing," and their references to "peace" are significant.

Peace, it seems, is merely the absence of fighting. The country is full of partisan debate about foreign policy, but most of the time it ends very quickly with the statement that "Ike ended the Korean war."

The voters are impressed, too, by the images of family life around the President. They talk a great deal about the President's attentiveness to his wife, of his handsome son and daughter-in-law and his grandchildren.

Everywhere one goes, Stevenson comes out badly in this personality race. The voters concede he is intelligent, that he has "ideas," but they complain about his "manner": too formal, too "Eastern," they say out here, and sometimes too "English."

In this part of the country nothing carries more weight than the carefully calculated image of "Eisenhower the peacemaker."

It is widely accepted, not only that Eisenhower "stopped the killing in Korea," but that he has the Communists on the run. He was responsible, many people feel, for forcing the Soviet Union and Communist China to change their tune.

He "avoided war" in Indochina. He went to Geneva and "reached an understanding" with the Soviet leaders, and in recent days he has "taken care of the situation" in Suez.

This argument is Stevenson's greatest frustration. He knows the record well. He knows that the change in the Soviet tactics came at the Nineteenth Communist Party Congress in Moscow before Eisenhower ever entered the White House. He knows that the Russians have been trying to get a foothold in the Mediterranean for two hundred years and that they have made more progress toward that goal in the last four years than at any time in this century.

He has not, however, been able to make much progress with this serious and ominous development in our foreign relations, and therefore he has concentrated his fire on issues which he thinks the people will listen to, even though his arguments in these other fields are not so valid.

Stevenson is now concentrating almost entirely on trying to cut down Eisenhower's popularity by associating him with the unpopularity of the Administration among certain classes of voters.

He is trying to put together a coalition of states where there is either an anti-Republican Party tradition or a current grievance against some of the Republican policies.

He is confident that the South will go solidly Democratic this time, and he hopes that he can pick up the additional 100-odd electoral votes necessary to win by concentrating on Northern states in which he believes there has been a powerful defection in the Republican ranks.

The campaigning Stevenson did not relax easily. Unlike Kefauver, for instance, who could board a plane, pull off his shoes and fall asleep, Stevenson spent most of his flight time working on speeches or correspondence. He never dictated a speech, but wrote them in longhand. If he was in a hotel, he would slip into his bedroom, remove his coat and tie, roll up his sleeves and write at a desk.

Stevenson's traveling arrangements were simple. He carried only one suitcase—a battered tan calfskin bag that he packed himself. His only other piece of luggage was a bulging, rump-sprung briefcase that was splitting its seams. Generally he carried it himself, to and from the airplanes he was constantly boarding and debarking.

He always had three suits with him. If he had time before an evening appearance, he would take a shower and change clothes. While he showered, his nephew Tim Ives or a secretary would have a suit pressed. He had his hair cut every two weeks, preferring to drop in at the barbershop of the hotel rather than have a barber come to his suite. He had his shoes shined while his hair was being cut. Not infrequently it was the last professional shine until he got his next haircut. In between he would give the shoes a swipe with a towel.

After an evening speech, Stevenson usually spent an hour or so with his staff and with local politicians. Often he had a highball. After some talk, he would retire to his bedroom and work on speeches or correspondence. Although he seldom got to bed before 1:30 or 2:00 A.M., he usually was up at 6:45 A.M. Then he would take a quick shower and have breakfast in his room with aides or local political figures.

Despite the rigors of the campaign he never lost weight. Stevenson was a nibbler. He helped himself each time the airplane hostess passed a snack tray, and there were always fruits, nuts and mints in his hotel room. And despite the tensions he eschewed both sleeping pills and stay-awake medicaments. Nor did he use gargles or cough drops, even after a hard day in which eight or nine speeches had roughened his throat.

Stevenson got almost no exercise and few intervals for relaxation while on a tour. Nevertheless, he usually had a fine tan. He had acquired it, he was fond of telling audiences, "not on the golf links but standing in public places delivering speeches."

Increasingly in the last month of the campaign the speeches concerned foreign and defense policy. Stevenson had first mentioned the hydrogen bomb issue in a speech in April of 1956 after he became convinced that the radiation problem was becoming dangerous and that the suspension of testing would leave the United States in a more favorable position than the Soviet Union. In the campaign he found that the issue had some appeal in the West but apparently very little in the East. However, Eisenhower's refusal to debate the question and Republican allegations that Stevenson was simply advocating unilateral disarmament led him to elaborate his proposal.

To be understood, the controversy has to be read against its background. In March, 1951, a preliminary test in the development of the hydrogren bomb was held at Eniwetok in the Pacific. The following June, Gordon Dean, then head of the Atomic Energy Commission, reported to President Truman that, if he approved, the first test of a hydrogen bomb could be held in the fall of 1952.

Truman did approve and, after checking weather conditions, November 1, 1952, was selected as the date. This, however, was only three days before the election, and Dean subsequently suggested to the White House that it might be better to delay the test so that it would not be judged a "political maneuver."

Meanwhile, Vannevar Bush, former chairman of the Research and Development Board at the Pentagon, urged Secretary of State Acheson to delay the test while another attempt was made to negotiate an agreement with the other atomic powers.

This was in the first week of October, 1952, less than a month before the election. Bush argued that there was a better chance of an international agreement if the bomb was not tested. Once a major power made a test, he said, the others could not refrain from doing so. But by then the complicated apparatus for the test was already on the way to Eniwetok.

Truman accordingly told Dean and the Pentagon to proceed, and the first hydrogen bomb was exploded on schedule, November 1, 1952. Then, as Bush had feared, the Russians exploded their first hydrogen bomb the following August. Since then there had been no progress in negotiating an agreement on the production, testing or use of the bombs.

In 1956 the Eisenhower Administration did what the Truman Administration had done in 1952: both heard arguments in favor of a moratorium on testing; both rejected them. By 1956, however, both the United States and the Soviet Union had a supply of bombs, and the British were preparing to explode their bomb. Stevenson was arguing that the Administration should take the initiative in ending the tests.

By doing this, he said, the United States could make progress in the cold war, help to prevent the contamination of the atmosphere, and could lessen the chances of the H-bomb's falling into the hands of, say, a Nasser or a Perón.

History would uphold Stevenson. Indeed, in March, 1957, at a Bermuda conference with Prime Minister Macmillan of Britain, Eisenhower tacitly conceded that there was a radiological hazard involved in unlimited testing. The final vindication for Stevenson came in 1963, when Britain, the Soviet Union and the United States concluded an agreement to ban all forms of testing except those underground.

Stevenson was still hard put to explain his position in 1956, however, and in a speech in Chicago he sought to make his stand clear:

> We are caught up today, along with the rest of the world, in an arms race that threatens mankind with stark, merciless, bleak catastrophe.
>
> It is no accident that the instinct of survival which is common to all men and to all nations is slowly but surely compelling the most practical and hardheaded statesmen to give increasing heed to the prevention and abolition of war. In this nuclear age peace is no longer merely a visionary ideal, it has become an urgent and practical necessity.
>
> Yet we dare not tear down and abandon our armed deterrents to war before we devise and secure other more effective guarantees of peace. Great and law-abiding nations cannot leave their security to the mercy of others. We have learned that unilateral disarmament invites rather than deters aggression....
>
> Yet if we are going to make any progress, we must . . . come forward with proposals which will bear witness to our desire to move toward—and not away from—disarmament.
>
> It was with this hard and urgent need in mind that I proposed last spring that all countries concerned halt further tests of large-size nuclear weapons—what we usually call H-bombs. And I proposed that the United States take the lead in establishing this world policy.
>
> I deliberately chose to make this proposal as far removed as possible from the political arena. It was made four months before the

party conventions. It was made to the American Society of Newspaper Editors. It was made without criticism of the present Administration's policy of H-bomb development.

Others—and not I—have chosen to make this proposal for peace a political issue. But I think this is good. After all, the issue is mankind's survival, and man should debate it, fully, openly and in accordance with democracy's processes.

Because there has been only negative criticism of this proposal from the Republican candidates in this campaign, I want—I must—return to it tonight.

These are the reasons—let me list them—why I think the time is ripe and that there is insistent necessity for the world to stop at least the testing of these terrifying weapons.

First, the H-bomb is already so powerful that a single bomb could destroy the largest city in the world—a single bomb. If every man, woman and child in the whole world were each carrying a sixteen-pound bundle of dynamite—enough to blow him to smithereens and then some—the destructive force in their arms—all the people in the world—would be equal to the force of one twenty-megaton hydrogen bomb, which has already been exploded.

Second, the testing of an H-bomb anywhere can be quickly detected. You can't hide the explosion any more than you can hide an earthquake. . . .

Now this means that if any country broke its pledge we would know it and could promptly resume our own testing.

Third, these tests themselves cause the human race unmeasured damage.

With every explosion of a super-bomb huge quantities of radioactive materials are thrown up into the air—pumped into the air currents of the world at all altitudes—and later on they fall to earth as dust or in rain. This radioactive fallout, as it is called, carries something that's called strontium 90, which is the most dreadful poison in the world. For only one tablespoon equally shared by all the members of the human race could produce a dangerous level of radioactivity in the bones of every individual. In sufficient concentrations it can cause bone cancer and dangerously affect the reproductive processes.

Now prior to the atomic age, radioactive strontium was practically nonexistent in the world. Careful studies show that today all of us—all over the world—have some of this substance in our bones. It enters our bodies through the foodstuffs grown in soil on which the bomb dust has fallen. And that's everywhere.

I don't wish to be an alarmist and I'm not asserting that the present levels of radioactivity are dangerous. Scientists don't know exactly how dangerous the threat is, but they do know that the threat will increase if we go on testing. And we should remember that less than half of this substance created by past tests by Russia and the United States has yet fallen to earth from the stratosphere.

So it seems clear to me that if it is humanly possible we should stop sending this dangerous material into the air just as soon as we possibly can.

Now fourth. The dangers of testing by three powers are ominous enough, but there is another reason why I think it's important to act now. Last May, Mr. Stassen, the President's disarmanent assistant, said that within a year the secret of making the H-bomb would spread all around the world. Think what would happen if a maniac, another Hitler, had the hydrogen bomb, and imagine what the consequences would be if a dozen nations were conducting hydrogen bomb experiments and wantonly thrusting radioactive matter into the atmosphere.

These are the reasons why it seems to me imperative that a world policy of stopping these tests be established at the very first possible moment.

I proposed last April that the United States take the initiative toward this end by announcing our willingness to stop these tests, and calling upon other nations to follow our lead, and making it clear that unless they did we would have to resume our experiments, too. That was my proposal. It was simple. It was safe. It was workable.

And since that time both Russia and Great Britain have declared their willingness to join us in trying to establish that kind of a policy.

So I say, what are we waiting for? ...

Therefore, if elected President, I would count it about the first order of business to follow up on the opportunity presented now by the other atomic powers. I would do this by conference and by consultation at whatever level—in whatever place—that the circumstances might suggest would be most fruitful.

The campaign drew near an end with few other telling issues raised. In the wake of the Suez crisis Stevenson charged that Eisenhower had given the nation assurances about the Middle East that had been "tragically less than the truth." "I deeply believe," he said, "that we cannot afford another four years under a part-time leader of a party which will not plan, which will not create, which will not dare to see the vision of a new America and make that vision come true.

"As a campaigning politician there is none better. It is as a performing politician, as a President who knows how to control his own party, who knows how to grasp the reins of government that he fails."

It was only at the end of October that foreign policy occupied the entire political dialogue. And then only because of the invasion of Egypt by Britain, France and Israel and the disturbances in Hungary and Poland. The keenest observers thought that these, no matter how diligently Stevenson sought to associate them with Republican policy failures, would lose, not gain, votes for the challenger. Americans had always shown a tendency in periods of crisis to resolve doubts in favor of an Administration.

On election night James Reston wrote the lead story for *The Times*. It began:

Dwight David Eisenhower won yesterday the most spectacular Presidential election victory since Franklin D. Roosevelt submerged Alfred M. Landon in 1936.

The smiling sixty-six-year-old hero of the Normandy invasion, who was in a Denver hospital recuperating from a heart attack just a year ago today, thus became the first Republican in this century to win two successive Presidential elections. William McKinley did it in 1896 and 1900.

Adlai E. Stevenson of Illinois, who lost to Mr. Eisenhower four years ago, thirty-nine states to nine, conceded defeat at 1:25 this morning.

At 4:45 A.M. President Eisenhower had won forty-one states to seven for Mr. Stevenson. His electoral lead at that time was 457 to 74 for Stevenson, and his popular vote was 25,071,331 to 18,337,434 —up 2 percent over 1952. Two hundred and sixty-six electoral votes are needed for election.

This was a national victory in every conceivable way. It started in Connecticut. It swept every state in New England. It took New York by a plurality of more than 1,500,000. It carried all the Middle Atlantic states, all the Midwest, all the Rocky Mountain states and everything beyond the Rockies.

More than that, the Republican tide swept along the Border states and to the South, carried all the states won by the G.O.P. there in 1952—Virginia, Texas, Tennessee and Florida—and even took Louisiana for the first time since the Hayes-Tilden election of 1876.

Stevenson read his telegram of concession and his statement on the election to about two hundred supporters who had gathered in the grand ballroom of the Conrad Hilton Hotel. He had spent the evening with close friends and associates in the Presidential suite of the Sheraton-Blackstone Hotel across the street.

He appeared relaxed, showing no bitterness or disappointment. He congratulated the President for having won the "great confidence of the American people" and he pledged him his support. Then he said:

And now let me say a word to you, my supporters and friends, all over the country.

First, I want to express my respect and thanks to a gallant partner in this great adventure—Estes Kefauver.

I wish there was some way I could properly thank you, one by one. I wish there was some way I could make you feel my gratitude for the support, the encouragement, the confidence that have sustained me through these weeks and months and years that I have been privileged to be your leader.

Thanks to many of you, I have twice had the proud experience of being selected by the Democratic Party as its nominee for the most exalted office on earth. Once again I have tried hard to express my views and make clear my party's hopes for our beloved country. To you who are disappointed tonight, let me confess that I am too! But we must not be downhearted, for "there is radiance and glory in the darkness, could we but see, and to see, we have only to look."

For here, in America, the people have made their choice in a vigorous partisan contest that has affirmed again the vitality of the democratic process. And I say God bless partisanship, for this is democracy's lifeblood.

But beyond the seas, in much of the world, in Russia, in China, in Hungary, in all the trembling satellites, partisan controversy is forbidden and dissent suppressed.

So I say to you, my dear and loyal friends, take heart—there are things more precious than political victory; there is the right to political contest. And who knows better how vigorous and alive it is than you who bear the fresh, painful wounds of battle.

Let me add another thought for you who have traveled with me on this great journey:

I have tried to chart the road to a new and better America. I want to say to all of you who have followed me that, while we have lost a battle, I am supremely confident that our cause will ultimately prevail, for America can only go forward. It cannot go backward or stand still.

But even more urgent is the hope that our leaders will recognize that America wants to face up squarely to the facts of today's world. We don't want to draw back from them. We can't. We are ready for the test that we know history has set for us.

And, finally, the will of our society is announced by the majority.

And if other nations have thought in the past few weeks that we were looking the other way and too divided to act, they will learn otherwise. What unites us is deeper than what divides us—love of freedom, love of justice, love of peace.

May America continue, under God, to be the shield and spear of democracy. And let us give the Administration all responsible support in the troubled times ahead.

Now I bid you good night, with a full heart and a fervent prayer that we will meet often again in the liberals' everlasting battle against ignorance, poverty, misery and war.

Be of good cheer. And remember, my dear friends, what a wise man said: "A merry heart doeth good like a medicine, but a broken spirit dryeth the bones."

The election was a sizable Democratic defeat. Stevenson was reduced to two Border states and six in the South. The electoral vote was Eisenhower 457 and Stevenson 74. Stevenson even showed a decline from 1952 in the popular vote, winning 26,031,322 votes to Eisenhower's 35,581,003.

Stevenson himself thought that the foreign crises that broke out late in the campaign—the march into Egypt, the Soviet satellite rebellions—had determined the size of Eisenhower's plurality. The President had presented himself as the architect of peace, and at the same time he stood out in the public mind as the man to win a war.

Others noted that the mass media of the country were dominated by Republicans. In the ten largest cities of the nation, for instance, thirty-two newspapers supported Eisenhower, while only two supported Stevenson. The superior wealth of the Republican Party was also cited. In a report on the campaign a Senate subcommittee said the Republicans had reported expenditures of $20.69 million, the Democrats $11 million.

All this played a part. But most important, Eisenhower,

with his enormous personal popularity, was probably the beneficiary of a great weariness toward politics by the American people. Since the Depression the electorate had been faced with a series of crises. From 1932 to 1952 two Presidents had presented the people with urgent, insistent questions. In 1952 Americans elected a Republican President who appeared to be above party, who could calm and unify a nation, who, with the assistance of Congressional Democrats, could present himself as a national, not a partisan, leader.

CHAPTER VI

---∞---

FROM POLITICIAN TO DIPLOMAT

As crushing as was Stevenson's defeat and as much as his pride was bruised, he refrained from any outward display of rancor. He might well have desired, however, to step gracefully out of the limelight, to become a party counselor or even an elder statesman—that shadowy role to which the defeated are so often assigned as a sop or as a way of edging them off stage. But the curious fact is that in defeat he had not lost his enchantment for many Democrats; nor had he lost his own enchantment with public life. He might seek to take things easy, but not to the point of entering obscurity.

Thus, although Stevenson received many invitations to speak, he accepted only a few, but enough to keep his name current in the news. He also expressed a desire to travel and to practice law. And he began to spend some time at his Libertyville farm, where he played tennis, rode and hunted. Nonetheless, he did not arrive at a clear definition of his future, nor did he really know what choices to make, where to commit himself. But in the spring of 1957 a tentative outline took shape.

On April 9, 1957, Stevenson accepted one of the dozens of positions offered to him—the chairmanship of the advisory board of Encyclopaedia Britannica Films, whose headquarters was at Wilmette, Illinois. His work there was to view and help evaluate documentary and educational films for schools and other groups. The work required his attention only a few weeks a year.

Several weeks after this announcement, Stevenson accepted a partnership in the New York City law firm of Paul, Weiss, Rifkind, Wharton & Garrison. The firm promptly reorganized and established offices in Chicago and Washington, with Stevenson devoting himself mainly to the Chicago office.

At the time of the announcement, Stevenson told reporters that he would soon leave on a European business trip for the law firm and said he expected to "traverse the Belgian Congo and visit my friend, Albert Schweitzer, at Lambaréné."

As titular head of the Democratic Party, Stevenson maintained informal contact with its leaders on Capitol Hill and across the country. His following remained remarkably strong. And his appearances and dinner speeches were still front-page news.

At a Democratic Party conference in San Francisco in February he urged an end to the Eisenhower Administration's "rock and roll diplomacy," saying that its foreign policy was marked by "vote-catching boasts" and reversals that had brought the country "perilously close" to disaster.

He coupled the attack with a plea to the Democrats on their responsibilities as an opposition party—a plea he was to reiterate again and again in the following years.

"Our duty as Democrats is identical with our duty as Americans," he said. "It is to face into the future, to ask hard and searching questions about where we are going, to help provide wise answers, and to help develop policies that will restore American leadership in the world."

"Two fallacies" about the party's future, Stevenson observed, spelled trouble for the Democrats.

One was "that we can win in 1958 and 1960 by a base on balls." This fallacy stemmed, he said, from the thought that the Presidential victory in November was "just an Eisenhower victory, a purely personal triumph," and that once the President retired it would be easy for the Democrats to capture the White House.

The other fallacy, Stevenson said, was a belief that "if we undertake a policy of vigorous opposition to the party in power, that opposition must, of necessity, be sterile, negative and destructive."

"We can show the nation what a creative opposition really is," he continued. "We can show that opposition means not picking at wounds but healing them; not destroying private reputations but rescuing America's reputation. We can demonstrate that a truly responsible opposition party need not substitute fanaticism for faith, vehemence for vigilance, or slander for truth."

Through 1957 Stevenson kept up a sharp, sporadic attack on the Eisenhower foreign policy, especially in the Middle East. In November, however, he became an Administration "consultant" to help provide "ideas" in shaping a program for the heads-of-government meeting of the North Atlantic Council in Paris in December.

The original proposal to Stevenson was that he head a

small group that would draft new proposals for the meeting. Stevenson rejected this. Instead, it was explained, Stevenson was to be kept informed of policy proposals as they developed. He was to be asked to give his comments either orally or in writing before final decisions were made.

For his part, Stevenson said that "the gravity of our situation in the world" had impelled him to accede to this extent to the administration "regardless of partisanship or personal convenience."

Stevenson's acceptance of a position within the Eisenhower Administration startled many Democrats and delighted many observers. "Stevenson's acceptance . . . established an interparty relationship on foreign policy that is a precedent in modern politics," wrote Arthur Krock.

Republicans have served Democratic Presidents in this area, and vice versa. But it may be the first time in at least a century when the counsel in foreign policy-making of the defeated candidate for President was sought by the Administration of his successful opponent. The nearest parallel generally recalled was President F. D. Roosevelt's invitation to Alf M. Landon, after the outbreak in Europe of what became the Second World War, to enter his cabinet as Secretary of the Navy. This Landon declined.

Among grumbling Democrats, however, including two or three on whom President Truman had greatly depended for counsel on foreign relations, there were private complaints that the Administration was primarily interested in bailing out its foreign policy by associating the Democratic Party with it. But Stevenson's close friend, Eleanor Roosevelt, in her syndicated column, suggested another interpretation that was simple, dead-pan and very tongue-in-cheek.

"I surmise," she wrote, "that the Administration in persuading Adlai Stevenson to act in a consultative capacity on foreign relation policies hopes that he will help regain the ground lost with our allies and uncommitted nations throughout the world.

"This cannot be accomplished, however, by calling in bipartisan help at this stage. There would have to be deeds," she added.

Two weeks before the scheduled meeting in Paris—and two weeks after Stevenson had started working in the State Department—the Democratic nominee in 1952 and 1956 met his former Republican opponent at a brief session in the White House. It was their first meeting in four years.

The President greeted Stevenson cordially in his office. Eisenhower quietly discussed his health problems—he had suffered a mild stroke a week earlier—and expressed his annoyance at a speech difficulty.

The President then thanked Stevenson for helping with preparations for the Paris conference and emphasized that the situation in the world was too grave to permit partisan approaches. He said that what was needed was not "party policies" but American policy. With this, Stevenson agreed.

Eisenhower then said he would be happy if Stevenson could go to Paris with the United States delegation. Stevenson replied that he would like to think about it.

What followed was the type of guessing game that the Washington cocktail party circuit adores and gossips about for days. More important, however, it was indicative of the ambivalence Stevenson obviously felt in his delicate "consultant" role.

Stevenson ultimately turned down the invitation, saying that membership in the United States delegation would put him in a position "without authority and necessarily identified with decisions I might not always agree with and could not publicly oppose."

He then declared that he would end his assignment as consultant as soon as he had "studied all the proposals, expressed my views and made my recommendations to Secretary Dulles."

"I am grateful to the President and the Secretary of State for this opportunity to be of service and for the further confidence implicit in the President's suggestion that I attend the NATO meeting in Paris," Stevenson told reporters.

Although most comments were laudatory and friendly—both Dulles and Eisenhower publicly expressed their appreciation to Stevenson—the feeling persisted that the bipartisan effort had not been handled too smoothly.

"Some Administration officials believed that while there still was doubt that the President would himself head the Paris delegation, Mr. Stevenson did not wish to put himself in a position to serve as a subordinate to Vice President Nixon, with whom he had sharper personal political differences than he had with the President," wrote W. H. Lawrence of *The Times*. "On the other hand, there were some who thought that the Administration's invitation to Mr. Stevenson to be a member of the United States delegation had been extended only belatedly and then in a not-too-hearty fashion by President Eisenhower."

"Whatever his reasons," Arthur Krock wrote,

Stevenson served the principle of bipartisanship in foreign affairs to the full extent of his commitment and usefulness. He is not a member of Congress, where the national security and foreign policy record will be made. At the Capitol, he is listened to with respect, but the group is small which would follow his counsel if it differed with that of the party leaders in Congress. And few, if any, Democrats rode to national office on Stevenson's coattails in 1952 or 1956.

Shortly before he wound up his three-and-a-half-week assignment, Stevenson made his suggestions to the Administration. He urged the President to enlist the cooperation of the other North Atlantic Treaty powers in a new effort to negotiate a general peace in the Middle East. And he proposed that the Atlantic powers consider guaranteeing the Arab-Israeli boundaries and armistice lines against armed aggression.

He also suggested that the Administration give serious consideration to the Soviet proposal to stop shipping arms from all quarters into the Middle East.

For its part, the Administration said it was "interested" in Stevenson's guarantee idea, but did not think the NATO meeting was the proper forum for discussing it. On the boundary proposal, the Administration said it did not believe a guarantee was "practicable" until Israel and her Arab neighbors had agreed on permanent boundaries.

If Stevenson felt frustrated in his brief role within the Administration, it was unapparent to most observers. A day before he left the State Department, Stevenson greeted Dulles warmly, chatted and, of course, quipped.

As Stevenson, Dulles and Theodore E. Green, the Rhode Island Democrat and chairman of the Senate Foreign Relations Committee, met reporters, a handful of photographers asked the three to pose together.

"You've got me surrounded by Democrats here," said Dulles.

"This is what is called 'containment,' gentlemen," Stevenson remarked.

A few days later Stevenson left Washington. As he departed, he reflected that what he found most lacking was "a sense of urgency." He had "deep misgivings about the Administration's overemphasis on the military and underemphasis on the economic-political war around the world."

Important as arms may be, he felt, there was a great opportunity at the time "to go beyond the everlasting chatter about arms."

So, by the end of 1957, Adlai Stevenson had returned permanently—and irrevocably—into the spotlight.

"Stevenson's influence abroad is probably greater now than it is at home," wrote John B. Oakes, now editorial page editor of *The Times,* in an article in December, 1957.

Here he's still the twice-defeated Democratic candidate, and there he's the Leader of the Opposition. Here he's the titular head of the Democratic Party, and not more than that; there—because European constitutional systems are so different from ours—he's billed in the popular mind as the official spokesman for the party of Roosevelt and Truman, the party that had traditionally had the more sympathetic approach to foreign affairs and America's relationship to Europe. Here he is a respected figure whose political future is at best highly precarious; there he's a powerful representative of a major segment of public opinion.

Mr. Stevenson now says he wants to resume his law business "and earn a living." He freely admits that it was a combination of "duty and desire" that impelled him to go to Washington at Mr. Dulles' request. . . . It is quite possible, now that he has returned to public life, that he will be heard more frequently than in the recent past on various aspects of his favorite subject, foreign affairs. And it is not difficult to get the feeling as one talks to him that, should the occasion arise next year or in some future year, he wouldn't mind being invited back to Washington for consultation—or something far more important than that—once again.

In the early months of 1958 Stevenson stepped up his

speaking schedule. At a dinner sponsored by the Americans for Democratic Action, he suggested that the Secretary General of the United Nations select a group of private citizens from all over the world to evaluate disarmament recommendations so as "to clear the air of all the bunk and phony proposals."

In a speech to the United Parents Association, Stevenson said vehemently:

The softness which has crept into our educational system is a reflection of something much broader, of a national complacency, if you will, of a confusion of the priorities of the body, the mind and the spirit.

The imperative today, in my judgment, is that we reassert—so that every person in this country is not left in any doubt about it—every man and woman, every politician, yes, and every teacher and every child—our conviction that children's needs have first priority over all other civilian wants.

We have lacked, I fear, the deep inner conviction that education in its broadest sense unlocks the door of our future, and that it gives us the tools without which "the pursuit of happiness" becomes a hollow chasing after triviality, a mindless boredom relieved only by the stimulus of sensationalism or quenched with a tranquilizer pill.

And pray, let there be no more derision of the nonconformist; rather let them be encouraged to speak their minds, to criticize and question. The deprecation of the intelligence, the ridicule of the intellectual, has been too often the stock in trade of our demagogues and the easy fashion of our times. If the Sputniks have helped in any measure toward change in this respect, we may yet live to hail Khrushchev as an educational reformer. But the change will not last if it is merely external. Respect for excellence—an idea which we can confidently draw from our classical heritage of freedom—this respect we must learn for ourselves.

And in what James Reston called a "remarkable and largely ignored speech," Stevenson addressed a group at the

University of Louisville on East-West economics. "We are witnessing," Stevenson said, "the last stages of the old world-wide, self-regulating, international trade and investment system, which we in America have largely taken for granted.

"At the same time, as it recedes, we see, expanding and eager to take its place, the new Communist techniques of grants, gifts, loans, trade, aid, barter, technical assistance, raw materials at cost or plain dumping, all bent to the same purpose—the reinforcement of Communist power."

He noted that all this was taking place just at the time when the United States' need for secure trade abroad and for steady access to foreign materials was growing in proportion to its soaring population and diminishing resources.

"We are heading for a new crisis," he proclaimed, "one no less dire than the crisis of 1947, and no less certain to lead to catastrophe unless we act in time."

Accordingly, he called for the creation of a committee of experts, similar to the one that laid the groundwork for the Marshall Plan eleven years earlier. This, he proposed, should work out, not a European recovery plan, but a long-range economic recovery plan, to secure in the whole free world sustained economic growth, joint negotiations for a low tariff or free-trade area, joint undertakings of a long-range aid and investment program, and joint agreement on adequate working capital for world trade and convertibility.

Then in June Stevenson left on a three-month tour of Eastern and Western Europe and parts of Asia and Africa. Upon his return, he told newsmen that he had noted an "undertone of great anxiety of conflict between East and West."

He also said he had observed a disposition to "look to the

United States for leadership, wisdom and support—and to blame the United States for everything."

Even before his return, however, the first of a series of extensively read articles by Stevenson on his visit to Eastern Europe appeared in *The New York Times*. The articles were copyrighted by the North American Newspaper Alliance and later turned into a book, *Friends and Enemies*, published by Harper & Row.

Deftly painting a broad picture of life in the Communist camp, Stevenson used swift, artful strokes in his delineation of the leaders and the people of Eastern Europe:

"Men working," is the symbol of the Soviet Union today as I saw it over seven thousand miles, from the Gulf of Finland through Siberia to Central Asia and the Chinese border. We visited huge farms and factories, government officials and scientific centers, schools and universities, power stations and housing projects and talked with many people in many different walks of life.

I bring back with me an image of a vast, rich underdeveloped country, hard at work with single-minded purpose to build itself to challenge the United States' world leadership.

In his first article Stevenson briefly discussed his two-and-a-half-hour conversation with Khrushchev ("He looked tired and lacked the bounce I had expected") and outlined the points of agreement and disagreement between himself and the Soviet leader.

When I said that peace depends on the security of all nations from outside interference, that the United States was not in Lebanon to please Arab opinion but to protect an Arab country at its request, he [Khrushchev] said he was "astonished" and "surprised" and that "public opinion must be respected."

"See how far we stand from one another," he added in a melancholy tone, "at opposite poles."

I could hardly believe my ears—the Premier of the Soviet dicta-torship, which tolerates no criticism, was lecturing me on democ-racy and the sovereignty of public opinion!

But I think he was saying something significant—the present So-viet leadership does consider opinion, for its foreign policy relies, in part at least, on persuasion rather than coercion alone as in Stalin's day.

Stevenson said he and Khrushchev heartily agreed that big nations should not interfere in the internal affairs of smaller nations. But "when I asked whether that had been the Soviet Union's attitude at the time of the armed inter-vention in Hungary and the recent denunciation of Marshal Tito of Yugoslavia, he let me have it.

"Following the familiar Communist debating tactic of at-tack, Mr. Khrushchev assailed the United States and its ac-tions around the world—in Lebanon, Jordan, Guatemala—even Cuba!

" 'The trouble is that Americans poke their noses where they should not,' " he complained.

Khrushchev, by implication at least, then insisted that whatever went on in the Communist world was a family affair and did not concern outsiders; that Soviet suppression of the uprising in Hungary in 1956 was not interference; and that Soviet pressure on Yugoslavia to conform to Moscow was not a case of meddling in another country's affairs.

In his second article Stevenson wrote that United States security measures appeared uppermost among the Soviet Union's fears.

"We see ourselves encircled by your bases," Khrushchev said. "There are no Soviet troops in the Near and Middle East, but the Americans have bases in Britain, Turkey and Greece, and I do not know where they do not have them.

"What would you Americans think if we set up bases in Mexico, or some such place? How would you feel?"

The policy of Secretary of State Dulles, he went on, was one of "rollback."

"But history will roll him back," Khrushchev said. "The policy of rollback must be rolled back. You cannot roll us back from your country. On this basis, there not only cannot be friendship, there cannot even be good relations."

Stevenson replied that United States policy had not been aggressive or expansive but had been designed to defend its security and the right of all countries to go their way, unmolested and secure.

"Mr. Premier," Stevenson said, "there should not be conflicts between us. We each have enough territory and resources. Our troubles arise from the outside. Maybe we Americans have made mistakes, but this is the way we see things, and I am sure my countrymen are very eager to find a way to settle the conflicts that divide us."

"This I believe," Khrushchev answered. "I have read your speeches. Some things in them are wrong and even offensive ["Sounded like campaign time at home," Stevenson wrote], but on the whole I think you stand for improving relations and we welcome it."

Stevenson wrote at this point: "And then he [Khrushchev] went on to say something about Soviet attitudes that I think is little understood among us Americans."

Khrushchev said frankly and confidently that the world was inexorably going Communist.

"You must understand, Mr. Stevenson, that we live in an epoch when one system is giving way to another. When you established your republican system in the eighteenth century, the English did not like it. Now, too, a process is taking place in which the people want to live under a new system of society; and it is necessary that one agree and reconcile himself with this fact. The process should take place without interference. If this principle [of noninterference] were accepted, it would improve the international climate and we would welcome it."

Stevenson's visit with Khrushchev had its lighter moments, too. At one point, Khrushchev confided to Stevenson that when the leaders of the Communist countries got together, they always toasted their best friend, the Secretary of State of the United States.

"We say: 'We will regret it if President Eisenhower's Sputnik leaves the State Department for he helps us so. We will hardly get a more useful opponent.'"

At another stage, the Soviet leader suggested that Stevenson's two sons who accompanied him on the trip, Borden and John Fell, come back and marry Russian girls.

"That would be a contribution to Russian-American relations!" Khrushchev said jovially.

The boys were noncommittal.

In later articles Stevenson wrote vividly of the changes enveloping Eastern Europe, especially in Poland. "The first thing that strikes you is Warsaw itself," he said. "Miraculously, the ancient, beautiful city has risen from its ashes. Methodically destroyed, building by building by the Nazis, it is being rebuilt, stone by stone, by loving Poles exactly as it was."

Stevenson wrote, too, of Russian willingness to expand trade with the West, of Kremlin nervousness over Communist China, of the Soviet drive to develop the riches of Siberia and of the ordinary people, the workers, in the Soviet Union.

"Their hair was long, their clothes poor," observed Stevenson after a group of students and workers had gathered in front of his Leningrad hotel, not to see Stevenson, but to examine a strange and wonderful sight—a 1956 Buick.

"But they were friendly and good-humored," Stevenson continued, "with a ready laugh when I said we hoped to go to Siberia—and also to return. They were intensely curious about America, our education and living conditions."

Stevenson noted the striking contrast between the savage propaganda against the West and the friendship that people felt for Westerners.

"Why didn't they knock us down instead of embracing us?" Stevenson asked.

No one is too confident of the answer. Some Russians say their criticism is just of "your ruling clique." But there must be some immunity to propaganda after forty years, together with an abiding admiration for the United States as the most "advanced" country, and also gratitude for our help in the war.

After seeing the anti-American headlines and hearing the radio attacks in a distant place one night, my notes conclude: "If this has been going on for twenty years it is a wonder that we are still at peace." And it is.

In his concluding article Stevenson strongly discounted any notion that Communism, Soviet style, was unstable.

When I say the Soviet regime is stable, I don't mean there is no internal dissension. I have no doubt there is bitter controversy over policy and sinister plotting for power in the Kremlin. One of the worst indictments of the Soviet system is that after forty years they have not yet worked out a means of transferring power without conspiracy, exile and violence.

What I mean by stability is that if life is austere and hard, at least it is getting better and there are no signs of rebellion. That does not mean that all Russians are devout Communists. Actually, only a fraction of the adults belong to the Communist Party. . . .

I have seen the Russians close up. They are tough, fearful and going places. But they are also very human. Their hopes and desires are for peace and an apartment. Even Mr. Khrushchev wants to attain the American standard of living. And we still have the supreme advantage of living under the system most people want if they can get it and afford it.

This should give us calm and final confidence.

Upon his return, and through the winter, spring and summer of 1959, Stevenson, with an eye on 1960, was speaking a great deal. In Washington he told an audience that the Soviet Union had created an "iron, forceful and even formidable" way of life that was making great advances in competition with the "sluggish" pace of the United States and other Western democracies.

In Boston he called for unity in the Berlin crisis and asserted that "when the President says we will not give in to force, he speaks for all of us."

And in Cambridge, Massachusetts, he warned American businessmen that the nation's economic system "was on trial for its life."

"A realistic re-examination of our economic system and its state of readiness," Stevenson said, "is a responsibility business cannot, must not, evade."

In May Stevenson made a highly publicized speech at McGill University, declaring that the disparity of living conditions between developed and underdeveloped nations was "the most important and fateful fact in the world today."

He added that raising the living standards of the poorer nations was possibly a more urgent matter than direct national defense measures.

"The rich are getting richer and the poor poorer as population grows faster than production in the poor areas," he observed. "The precondition of any effective world policies in the West is an imaginative understanding of the implications of this race between resources and population; of this growing gap between a small wealthy white Western minority who have modernized and the vast majority of mankind who have not."

Stevenson was to repeat this theme again and again in his later years at the United Nations.

With uncanny prescience, Stevenson wrote an article a short time later for *The New York Times Magazine* on what Khrushchev should see in the United States if he ever decided to visit. Two months after the article was published, the Soviet leader announced that he would visit this country.

What Mr. Khrushchev must see, if he comes to the United States, Stevenson wrote,

is not so much the size of our accomplishments as the capability of change and growth which makes our civilization viable and exciting. It will be more important for him to see America *in the process* of meeting its serious problems in the democratic way, correcting its faults, striving to make its ideals meaningful, facing up to its deficiencies. Not a country with its problems all solved, but one with the manifest capacity to solve them, and to do this within the framework of the democratic way.

What specifically should Khrushchev—or for that matter any other Soviet leader—see on a visit to the United States?

Stevenson suggested a session of Congress or a legislative committee hearing, a school in the process of integration, a housing development, the Tennessee Valley Authority, the International Harvester Company, a state fair, a campus and a corn farm in downstate Illinois.

Two months after the suggestions were made, Stevenson and Khrushchev discussed world problems under a brown county fair tent on a sprawling corn farm—not in downstate Illinois, but in Coon Rapids, Iowa.

The two men, on the farm of Roswell Garst, Iowa's great advocate of hybrid corn, ate home-fried chicken and barbecued ribs and discussed disarmament, economics, ideology, trade and world health problems.

It was for Khrushchev his most folksy day in the United States. And for Stevenson it was a day that he would recall to friends and associates many times in later years.

"He [Khrushchev] is extremely smart," Stevenson told reporters on the farm. "He has changed a little since I saw him last summer. I feel better about him now as a result of this talk with him than I did after talking with him in the Soviet Union a year ago."

The conversation was not entirely serious, of course.

"I told him," Stevenson said, "that I am not as good a campaigner as he is. I told him that if he ever found himself out of a job to come over here and I would give him one."

Khrushchev was asked whether Stevenson had told him that he (Stevenson) was a retired politician.

"Can I repeat that little conversation?" Khrushchev asked Stevenson. "It won't reveal any secret? You will not be investigated by the Bureau on Un-American Affairs? I will not be investigated, of course, because I am carrying a diplomatic passport."

"You are at liberty to reveal my deepest secret," Stevenson laughed.

"Mr. Stevenson said that he was a politician in retirement," Khrushchev resumed. "But in politics it often happens that a person retires today and tomorrow he may be in the first rank. It all depends on the people."

"It depends how many times you can retire," Stevenson said.

"Honest effort is always rewarded," Khrushchev replied.

"My efforts have always been honest, but they have not always been rewarded," Stevenson observed.

"One must never be discouraged," Khrushchev said with a smile.

"I never knew what it was to be happy until I was retired," Stevenson said. "But I don't wish that upon the Chairman. But if he ever retires and wants something to do, let me know. Come and live on my farm in Illinois."

"Do you have a fish pond?" Khrushchev asked.

"No, but I'll dig one for you."

"Don't hurry," Khrushchev said, "I'm not retiring for the time being. I am not ready for fishing yet. Maybe we'll grow some flowers."

Stevenson and Khrushchev got into a talk about what kind of fish was best for stocking ponds. Stevenson made a reference to sturgeon, to which Khrushchev quickly said: "I can get you some sturgeon even while I am on my visit here. I just have to call up Moscow and tell them to send some on the next plane. The sturgeon will be here tomorrow."

Stevenson said, "Fine," and added that he would come to eat the sturgeon and bring his fork.

"Bring a big fork," Khrushchev said.

The fact was, Stevenson observed, he would much prefer caviar.

Later, Stevenson wrote:

During my day with him in Iowa, he [Khrushchev] emphasized

the same theme: reduce the arms burden, increase trade, keep talking! And what a day it was—of simple, warmhearted hospitality, amid pandemonium. Walking across the famous farm of my friend, Roswell Garst, the champion corn producer, Mrs. Khrushchev said to me in her best English:

"The grass it will be hurt."

For temperate understatement, I would recommend Mrs. Khrushchev to Mr. Khrushchev.

Stevenson was especially fond of Khrushchev's farewell remark to his hosts—a remark, Stevenson felt, that was more than a good-humored jest.

"I have seen how the slaves of capitalism live, and they live pretty well," the Soviet leader said. "The slaves of Communism live pretty well, too, so let's all live the way we want to live and be friends."

With the departure of Khrushchev, Stevenson returned to his farm in Libertyville. He loved to stroll alone near the grazing, black-faced sheep, to sit in his library in the autumn and look out over the gold and scarlet maples, to don Bermuda shorts and blue sneakers and sun himself on the lawn in the summer.

"He loved that house more than anything else in the world," a close friend at the United Nations said years later. "It really wasn't much of a house but it was the one place he could relax in."

To the house came a steady stream of Stevenson's close friends—lawyers, a handful of politicians, some businessmen, columnists and such writers as John Steinbeck, Archibald MacLeish and Barbara Ward.

They discussed Khrushchev and Stevenson's travels and Eisenhower and books (Stevenson had virtually stopped reading novels and concentrated on philosophy and books on public affairs), and then, in the winter of 1959, came the stirrings of Stevenson's possible re-entry into politics.

One month after the 1956 election, Stevenson had said: "I will not run again for the Presidency."

In June, 1959, he told reporters at an informal news conference during sessions of the Democratic Advisory Council: "I will not be the nominee."

Yet Stevenson's supporters—and possibly even Stevenson himself—did not take this too seriously. "He wanted a draft," said a friend in New York later. "He wanted the convention to come to him. He felt that he was somehow bound by that pledge about not running. I told him that politics changes, you can say one thing today and change your mind tomorrow. But he wouldn't change. He wouldn't announce himself, yet he wanted it."

Slowly and spontaneously, the Stevenson boom began— puzzling the professional politicians, dismaying the hard-driving candidates and surprising, and probably delighting, Adlai Stevenson.

"Mr. Stevenson is in the bullpen," wrote a *Times* reporter in November, 1959, "but his followers are doing the warming up."

"He is in an odd and interesting situation," wrote James Reston from Libertyville, Illinois.

Four years ago and eight years ago he was rushing out from here to see other influential Democratic politicians. Now they seem to be making their way here to see him.

This is not arranged by Stevenson. He is inviting nobody. He is initiating nothing. In fact, he is spending a good deal of his time explaining why he cannot accept invitations to speak to this Democratic rally here or that Democratic fund-raising dinner some place else. Nevertheless, he is available to anybody who wants to talk to him, just as he was this week when Governor Pat Brown of California came by for lunch.

What is odd about this is that there is little or no enthusiasm among the professional politicians for another Stevenson nomination. Many of the pros say quite frankly that they do not want him. Many more say that, if somehow they could wish him into the White House, they would gladly do so, but that they cannot look forward happily to another campaign of iambic pentameter.

As the autumn turned to winter and as the candidacies of Hubert H. Humphrey and John F. Kennedy were announced, the pressures on Stevenson mounted. He remained adamant; he would not seek the nomination.

So far as the other Democratic possibilities went, he told a panel of five college and graduate students on a television interview in December, he was not leaning toward anybody but "trying to maintain an attitude of vertical neutrality."

During the program Stevenson was obviously taken aback when David Dulles, a Harvard law student and nephew of John Foster Dulles, asked whether he had ever refused any position, such as the presidency of a corporation, lest it preclude his running again for President.

After a long pause and a couple of inarticulate noises, Stevenson repeated the question. Then he said hesitantly: "Well, I don't know, really. They never were posed in that form, but maybe so, maybe so. I think they have been mostly academic, however, not business."

As the next question was asked, the former Governor turned back to young Dulles and said: "It's a very good question. I should have thought of that sooner."

Stevenson "is spending most of his time writing rejection notes to speaking invitations and imploring disciples to keep his name out of the Oregon and District of Columbia primaries," James Reston wrote in December.

Every once in a while, however, he shows up at a party rally, as he did in New York last week, just to demonstrate that he can still make the other Democratic candidates look like a band of high school debaters.

Also, when he does talk, he seems to feel obliged to say something. Thus, he came to grips last week with the steel-strike issue [Stevenson had proposed a new labor law that would recognize the public welfare and give the President far greater powers than under the Taft-Hartley Law] and put himself on record as favoring compulsory arbitration, if necessary, to avoid nationwide strikes in basic industries.

But this happens seldom. He is very quiet. He is biding, and, like Nixon, assuming that the trend of politics is moving his way.

For Stevenson, this procedure is likely to last until summer with occasional major policy statements breaking his silence, for he will accept defeat rather than wage an open campaign.

At the end of January Stevenson set out on a two-month business and sight-seeing tour of South America. As a member of the board of directors of the Encyclopedia Britannica he had some legal work there in preparation for the Spanish edition. And for his law firm he was a counsel to Reynolds Metals, which also involved some work in South America.

His departure, as the primaries approached, left Stevenson's supporters unshaken.

Organized boomlets were spreading across the country —with leaders as confident and self-assured as Stevenson was guarded and uncertain. By November, a *Times* survey showed that loosely coordinated draft-the-reluctant-Stevenson groups existed in Ohio, Oregon, Washington, California, Missouri, Texas and Washington, D.C.

By December, there were four focal points of the campaign. In New York a reform group retained the offices of William Attwood to prepare speeches and research. In Madison, Wisconsin, James Doyle, former Democratic state chairman, was hired by Stevenson friends to watch over the growing number of volunteer groups. In Los Angeles a fund-raising campaign began, under the producer Dore Schary. And in Washington a behind-the-scenes strategy center was set up, whose leaders included George Ball and Senator Mike Monroney.

Before—and during—his South American trip, Stevenson skipped nimbly around questions on whether he had given up all thought of being President.

Upon his return, however, Stevenson held a news conference at which he declared that he did not want to be a "draft evader." But he added that he neither hoped nor expected to be a third-time Democratic candidate for the Presidency.

The news conference, at the Savoy Hilton in New York, was relaxed and informal. Stevenson was tanned and somewhat thinner. He smiled and joked with reporters, and parried questions about himself with a skill he defined as that of an "old fox."

He started by reading a prepared statement saying that he was not a candidate for the Democratic nomination, but would make speeches for "a liberal program." Then he was asked if he would accept a nomination if a deadlocked convention turned to him.

"If I told you that I would accept a draft," Stevenson rejoined, "I would be courting a draft, which was the same dilemma I was in in 1952. And if I said I would refuse a draft, I would be a draft evader. So I just don't say anything at all."

Although Stevenson tried hard to turn the conference to other questions, and once plaintively asked if anybody was interested in Latin America, the reporters pressed him on the nomination.

At one point, one long question mentioned the thought

that the world might be exterminated at any moment, and in view of such dangers asked whom Stevenson would like to see as President.

"It might sound irreverent if I suggested—" Stevenson started, and stopped when the audience burst into laughter. Then he went on: "Short of that, I should like to say any of the Democratic candidates who are competing for the Presidency or appear to be."

Another question evoked recollections of the late Senator McCarthy of Wisconsin. The questioner said Stevenson in 1954 called Nixon "McCarthy in a white collar."

"Not bad," Stevenson commented.

"Have you observed any great change?"

"I should prefer not to go into that," Stevenson replied. "I believe in the redemption of souls."

Stevenson's highly publicized news conference raised new speculation among Democrats, especially about the possibility of a Stevenson-Kennedy ticket.

One day after the conference, James Reston wrote:

This [the possibility of a Stevenson-Kennedy ticket] is a remarkable tribute to Stevenson as well as an indication of the perplexity of the voters about the other candidates. He has gone through eight hard years. He is a proud and lonely man. There have been times during this period when it almost seemed that he was defeated in his soul. For a time he had nothing to say to the country. After the second defeat he did not even seem to be keeping abreast of many major world developments.

Even when this mood passed, and he came back into public view again with his trips to the Soviet Union and Africa, his speeches, while still full of the old poetry, had a melancholy ring. They seemed possessed with the tragedy of life, and dwelled at length on the decline of American moral values.

The Stevenson who returned to New York yesterday was much more optimistic and ebullient. . . . His sense of humor and his sense of history and proportion have revived. He is suffering from a painful infection in his right ear, but he is thinner and more serene.

When he says, as he did yesterday, "I neither seek [the nomination], nor hope for it, nor expect it," he is about two-thirds right. He is not seeking it, and he really doesn't expect it, but he has his hopes. He is available.

While the others are tossing in the political storm, he has come out into calm water where he can see the longer horizons, and he is writing as well as he ever did, which is pretty good. If the long odds do go this way, this will be a hard and lively campaign.

"His [Stevenson's] is a course not open to any of the others," wrote Arthur Krock several days later.

As top runner, Senator Kennedy must contest the primaries, and win the hard ones if he is to retain this status. Senator Symington must somehow overcome the strategy of staying out of the primaries if Kennedy succeeds in making this an adverse factor in the national convention. Senator Johnson, though his daily obligations as majority leader make him reasonably immune from the operation of this factor, must surmount the high obstacles of being a Southerner, a moderate on equal rights . . . and a statesman whose policy is to get a good half-loaf of legislation instead of losing a whole loaf by Presidential veto.

As the convention approached, as Stevenson generated more publicity, the Democratic leader was jesting more, traveling more and obviously having a good time.

At a speech before a gathering of one thousand newspaper editors in Washington in late April, he shared a panel with Hugh Gaitskell, leader of the British Labour Party, and Lester B. Pearson, leader of the Canadian Liberal Party.

"As my two honorable friends and I share this platform," Stevenson began, "it will no doubt cross the minds of some of you that we have something in common: we are demonstrably out of office! However, like George Orwell's pigs, some of whom were more equal than others, I will yield to no one in my claim that I am more out of office than anyone else.

"This is partly due to the fact that they are in Parliament and are the chosen leaders of their parties, and that they confidently expect at some point or other to take over the political leadership of their nations. And I do not."

Stevenson then apologized to his audience for being late, but explained that his airplane had been delayed at the airport by the ceremonies welcoming President de Gaulle of France.

"It's a curious thing," Stevenson said, "how often some national hero seems to be in my way."

The audience roared.

Stepping up his statements on foreign policy, Stevenson, in May, assailed the recent United States U-2 reconnaissance flight over the Soviet Union as a blunder in timing. He added, however, that "no one questions the necessity of gathering intelligence for our security."

"This is no time for partisan criticism," he said. But he asked whether such a blunder might not "carelessly, accidentally trigger the holocaust."

Several days later, Stevenson asserted that Khrushchev had wrecked the Paris summit conference (the Soviet leader had refused to attend after the U-2 plane incident) but that the United States had handed him "the crowbar and the sledgehammer to do it."

As the nation's responsible opposition, he said, the Democratic Party had an obligation to the country and to its allies to expose and criticize the Administration's carelessness and mistakes.

There is too much at stake "to sweep this whole sorry mess under the rug in the name of national unity," he added. "We

Democrats know how clumsy this Administration can be. We are not likely to forget the fumbles that preceded the Suez crisis on the eve of the 1956 election."

And on June 1 Stevenson called for a permanent special peace and disarmament agency under the Secretary of State as a "symbol of our determination to lead the world away from madness." It was part of a five-point strategy he presented as a "grand strategy for peace."

Stevenson deplored what he called Republican implications that it was impossible to negotiate with Soviet leaders. "We shall," he said, "have to talk and bargain with the Communist countries for many years to come."

"Instead of always worrying about what Russia will do next, let's concentrate on what we can do next," he said.

At one point in his speech, Stevenson asked who in Washington was "doing his homework for peace," and answered by charging that the problem had been handled as a "series of improvised efforts."

"Our approach to disarmament had been: 'Yes but.' It ought to be: 'Why not?'"

Meanwhile, full-page ads were being placed in major newspapers around the country, urging a Stevenson nomination. Financial support—even heavier than in 1952 and 1956—rolled in. Pressure increased on Stevenson to step openly into the race.

By early June, the Stevenson drive covered forty-two states. In Washington James Doyle officially announced the start of the "Draft Stevenson" movement. Soon mail, posters and brochures began blanketing major cities.

In Los Angeles a hundred-foot-long, nine-foot-high banner reading, "Draft Stevenson," went up near convention headquarters. Planes carried "Draft Stevenson" banners over

Coney Island, the Rockaways and Fire Island.

The Stevenson camp was counting on a stalemate, a dead-lock among Kennedy, Johnson and Symington. "We're not out to stop anyone," said Russell D. Hemenway, deputy chairman of the group seeking to engineer a Stevenson draft.

"We want everyone to have a free and clear run for the nomination. We think Senator Kennedy will have the first run, Senator Johnson the second and Senator Symington the third.

"It is our belief that none of them can get the necessary convention majority to be nominated and that the convention will turn to Stevenson."

From the Kennedy side came feelers to Stevenson to support, perhaps even nominate, the Massachussetts Senator. "Stevenson," said a close friend five years later, "could have had anything if he had supported Jack then. He could have been Secretary of State. He could have even been Vice President."

At that moment Kennedy was not only uncertain of his convention delegate strength, but he was also unsure of his following among those independent voters who had in the past rallied to Stevenson.

It was a time for Stevenson to weigh his chances, to make an advantageous deal for himself, to get out of the way of Kennedy's bandwagon by hopping onto it. It must have been a tempting opportunity, but Stevenson foreclosed it on at least two grounds. The first was that he thought the nomination might come to him—surely a misjudgment so palpable that it could only have been based on an intense desire to run again. The second ground was distaste for Kennedy, whom Stevenson considered a parvenu. Moreover, Kennedy seemed to Stevenson calculating and cocksure. This was a view that Stevenson was not careful enough to keep to himself, and his remarks to friends and at cocktail parties worried some of his admirers. Of course Stevenson's talk got back to Kennedy, and relations between the two were never more than superficially cordial, even when Stevenson was a member of the Kennedy Cabinet.

So, instead of bowing out of the Presidential race, Stevenson kept himself in by not backing anyone.

"I have no plans for an endorsement of any candidate," he said in a telephone interview with W. H. Lawrence in May.

Several weeks later, confusion and a virtual comic opera situation arose. Mrs. Franklin D. Roosevelt said flatly that Stevenson was a candidate for President. Stevenson promptly replied that he was not.

This followed the defection of a group of liberal Democrats from Stevenson's camp, who said that although they preferred Stevenson for President, it was too late to campaign for the nomination. This group included Arthur M. Schlesinger, Jr., the historian; John Kenneth Galbraith, the economist; Henry Steele Commager, the Amherst professor; and Joseph L. Rauh, Jr., the Washington lawyer and a leader of the Americans for Democratic Action.

Seeking to clear up what Mrs. Roosevelt termed a "misunderstanding which seemed to exist . . . as to whether he could be a candidate or not," the former First Lady phoned Stevenson and received a statement that said, in part, that although he would not seek the nomination, "I will serve my country and my party whenever called upon."

"From this statement," Mrs. Roosevelt said, "I think you will find it clear that Mr. Stevenson is a candidate."

Reached at his home in Libertyville, Stevenson said: "My message to Mrs. Roosevelt speaks for itself. I reiterated the position I have taken for several years that I will not seek the nomination for President at the convention. Therefore, I am not a candidate."

When this was read back to him for confirmation, Stevenson added, as though to himself: "Oh, dear. I suppose that will get me into it with Eleanor, won't it?"

One week before the convention, Stevenson's statements became more explicit. On July 7 he said on a television program that it was "possible but not probable" that he would get the Democratic nomination for the third time.

"I have read my epitaph so many times," he said, "that I thought I was dead and then, when I wake up in the morning and find I am alive, it is a matter of delight, I must confess."

The next day Stevenson said he would accept a draft and "do my utmost to win."

The statement cheered his supporters gathering in Los Angeles. Senator Monroney, the Democrat of Oklahoma who led the Stevenson draft effort at the convention, said with unabashed optimism: "We have the greatest growth potential of any candidate."

Stevenson later recalled with some amusement that prior to his draft announcement Lyndon Johnson, in a series of profane discussions, had tried to form a political alliance. Together, Johnson said in Stevenson's recollection of these talks, they could "take" Kennedy. Stevenson, who had no great personal admiration for Kennedy, nonetheless declined to join Johnson's stop-Kennedy movement.

On the first day of the convention the Stevenson forces received a not unexpected blow. The powerful delegations from Pennsylvania and Illinois—both former strongholds for Stevenson—declared themselves in a strong majority for Kennedy. A victory by the youthful Massachusetts Senator —who had won primaries in New Hampshire, Wisconsin, West Virginia and other states—was now very much within reach.

Then on Tuesday the convention became a setting for a rapidly unfolding drama that reached a sweeping climax the following night.

That morning the spotlight focused on two delegations, Minnesota and California. Both were strong, both were influential, both had not yet made up their minds.

First, the 31-man Minnesota delegation, badly split, caucused, but made no decision. They listened to G. Mennen Williams plead for Kennedy. They heard Herbert H. Lehman and Mrs. Roosevelt plead for Stevenson. Even the leaders of the delegation were split—Senator Eugene McCarthy would nominate Stevenson, Governor Orville Freeman would nominate Kennedy.

On Tuesday afternoon the California Democratic delegation, spurred by the chants, banners and pleas of Stevenson supporters, deluged with letters, telegrams and phone calls, gave Stevenson one more vote than Kennedy at a three-hour caucus. The Kennedy forces had hoped to obtain as many as 50 votes. Instead, they received 30½ and were obviously shaken.

Stevenson, meanwhile, was being pressured to act, to end his Hamlet-like indecision, to announce once and for all that he was a candidate. That night Stevenson emerged from his hotel suite to take his seat at the convention with the Illinois delegation. His appearance threw the arena into an uproar.

"We want Stevenson!" howled the galleries and delegates in unison while convention chairman, Governor LeRoy Collins of Florida, pleaded for order. "We want Stevenson!" screamed thousands of marchers outside the sports arena. "We want Stevenson!" blared the banners, the buttons, the flags inside and outside the convention.

As soon as Stevenson appeared, he was engulfed in the swarming, screaming mob. For a time, he seemed in danger of being crushed, as, with several muscular men trying to shield him, he was pushed, pulled and squeezed from his place in the Illinois delegation to the platform.

It took twelve minutes of shoving and pushing to get Stevenson there. Then the cries of "We want Stevenson!" broke out all over again.

Stevenson smiled, waved and said: "I won't attempt to tell you how grateful I am for this tumultuous welcome to the 1960 Democratic convention. I have, however, one observation—after getting in and out of the Biltmore Hotel and this hall, I know whom you are going to nominate. It will be the last survivor."

The crowd roared. "More, more," they yelled, but Stevenson turned and left the convention.

"He could have stepped up there and gotten the nomination," said Roger Kent, Northern California Democratic vice chairman and a Kennedy supporter.

"After about eight minutes," Representative Stewart Udall of Arizona remarked, "some of us got a funny feeling in the stomach that it might be Willkie [the 1940 Republican nominee] all over again."

On Wednesday the nominations began. Slowly and tediously, the speeches and demonstrations and hoopla droned on. As the morning stretched to afternoon, however, as the afternoon yielded to evening, a tension and excitement gripped the arena.

The galleries were filling with youthful Stevenson supporters, clutching banners, chatting, waiting. Telegrams were pouring into delegations' headquarters in a telegraphic blitz for Stevenson. Outside, swarms of Stevenson fans began gathering at 2 P.M.—seven hours before the convention.

Under convention rules, a maximum of 125 persons, including bands, was allowed admittance from the outside for each candidate. The Stevenson group passed entry badges back and forth until nearly five hundred outsiders had slipped in, and then tried to crash through without any kind of passes, forcing an emergency call for more policemen.

With the convention packed and tense, Senator Eugene J. McCarthy stepped up to the podium Wednesday night and, in a quavering voice, began the most emotional, dramatic speech of the convention.

Mr. Chairman [he began], Democratic delegates at this great convention, we now approach the hour of all-important decision. You are the chosen people out of 172 million Americans, the chosen of the Democratic Party, come here to Los Angeles to choose a man to lead this Democratic Party in the campaign of this fall and this November, but to choose a man whom we hope will lead this country and all of our friends and all of those peoples who look to us for help, who look to us for understanding, who look to us for leadership. . . .

Let me ask you at this time to put aside all of your prejudices, to put aside any kind of unwarranted regional loyalties, to put aside for the time being preferences which are based purely upon questions of personality. Put aside, if you can, early decisions—decisions which were made before all of the candidates were in the race, decisions which were made when the issues were not clear, as they are today.

I say to those of you candidates and spokesmen for candidates who say you are confident of the strength that you have at this convention, who say that you are confident and believe in democracy—let this go to a second ballot.

I say let this go to a second ballot, when every delegate who is here will be as free as he can be free to make a decision.

Let us strike off the fetters of instructed delegations. Let governors say to their people: This is the moment of decision and we want you to make it as free Americans, responsible to your own conscience and to the people of the state that sent you here, and to the people of this country.

This I say is the real test of democracy. Do you have confidence in the people of this convention to make a fair and responsible choice, or do you not have that confidence? . . .

There's demagoguery abroad in the land at all times, and demagoguery, I say to you, takes many forms. There's that which says "Here is wealth and here is material comfort." We suffer little from that in the United States.

There's demagoguery which promises people power, which is used for improper purposes and ends. And we have seen in this century and in this generation what happens when power is abused.

I say to you there's a subtle kind of demagoguery which erodes the spirit. And this is the demagoguery which has affected this United States in the last eight years.

What are we told? What have we been told? We've been told that we can be strong without sacrifice. This is what we've been told. We've been told that we can be good without any kind of discipline if we just say we're humble and sincere—this is in the nature of goodness. We've been told that we can be wise without reflection. We can be wise without study, we've been told. I say this is the erosion of the spirit which has taken place in this United States in the last eight years.

And I say to you that the time has come to raise again the cry of the ancient prophet, and what did he say? He said, "The prophets prophesy falsely. And the high priests," he said, "rule by their words. And my people love to have it so. But what will be the end thereof?"

I say to you the political prophets have prophesied falsely in these eight years. And the high priests of government have ruled by that false prophecy. And the people seem to have loved it so.

But there was one man—there was one man who did not prophesy falsely, let me remind you. There was one man who said: Let's talk sense to the American people.

What did the scoffers say? The scoffers said: Nonsense. They said: Catastrophic nonsense. But we know it was the essential and the basic and the fundamental truth that he spoke to us.

This was the man who talked sense to the American people. There was one man who said: This is a time for self-examination. This is a time for us to take stock, he said. This is a time to decide where we are and where we're going.

This, he said, is a time for virtue. But what virtues did he say we needed? Oh, yes, he said, we need the heroic virtues—we always do. We need fortitude; we need courage; we need justice. And everyone cheers when you speak out for those virtues.

But what did he say in addition to that? He said we need the unheroic virtues in America. We need the virtue, he said, of patience. There were those who said we've had too much of patience.

We need, he said, the virtue of tolerance. We need the virtue of forbearance. We need the virtue of patient understanding.

This was what the prophet said. This is what he said to the American people. I ask you, did he prophesy falsely? Did he prophesy falsely?

He said, this is a time for greatness for America. He did not say he possessed it. He did not even say he was destined for it. He did say that the heritage of America is one of greatness.

And he described that heritage to us. And he said the promise of America is a promise of greatness. And he said this promise we must fulfill.

This was his call to greatness. This was the call to greatness that was issued to 1952. He did not seek power for himself in 1952. He did not seek power in 1956.

He does not seek it for himself today.

This man knows, as all of us do from history, that power often comes to those who seek it. But history does not prove that power is always well used by those who seek it.

On the contrary, the whole history of Democratic politics is to this end, that power is best exercised by those who are sought out by the people, by those to whom power is given by a free people.

And so I say to you Democrats here assembled: Do not turn away from this man. Do not reject this man. He has fought gallantly. He has fought courageously. He has fought honorably. In 1952 in the great battle. In 1956 he fought bravely. And between those years and since, he has stood off the guerrilla attacks of his enemies and the sniping attacks of those who should have been his friends. Do not reject this man who made us all proud to be called Democrats. Do not reject this man who, his enemies said, spoke above the heads of the people, but they said it only because they didn't want the people to listen. He spoke to the people. He moved their minds and stirred their hearts, and this was what was objected to. Do not leave this prophet without honor in his own party. Do not reject this man.

I submit to you a man who is not the favorite son of any one state. I submit to you the man who is the favorite son of fifty states.

And not only of fifty states but the favorite son of every country in the world in which he is known—of every country in which he is unknown but in which some spark, even though unexpressed, of desire for liberty and freedom still lives.

This favorite son I submit to you: Adlai E. Stevenson of Illinois.

The speech's effect was electric. The convention erupted in a screaming roar. Chanting, placard-waving demonstrators jammed the aisles while the galleries suddenly came alive with Stevenson supporters going round and round in a deafening din.

For twenty-five minutes, the bobbing, weaving demonstrators shook the convention in a wild, emotional outburst. Banners were unfurled everywhere, reading, "We Want Stevenson." A giant papier-mâché ball bounded through the air reading, "Draft Stevenson." The convention chairman pleaded for order. Senator McCarthy pleaded for order. But the pandemonium continued.

At his hotel, Stevenson said he was "deeply touched" by the speech and demonstration. But even as he made the comment, even as the galleries chanted, "We want Stevenson," the smoothly run Kennedy organization was driving forward toward a smashing victory.

As the roll-call began, Stevenson and his aides realized at once that, although the galleries favored him, the delegates were bound to Kennedy. By eleven o'clock that night, the race for the nomination was over. Kennedy overwhelmed his opposition, piling up 806 votes to 409 ballots for Lyndon B. Johnson. Stevenson had only 79½ votes, slightly fewer than the 86 cast for Senator Symington.

After the convention, James Reston wrote:

Adlai Stevenson is free at last of the long anguish of Presidential politics, but he is still not entirely at peace.

He came here today from the Democratic convention in Los Angeles, relieved in one way that he escaped a third Presidential campaign, grateful for the enthusiastic support he did receive, but still wondering about the mysteries of American politics.

Did he let his supporters down? Did he underestimate his popular strength in the country? Why did his own state of Illinois not support its only Presidential nominee since Lincoln?

He is not complaining; just puzzling, as usual. In 1952 he did not want to be drafted and was. In 1960 he wanted to be drafted and was not.

What consoles him in all this are the obviously sincere expressions of sentiment and even affection by his backers in Los Angeles. But outside of this enthusiastic minority support the picture was more confused.

At the end, he finds himself once more at odds with the spirit of the professional politicians and, surprisingly, even with many of his old intellectual backers.

The pros thought he should have gone much further than he did in seeking the nomination if he wanted to be considered. . . .

Even many of his intellectual friends thought he should have done more to fight for the nomination and, paradoxically, some of them thought he should have done less.

Thus some of his old friends now in the Kennedy camp argued that, if he was not going to get all the way into the battle, he should have stayed all the way out.

Half in, he seemed to the Kennedy backers a potential threat. Half out, he seemed to his own supporters a reluctant and ineffective instrument in the convention struggle.

Nevertheless, he still has an extremely important role to play. . .

The Republican argument will be that the conduct of foreign affairs is the central issue of the campaign and that the choice before the country is between the experienced Republicans and the inexperienced Democrats.

Stevenson's active support of Kennedy is widely regarded as a useful counter to this argument. He carries more weight in both the Allied and the Communist worlds than Kennedy, Nixon or Lodge. He is more experienced and more articulate in this field than either candidate, which is why Kennedy said during the primary campaign that he "assumed" any Democratic President would nominate Stevenson as Secretary of State.

There is, however, no commitment to Stevenson on this score and much will depend on the relations between the two men in the next few months. . . .

His Presidential career, therefore, is at an end but his diplomatic career may just be beginning—and he has always been more at home in diplomacy than he was in politics.

Stevenson left Los Angeles with, typically, an outwardly broad smile and a word of cheer for his disheartened supporters.

Fans swarmed around him as he made his way through the lobby of his hotel to a car waiting to take him on a trip through California and the Pacific Northwest.

"I don't know why you are all so sorry," Stevenson said. "I had no expectation of ever being a candidate again. You made me one, and it was a very happy, happy experience."

CHAPTER VII

------··✠··------

AN AMERICAN AT THE
UNITED NATIONS

ON DECEMBER 8, 1960, President-elect John F. Kennedy
opened the door of his red-brick Georgetown home,
walked to the front stoop and told waiting newsmen that he
had asked Adlai E. Stevenson to head the United States
delegation at the United Nations.

From across the street, a pro-Stevenson crowd, largely
Georgetown University students, applauded. At the United
Nations delegates were pleased. Newspaper comment was
favorable.

Perhaps the only grumbles—and they were private—came
from a handful of liberal Democrats, such as Mrs. Eleanor
Roosevelt, who had urged Stevenson's appointment as Secretary of State. The President-elect had decided against this,
however, long before Election Day.

Relations between Stevenson and Kennedy, once cordial,
had cooled during the preconvention campaign when the
Massachusetts Senator, driving for a first-ballot nomination,

asked but was refused Stevenson's support. After the convention the two men maintained a surface peace, and Stevenson campaigned for Kennedy. Yet that December Stevenson-Kennedy news conference indicated that some tensions between the two men still persisted.

"I appreciate Senator Kennedy's confidence and I share his view about the difficulty and the importance of this assignment," Stevenson remarked, standing next to Kennedy. "The United Nations is the very center of our foreign policy and its effectiveness is indispensable to the peace and the security of the world."

"While I have not sought this assignment," Stevenson continued, "I want to be helpful. I have some matters both of organization of the work and of ways and means of strengthening it that I want to discuss with him [Kennedy] further. This I hope to do in the very near future."

"Governor," a newsman asked, "are we to understand you have not accepted it?"

"I have not accepted it, pending a further talk," Stevenson replied.

In deferring a firm acceptance, he left the impression that Kennedy had been unable to tell him his choice for Secretary of State. (Dean Rusk was named four days later.) "It was felt," reported W. H. Lawrence, "that the uncertainty about who would serve as his chief had been a factor in Mr. Stevenson's reluctance to accept at once."

Another factor was Stevenson's uncertainty about the role he would play in policy-making; he emphasized that he did not want to defend a policy without actually being involved in its making.

"I just don't know," he told a friend at the time. "I know everyone wants me to jump up and down with delight and say this is the thing I want to do more than anything else in the world, but I just don't know. I don't want to be a lawyer arguing a case whether he believes in it or not. I'm not interested in explaining or defending a policy; I want to be involved in the making of that policy."

Arthur Krock wrote after the news conference: "To some observers it seemed that, while Stevenson was at the microphone, the President-elect's facial expression betrayed an annoyance he had not quite been able to suppress. Certainly after Stevenson made his reply there were heard in quarters close to the Senator the familiar accusation of 'indecisiveness' against the former Democratic Presidential candidate."

The selection of Rusk, however, and the promise that Stevenson would "play a key role in the formulation of foreign policy" settled the matter, and Stevenson accepted the United Nations post, with Cabinet rank. But to a reporter who congratulated him in private he retorted, "You must be kidding."

At a joint news conference on December 15, Rusk paid a long tribute to the new United Nations Ambassador. Rusk said that Stevenson probably knew more about the United Nations than anyone else in the country and recalled Stevenson's links with the organization. "There is almost no phase of our foreign policy that does not come within the United Nations," he said.

On January 18, 1961, the Senate Foreign Relations Committee unanimously approved Stevenson's designation after a two-hour hearing in which he said that the United States would have to face the possibility of Communist China's admission to the United Nations.

"The identity of the United Nations with our deepest convictions about the nature and destiny of man is a central fact we need to keep in mind as we move through a period of relentless turmoil and travail," he said at one point. "The membership has almost doubled since my time, and we are likely to encounter some unaccustomed rebuffs and disappointments in that political area in the months ahead."

"At its best," he observed, the United Nations "is not a formula for 'stability' but a framework for change. All the world's tensions are not bad; some of the incentives of hope and the drives for self-expression and self-government are what makes the free world hum. It is a mistake, in my judgment, for us to see in the United Nations merely a desperate survival operation, without also exploiting its potential as a cooperative search for better answers to the overhanging question, 'After survival, what then?' Peoples are best cemented together, after all, not by mutual fear but by mutual hope."

Five days after his appearance before the committee—and three days after Kennedy was inaugurated—Stevenson stepped from a black limousine at the entrance to the United Nations Secretariat Building at noon during a whirling snowstorm. He then presented his credentials to Secretary General Dag Hammarskjöld, and took over his duties as United States Representative at the United Nations.

Later, he was conducted on a tour of the Security Council chamber. He spotted the United States name plate and was told that he was next in line for the Council's rotating presidency. Shaking his head, he remarked: "That's the way it is. When I want the Presidency, I can't have it; when I don't, I can."

In his first official appearance, February 1, Stevenson was greeted warmly as he took his seat at the Council's horseshoe-shaped table. He shook hands with diplomats near him and then he stood up and walked around the table to where

Valerian Zorin, the Soviet delegate, was sitting and greeted him.

Stevenson, who was afflicted with laryngitis, had come to the meeting from his doctor's office. After a round of speeches, he apologized for his hoarse voice, saying: "I wish I could say it was a casualty for the battle of peace instead of the New York weather."

Then, taking note of the speeches, the tributes and the applause from the galleries, he said with a smile: "I have sometimes said that flattery is all right, Mr. President, if you don't inhale. Well, you have made it very hard for me not to inhale, thanks to the charity and kindness which have touched me so deeply."

He then told the Council:

We are, to use the French phrase, the Nations United. Let us *be* united—united in a patient and persevering attempt to find the things we can agree upon and to build upon them a structure of understanding and cooperation against which whatever storms may be ahead shall beat in vain.

To one who has long been absent from these councils, it is striking and heartening that the United Nations has not only survived the turmoil and the conflict of the years, but has grown wiser, stronger and an ever more potent factor in the shaping of world events.

Protocol accomplished, Stevenson turned to a political crisis that was to occupy him countless times in the next four years—the Congo. During that first Council session, Secretary General Hammarskjöld asked it to widen his powers in the Congo so that he might stop factional fighting in the Congolese Army.

As Stevenson listened and took notes on a yellow scratch pad, Hammarskjöld warned that the weakening of the United Nations force by withdrawals of national contingents might require him to call for an end to the entire Congo operation—economic as well as military. If present trends continued, he said, there loomed "the threatening possibility of civil war."

Two weeks later, the Soviet Union, which had strongly opposed United Nations policy in the Congo, withdrew its recognition of Hammarskjöld as the Secretary General. Among other things, the Russians accused him of "organizing the murder" several days earlier of Patrice Lumumba, the deposed Congolese Premier.

After the Russian charge, Stevenson arose in the Security Council February 15 and delivered an impassioned speech on the Congolese crisis.

Within recent days we have seen the successive withdrawal of two national units of the United Nations forces [in the Congo], the violent death of former Prime Minister Patrice Lumumba, the reported recognition of the [Antoine] Gizenga regime in Stanleyville by the United Arab Republic and a threat by the U.S.S.R. to provide unilateral assistance outside the United Nations. . . .

What we decide here in the next few days may . . . determine whether the United Nations will be able to carry on its essential task of preserving the peace and protecting small nations.

Turning to the Soviet Union's accusations against Hammarskjöld, he remarked:

I pass lightly over the Soviet Government's petulant attack on Secretary General Dag Hammarskjöld and his great office. He needs no defense from me nor does his institution. His record is an open book, a book which all peace-loving peoples recognize as the record of a dedicated international civil servant whose only loyalty is to international justice and international peace.

Let the Soviet Government, if it wishes, pretend that he does not exist . . . it will find that peace-loving states will continue to support his patient search for the right road to security and peace in the Congo and for all peoples. The United Nations may have made mistakes in the Congo, as who has not, but nothing justifies an intemperate and unjustifiable attack on the integrity of the office of Secretary General. . . .

We regret that the Soviet Government has not as yet seen fit to cooperate with states which truly seek peace in attempting to work out constructive steps for the solution of the agonizing problems the Congolese people are now facing. Instead, the Soviet Government proposes the complete abandonment of the United Nations operation in the Congo. . . .

What does this mean? It means, my colleagues, not only the abandonment of the Congo to chaos and civil war—to, if you please, the cold war—it means abandonment of the principle of the United Nations itself.

Does anyone doubt it would mean chaos? Does this Council, the *Security* Council, favor abandoning security for insecurity and anarchy?

Do we want to withdraw the only elements that stand foursquare against civil war and tribal war? Does the Soviet Government really want Africans to kill Africans? The United States does not, and it devoutly hopes that the Soviet Government does not, too, and that it will join the United States and other peace-loving states in supporting and strengthening the only force that can prevent Congolese civil war—the United Nations.

The issue is simply this: Shall the United Nations survive? Shall the attempt to bring about peace by the concerted power of international understanding be discarded? Shall any pretense of an international order, of international law, be swept aside? Shall conflicts of naked power, awful in their potential, be permitted to rage in Africa or elsewhere, unchecked by international cooperation or authority?

Less than a week after that speech, the Security Council upheld the Secretary General and refused to condemn the actions of the United Nations Security Force in the Congo. The Council also told the United Nations command in the Congo to use force if necessary to prevent the outbreak of civil war.

In his first months Stevenson settled comfortably in his new role. Swinging his attaché case, walking briskly, conferring enthusiastically, he became a familiar sight in the corridors, at private luncheons and the cocktail parties of the United Nations.

One of his first tasks, he felt, was to meet as many heads of delegations as he could. He invited them to his office, sought them out and soon became a favorite, especially of the Afro-Asians.

"It took me two years to meet Lodge," one Arab delegate told a newsman. "Stevenson I met in two weeks."

To his eighteen-room, forty-second-floor suite at the Waldorf Towers, reserved for the chief of the United States Mission, Stevenson invited visiting dignitaries as well as friends. As the length of his working day increased, he spent most of his time away from the Towers and in the United States Mission or at the United Nations itself. And as each crisis or problem shifted, he became a focus of attention.

For months there had been rumors of a United States-backed invasion of Cuba to overthrow Fidel Castro.

According to several books published after the death of Kennedy, invasion plans had been set, in fact, by the Pentagon and the Central Intelligence Agency during the Eisenhower Administration. When Kennedy took over, this project moved "mysteriously and inexorably toward execution without either the President's being able to obtain a firm grip on it or reverse it," Theodore C. Sorensen wrote afterward.

In February, 1961, Cuba charged in the United Nations that the United States was planning "direct and unilateral intervention." Stevenson angrily denied the charge.

In the next two months, however, rumors persisted of a

United States drive to oust Castro, although the United States—in Washington and at the United Nations—still denied the reports.

Nevertheless, from Miami on April 12, Tad Szulc wrote:

Preparations for action against the Castro regime by Cuban exiles in the United States were reported . . . to be mounting steadily despite the reported indecision of the Kennedy Administration on how much to aid this undertaking.

Rebel leaders here have long been aware of the difference in Washington not only over the scope of such assistance but also over which of the many groups fighting the regime of Premier Fidel Castro should be particularly favored.

From Havana and at the United Nations, Cuba repeated her charges of aggression—even though Kennedy gave a firm pledge in April that the United States would not intervene in Cuba "under any conditions" to bring about Castro's downfall.

Then on the morning of April 15, three Cuban military air bases were attacked almost simultaneously by bombing planes. Castro immediately ordered a general mobilization of the armed forces and civilian militia, and declared: "If this air attack is a prelude to an invasion, the country, on a war basis, will resist and destroy with an iron hand any force which attempts to disembark on our soil."

At a hastily called meeting of the General Assembly's Political Committee, Cuba charged that the United States was wholly to blame for the bombings. This was denied by Stevenson.

"No United States personnel participated," he said. "No United States Government airplanes of any kind participated."

Two days later, rebel troops landed before dawn on the

swampy southern coast of Cuba in Las Villas Province. In Washington Rusk expressed sympathy for those who struck against Castroism but emphasized that "there is not and will not be any intervention there by United States forces." And at the United Nations Stevenson again denied Cuban charges of "aggression."

Kennedy meantime warned the Soviet Union that the United States would tolerate no outside military intervention in Cuba (Khrushchev had threatened to give the Castro regime "all necessary assistance" in repelling the attacks), and word was received that the Castro forces had opened a tank-led offensive against the rebels. That was on April 18.

Two days later, Castro announced that the Bay of Pigs invasion had been crushed.

"Tonight, after four days of uncertainty," wrote Wallace Carroll in *The Times*, "it is clear that the [Cuban] expedition had involved the United States in a disastrous loss of prestige and respect. Among high Administration officials there is recognition that a serious miscalculation was made. The nature of that miscalculation is now clear."

"It is now common knowledge," a *Times* editorial said, "that the United States played a considerable role in the preparations for the episode and that specifically the Central Intelligence Agency masterminded the operation for the American Government first during the Eisenhower Administration and then under President Kennedy. . . ."

"For the first time in his life, John F. Kennedy has taken a public licking," James Reston wrote. "He has faced illness and even death in his forty-three years, but defeat is something new to him, and Cuba was a clumsy and humiliating one, which makes it worse.

"How he reacts to it may very well be more important

than how he got into it. For this will be a critical test of the character and perspective of the new President, and of the brilliant young men he had brought to the pinnacle of political power."

For Stevenson, however, it was not only the defeat—and his repeated denials of any United States role in the invasion —but also the fact that he had been kept in the dark on United States plans that made the situation so humiliating. He was disheartened and hurt, even though the President was privately apologetic and promised that a similar incident would never recur.

At the United Nations, though, Stevenson's reputation remained high. Few delegates believed that his reputation had been seriously damaged and many sympathized with him. In fact, several had been involved in similar situations where they had not been notified of a policy decision or shift by their governments and had been left, in effect, with egg on their faces at the United Nations.

From his first days as the United States Ambassador during the Sixteenth General Assembly session until his final session, the Nineteenth in 1964, Stevenson was known as the "Housemother of the U.N." The sobriquet pleased him immensely, not only because it reflected the esteem and respect accorded him by his United Nations colleagues, but also because it acknowledged that Stevenson was their confidant and friend.

This was especially true among the African and Latin-American delegates, who came to Stevenson by day or at night with their problems, personal and official.

In conference, chatting privately or speaking publicly, Stevenson was unfailingly courteous and immensely charming. During sessions of the Security Council, visitors were more likely to recognize him, perhaps, than anyone else sitting about the sunken ring of the Security Council chamber. He appeared at once cheerfully energetic, animated, intense and involved. He seemed to listen more deeply than anyone to the translation that came to his right ear through a wire and a pink plug. He conferred more earnestly and laughed more easily during the long translations.

When he came to speak, he paid his auditors the compliment of choosing his words with great care, giving a cliché a personal phrasing so as never to convey even a hint that he had brushed off what was said to him. Fellow ambassadors liked to talk about "the tremendous humanity of the man."

Some of Stevenson's care in conversation and in his speeches reflected a shy pride, an insistence on putting a personal stamp on the common currency, but not everyone approved it, for Stevenson took endless hours polishing his speeches. Not everyone was enchanted by Stevenson's friendliness either. Some observers at the United Nations felt that he was less effective than he might have been because he was never willingly offensive, even to people who had behaved offensively to him or to his country. He was hurt, and showed it at times; but he rarely struck back.

Henry Cabot Lodge in similar situations would bully his way into the opposition, creating the impression that he had greater independent authority. Most observers believed, however, that Stevenson, if anything, had a touch more freedom than Lodge had—"the difference," one of them said in 1965, "between being able to call right through to Dulles and being able to call right through to Johnson." Stevenson merely chose to be quiet.

In addition to his gentility and gentleness, Stevenson was an entertaining companion, who liked to be quick on his feet and stimulated others to do the same. "I dined out with him the other day at one of the embassies," said a Secretariat member in 1965, "and the evening would have been insufferably stuffy without him."

He was in demand for parties not only because he represented the United States and gave the event a social tone, but also because he livened things up. Stevenson spent almost all his official working day in conferences, but he then went to an appalling number of parties—several hundred a year, for each of 115 national holidays, visits of foreign ministers and the like.

By universal agreement, United Nations parties were work, and although Stevenson never seemed to mind them, he once remarked that a diplomat's life was made up of three ingredients: protocol, Geritol and alcohol.

"Now you stick with me," Stevenson told a reporter in 1963, as both entered a party celebrating the admission of Kuwait to the United Nations. "I just go in there, hands open, ears open. Expect a concentrated period of handshaking and whispering."

As Stevenson stepped in, he was greeted informally and not in the usual diplomatic and protocol manner.

"Now I just let myself be drawn in here," Stevenson said after handshakes with several members of Kuwait's Mission. "Ah! Sir Muhammad Zafrulla Khan."

After greeting the then President of the General Assembly, Stevenson plunged into a conversation with several diplomats and then found himself chatting with a party crasher.

"Do you really listen to everybody?" Stevenson was asked when he finally turned from the crasher.

"I'm meat for these people," he said with a laugh.

"Don't you have bodyguards or something?" he was asked.

"I've never cared much for elbow men," he replied.

And then a young man came up and said quickly: "I merely want to say thanks for everything you've ever done, Mr. Stevenson—and I mean *everything!*"

A great deal of Stevenson's day was, simply, wasted. For the newer nations it constituted recognition to have an appointment with "the Governor"—and an insult to have to deal with the member of the United States Mission directly involved. Stevenson was therefore obliged every month to keep numerous appointments at which his prime function was to be gracious. The gossip and chatter of the delegates lounge was doubtless of great significance inside the United Nations, but its value in the colder world outside was considerably less.

A portrait of Stevenson at work would typically show a man waiting—waiting before a delayed meeting of the Security Council, waiting at a conference for someone to say something that directly touched the practical interests of the United States, waiting for an answer to a cable. But that was the nature of the job.

Stevenson appeared at times haggard and exhausted and paunchy—especially in his last months—but after returning from a vacation at his farm in Libertyville or in Palm Beach he looked bright and chipper. His face would be sunburned, his bald head freckled, his back hair freshly clipped, his eyes clear and blue.

When he first took over the United Nations post, Stevenson cheerfully discussed his new apartment 42A at the Waldorf Towers.

"My goodness! The things you have to do in order to live

here," he said. "Our government puts the Ambassador up in an apartment at the top of the Waldorf Towers. It's a handsome apartment. Very handsome. And equipped like an embassy abroad, with a living room, a dining room that will accommodate forty people, and—let's see—one, two, three, four, five bedrooms and five baths, and a full pantry and bar, and cabinets with beautiful china and all that."

Stevenson was asked whether he'd like living at the Waldorf. "I'm sure I'll love the view," he said. "I've never really enjoyed living in big cities. I'm a country boy. I love the feeling of the country. I love being on my farm, and I hope to be able to get back there occasionally for weekends. My children and grandchildren spend holidays with me at the farm. . . . I love to read to the two older grandchildren. They always ask me to read to them. I'm impressed with their power of concentration. I can't say I have any special favorites among the books at this stage. They're not old enough for me to read favorites like *The Wind in the Willows.*"

Four years later, Stevenson was asked at his Waldorf Towers apartment what he would like above all else to be doing at that moment.

"I'd like to be out on my farm in Libertyville, pruning trees," he said, and then, with a laugh added: "And I'd like an opportunity to get some rest. I've had about eleven days' vacation all told since I went into this job, four years ago. . . . But my first responsibility is to the President and to this job. I'd like to be useful as long as I can be. I've been so involved with affairs of my own generation I'd feel a little bereft if I were *not* involved. It's tempting sometimes to dream about a tranquil old age, but I think I'd be a little restive."

As a lonely man on the New Frontier and in the Great Society, Stevenson maintained, nevertheless, a strong and unwavering belief in the United Nations.

"Somehow, I still have a complete sense of the importance of the United Nations, in spite of the frustrations and the exhausting trivia," he remarked at one point. "I think of the United Nations, in the political field, as one of the great experiments of man. There's no issue in the world now that doesn't affect the United States. We're involved in everything. There are a hundred and ten other nations in the U.N., and I have to receive and talk with representatives of almost all of them, and there's no problem any more on which we can take the position that we're going to sit this one out.

"In my own day-to-day life, it's very much the way it was when I was campaigning for President; it's campaigning perpetually. The worst thing about running for President, for me, was that you had to shave twice a day, and you have to do that in this job, too."

In a long conversation with a friend at the American Embassy in London in May, 1964, Stevenson talked of the decision-making processes in government, of the complexity both of determining and executing United States policy and of the frustrations and satisfactions of diplomatic life.

Gazing outside the window over Grosvenor Square, Stevenson said: "One of my Latin-American colleagues told me the other day that my epitaph should be, 'Once upon a time there *was* an American diplomat....'"

Stevenson laughed and then added: "You know, I rather like that."

For Stevenson, the Cuban fiasco was the first of several humiliating experiences that led to private apologies from President Kennedy and a public show of support.

To show his faith in Stevenson, Kennedy asked him to go

on a goodwill tour of South America. The tour's key objective, however, was to help repair the prestige of the United States, damaged at the Bay of Pigs.

Stevenson left June 4, 1961, on his eighteen-day tour, and on his first stop in Caracas, Venezuela, was given a warm reception—as he was at most of his other stops.

As he stepped off a jet airliner at Maquetia Airport in Caracas, he beamed and waved his gray Homburg at the crowd that was shouting, *"Muy bien, Adlai"* ("Very good, Adlai").

There were similar friendly turnouts in Paraguay and Ecuador. In the bigger cities, Buenos Aires and São Paolo, people seemed indifferent or too busy to stand around for a glimpse of the visitor, but in Montevideo, Uruguay, and Santiago, Chile, crowds gathered to cheer Stevenson's arrival at government buildings.

Throughout the trip, however, there was an armed policeman between Stevenson and the people who craned their necks to see him. He was irked by the police guard—at times there was no chance to mingle with the people—and he said as much. All the governments were determined, however, that there should be no repetition of the violent incidents that had marred the Nixon visit to South America in 1958.

From his conversations with presidents, high officials, political leaders and, in some cases, students and labor groups, Stevenson came away with these dominant impressions and reported them to Kennedy:

In general, political and economic conditions had deteriorated since his private visit to South America in 1961. Inter-American relations were seriously damaged by the Cuban invasion. Social and economic unrest, fanned by Communist agitation, had reached the point in some countries where political instability was a serious problem.

There were significant differences in the way people in South America and the United States viewed the Cuban revolution. Many persons still saw it as a great social upheaval of the underprivileged, and not as a Communist beachhead in the Americas.

The possibility of more effective economic cooperation depended largely on the South American governments themselves. The adoption of needed economic and social reforms and the preparation of comprehensive development plans were "spotty and uneven." A great effort must be made to reach agreement on the nature of Latin America's development problems and to draft common action in this uncharted area.

After his report to the President, Stevenson made several speeches on his Latin-American visit and then flew to Europe for a three-week working vacation.

On the visit he discussed such problems as Berlin and Bizerte (in which France and Tunisia stood in uneasy truce over continuing French occupation of the North African base) with President de Gaulle and other leaders.

On his return in August—in the midst of the United States military build-up over Berlin—he remarked that Western Europe was far less jittery over the possibility that the crisis might lead to a shooting war than were many Americans.

He noted that he had not detected any "war jitters" in Europe and added that the consensus there was that the Berlin situation would not "degenerate into war because neither Mr. Khrushchev nor the West wants war."

For the remainder of August, Stevenson relaxed, prepared for the forthcoming session of the General Assembly and conferred several times with Kennedy—including one four-hour visit aboard the *Marlin,* the Kennedy family cruiser, on Nantucket Sound.

On September 17, two days before the opening of the General Assembly, Stevenson affirmed United States confidence that the United Nations could defeat Soviet attacks on its structure and policies.

"We believe the United States can and will keep on standing fast against the attacks from Moscow," he said, "until it is obvious that those attacks have defeated their own purpose and are given up."

At a reception by the American Association for the United Nations, Stevenson cited the Congo operation as a case that would go down in history to the credit of the United Nations, in spite of widespread criticism.

One day later, Stevenson, the United States and the entire United Nations were jolted by the news that Hammarskjöld had died in a plane crash close to Northern Rhodesia. Stevenson's shock and grief were obvious when he delivered his eulogy in the General Assembly.

"Dag Hammarskjöld was the embodiment of the international civil servant that the Secretary General of the United Nations should ideally and always be," he said. "He was resolutely impartial, resolutely even-handed and resolutely firm in carrying out the mandates with which he was entrusted. He never swerved from what he conceived to be his duty to the United Nations and to the cause of peace, and he never wavered under irresponsible invective and unjust criticism."

Hammarskjöld's death threw the United Nations into a constitutional crisis, with the Soviet Union urging a troika plan in which representatives of the Eastern, Western and neutral blocs would operate the Secretariat.

The proposal received little support outside the Soviet bloc and after seven weeks of negotiations, Stevenson announced, "There will be no troika and no veto in the Secretariat." U Thant was then selected Acting Secretary General.

A year later, when the word "acting" was removed from Thant's title, Stevenson lauded him before the General Assembly. "U Thant, as an international civil servant, has been devoted to the common good of all people," he said. "That so many nations have faith in him is testimony to his strength of mind, his clarity of purpose and, not least, his firm belief in the Charter and in the independence and integrity of the office he holds."

During the busy General Assembly, Stevenson was occupied with diplomatic issues that were to beset him for the remainder of his life: disarmament, the Congo, the peaceful uses of space, the admission of Communist China to the United Nations, the world organization's financing.

Two months after the Soviet Union suddenly resumed nuclear testing in 1961, Stevenson urged an immediate test ban treaty. The plea was ignored. But at the next General Assembly session he was the author of a proposal to outlaw all but underground testing. This eventually became the basis of the Treaty of Moscow.

Indeed, one of Stevenson's happier moments in his United Nations years was the signing, in 1963, of that treaty when he was a member of the United States delegation that went to Moscow for the ceremony. The treaty gave Stevenson all the more satisfaction because it reflected a proposal he had made in the 1956 campaign—a proposal that had been derided then as visionary.

For Stevenson, disarmament was the first order of business at the United Nations. He made one of his strongest and even poetic statements on it before the Assembly's Political Committee November 15, 1961, when he said:

War is one of the oldest institutions. It is deeply imbedded in the traditions, the folkways, the literature, even the values of almost all countries. It has engaged countless talented men and produced countless national heroes. At the same time, civilized men and women for centuries past have abhorred the immorality of organized killing of men.

Yet, let us confess at once, to our common shame, that this deep sense of revulsion has not averted wars, nor shortened one by a day.

While I do not say that all wars have been started for unworthy purposes, let us also confess, morality to the side, that almost all past wars have served to promote what was conceived to be the national or princely or religious interests of those who fought them—or at least those who won them.

For in past years there have been winners as well as losers, the victors and the vanquished, the decorated and the dead. In the end, valuable real estate and other riches have changed hands. Thrones have been won, regimes transferred, rules extended, religions and ideologies imposed, empires gained and lost, aggressions halted or advanced.

Thus wars in the past have sometimes been a means of settling international disputes, of changing political control, of inducing social transformation and even of stimulating science and technology. . . .

But war in the future would differ fundamentally from war in the past, not in degree but in kind. It is this which seems so difficult to grasp. Thermonuclear war cannot serve anyone's national interest—no matter how moral or immoral that interest may be, no matter how just or unjust, no matter how noble or ignoble, regardless of the nation's ideology, faith or social system.

It is no satisfaction to suggest that the issue of morality in war thus has become academic. Yet this is the fact and perhaps it will serve to clarify the dialogue of war and peace. For we can now free our collective conscience of nice ethical distinctions, and face the stark, amoral fact that war has ceased to be practical, that no nation can contemplate resort to modern war except in defense against intolerable exaction or aggression. Therefore we must abolish war to save our collective skins. For as long as this nuclear death dance continues, millions—tens of millions—perhaps hundreds of millions are living on borrowed time.

As the Sixteenth General Assembly continued, Stevenson offered a broad program for the peaceful uses of space—a program that, after minor changes, the Soviet Union eventually agreed to. He also spoke out strongly against the admission of Communist China, declaring that the issue was "whether it is right for the United Nations to drive the Republic of China from this organization in order to make room for a regime whose appetite seems to be insatiable." What heightened interest in this speech, however, was that it was the first time since the Communists gained control of the Chinese mainland in 1949 that the General Assembly had embarked on a full debate on who should represent China at the United Nations. Before 1961, the United States had countered resolutions to seat the Communists with the proposal that the issue be postponed.

Stevenson the diplomat drove himself hard, as Robert Conley reported in an article headlined "A 14-Hour Day With Stevenson":

Just about the busiest man around here these days is Adlai E. Stevenson, the chief United States delegate to the United Nations.

For example, his program today included these activities:

He met in the morning with Issoufou S. Djermakoye, Nigeria's chief delegate, went on to New York's City Hall to receive a distinguished service award from the National Bill of Rights Association, and attended a Canadian luncheon uptown and in the evening the annual reception of the Secretary General and the President of the General Assembly.

"My friends tell me I walk like a nervous rabbit," he said as he slipped into the flow of diplomats pouring into the General Assembly hall for the vote on whether to admit Communist China to membership this year.

Later Mr. Stevenson beamed. The United States had won a victory when the Assembly rejected a Soviet resolution calling for Peking's admission.

Elation was not always the case, though. Usually his day as the United States chief delegate has been more a diary of progress and frustration. It also has been an excursion into a world bounded by the clock and the telephone and infrequent moments alone.

On the surface it has been a glimpse of the hustling figure of Mr. Stevenson trailing a kite-tail of aides, unable to wait for a traffic light to change before crossing a street.

But underneath there has been an essay in "quiet diplomacy"—the grinding behind-the-scenes negotiations that have led to the brief dramas played out here on the floor of the General Assembly or the Security Council. . . .

On Wednesday Mr. Stevenson permitted a reporter and a photographer to accompany him on his rounds.

The work began when Mr. Stevenson left his official suite at the Waldorf Towers at 8:55 A.M., briefcase in hand and clutching a pair of left-behind rubbers to be returned to a friend. It went on with hardly a pause until 11:15 P.M., when he returned for the night. . . .

As this country's spokesman at the United Nations, Mr. Stevenson also presides over a delegation with a permanent diplomatic and administrative staff of 110, augmented during the Assembly by forty or more specialists from Washington in such areas as Africa, Asia, Latin America, economics, human rights, refugees and law.

The delegation headquarters is at United Nations Plaza and East Forty-fifth Street, behind a honeycomb-windowed façade.

Dr. V. K. Kyaruzi of Tanganyika arrived for an appointment. "Good to see you," Mr. Stevenson said and they talked for half an hour on the emerging African nation's new role as the 104th member of the United Nations.

Mr. Stevenson bustled to the United Nations to confer with Mongi Slim of Tunisia, the Assembly President, on the agenda schedule piling up in the rush toward next week's Assembly recess. They spoke in French.

The cocoa carpeting in the delegate's corridor hushed footfalls. Tinted window glass softened the glare of the city beyond. An aide drew Mr. Stevenson aside to mention an African development idea.

At 1 P.M. Mr. Stevenson gave a luncheon at his ten-room hotel suite high over the city for the Colombian Foreign Minister, José Joaquin Caicedo. An urgent message from Washington called him to the phone as the eleven guests gathered in the sun-filled living room. There was time for one drink and about an hour at the table before they all scattered again.

A friend joked with Mr. Stevenson in the elevator about the rush and asked about the job.

"It is something like asking the man burning at the stake how he feels," Mr. Stevenson quipped. "I'm having so much trouble putting out the fire I haven't had a chance to think about it."

Joseph B. Godber, Britain's Minister of State for Foreign Affairs, arrived at the delegation headquarters at 3:02 P.M. and was closeted with Mr. Stevenson for an hour on the Congo. Sir Patrick Dean, Britain's chief delegate, joined the two men as the pace stepped up.

Mr. Stevenson checked with the delegation's financial expert on the costs of the Congo military operation.

Reaching for his private telephone, marked with the gold and white Federal seal, he put in a call to Secretary of State Dean Rusk attending the conference of the foreign ministers of the North Atlantic Treaty Organization in Paris. It was 3:50 P.M. in New York and 8:50 P.M. in Paris.

Mr. Rusk was at a dinner, but was expected back in forty-five minutes. The British diplomats left.

An Algerian rebel group was downstairs.

Mr. Stevenson worked on his disarmament speech for that night, penciling in a marginal note to be developed, a point to be updated, from State Department messages and classified delegation memoranda.

At 4:50 P.M. Mr. Rusk was on the phone from Paris.

A message was laid on Mr. Stevenson's desk, reporting that the Acting Secretary General had just turned down the British request for an immediate cease-fire in Katanga.

Rosemary Spencer, his secretary, moved to a gray steel filing cabinet for a document. A red mushroom-shaped card with the word "Open" hung from the drawer pull. It was a standard warning to lock up before leaving.

George W. Ball, Acting Secretary of State in Mr. Rusk's absence, was called in Washington. A few floors below, in a guarded room behind a steel mesh gate, a Teletype whirred into activity with a coded message.

Mr. Thant phoned from the United Nations. Washington called to say Harland Cleveland, Assistant Secretary of State for International Organization Affairs, was catching the 6 P.M. shuttle plane for New York and would be at Mr. Stevenson's suite at 7:45 P.M. Mr. Ball was reached at the White House.

Armand Bérard, France's chief delegate, was shown in.

Word came that the forty-nine-nation Asian and African group at the United Nations had just commended the United States' stand on Katanga while being cool to the British.

Mr. Stevenson called Mr. Thant back. M. Bérard left.

The hall clock touched 7 as Mr. Stevenson left to change for the testimonial dinner for Mr. Thant, given by Paul G. Hoffman, director of the United Nations Special Fund, at the Four Seasons Restaurant.

There were four more hours before the limousine finally drove Mr. Stevenson home.

By then, Mr. Stevenson had delivered the disarmament speech, telling the other United Nations delegates that they had been given a "mandate from humanity" to preserve the world. . . .

Mr. Stevenson was visibly tired. He had forgotten to get a haircut that his housekeeper, Mrs. Viola Reardy, had reminded him of.

"Pick me up at 8:45, Danny," Mr. Stevenson told his chauffeur, Donato Tasto, at the hotel and went upstairs to let himself in. In the morning it would start all over again.

Despite the energy that Stevenson poured into the job, several friends and columnists observed that even in his first year he felt frustrated in his role and slightly out of step with Kennedy. As Stevenson had feared, several major foreign policy decisions had been made over his objections and even without his knowledge. And at times—especially in his last years—he was forced to defend tactics he did not like.

At one point, he was asked by a magazine editor to name a job—aside from his present post—that he wanted, provided all he had to do was wave a wand to get it.

"Other than the Presidency, of course," he replied with a smile, "I suppose it would be the job of Secretary of State. Assuming you could really be involved in making policy and not just be an administrator, the job, with its infinite complexities and challenges, is the one I would have to choose. Apart from that, I think I might like to be in your business, editing a newspaper or a magazine. You know, my father owned a small newspaper and I always felt that this was something I might like to return to at some time."

In the winter of 1961 Stevenson's private reservations about his United Nations post became public when he seriously considered a request by Mayor Richard J. Daley of Chicago to run for the Illinois Senate seat held by Everett M. Dirksen.

Following a first talk with Kennedy, Stevenson's public remarks suggested that the President had not made a strenuous effort to have him stay at the United Nations.

Several days later, however, Kennedy asked Stevenson to visit him at his Glen Ora estate in Virginia, where he strongly urged Stevenson to remain in New York. He bowed to the President's wishes and announced that "the President has greatly reinforced my view that I can best serve him and the country in the field of foreign policy." In reply, Kennedy said that he was "delighted" with the decision and that he hoped that Stevenson would "play an expanding role" in foreign policy. Nevertheless, relations between the two men remained cool.

The Seventeenth General Assembly had scarcely started in the fall of 1962 when another Cuban crisis developed. Smarting under its setback at the Bay of Pigs in 1961, the United States had kept the island of Cuba under air surveillance and had done its best to isolate Havana diplomatically. Cuba, for her part, was understandably apprehensive lest the United States again abet and encourage exile groups in their counterrevolutionary plans; and in self-defense she called upon the Soviet Union for military aid and took what she conceived to be her case against the United States to the United Nations. Thus on October 8 Osvaldo Dorticos Torrado, the President of Cuba, strode to the General Assembly rostrum to bid the world organization condemn "the American naval blockade" of his country. (There was no solid evidence of a blockade, although there was an uncommon amount of naval activity near the island.)

The explanation of the Cuban's diversionary appeal to the Assembly came two weeks later when the United States announced that Soviet missile emplacements and unmounted short-range missiles had been discovered in the island. Reaction in the United Nations was immediate, with Stevenson charging that the Soviet Union was converting Cuba into "a bridgehead and staging area" in the Western Hemisphere. He asked speedy removal of offensive weapons, including the disassembled missiles.

"We still hope, we still pray, that the worst may be avoided—that the Soviet leadership will call an end to this ominous adventure," he said. "The hopes of mankind are concentrated in this room. The action we take may determine the future of civilization."

Two days later, probably the most electric moment of any United Nations meeting took place in the Security Council chamber. After Soviet Ambassador Zorin had indicated that United States charges of Soviet aggression should not be believed, Stevenson said angrily:

I want to say to you, Mr. Zorin, that I do not have your talent for obfuscation, for distortion, for confusing language and for double-talk. And I must confess to you that I am glad that I do not!

But if I understood what you said, it was that my position had changed, that today I was defensive because we did not have the evidence to prove our assertions that your government had installed long-range missiles in Cuba.

Well, let me say something to you, Mr. Ambassador: We do have the evidence. We have it, and it is clear and it is incontrovertible. And let me say something else: Those weapons must be taken out of Cuba!

Next, if I understood you, you said—with a trespass on credibility that excels your best—that our position had changed since I spoke here the other day because of the pressures of world opinion and the majority of the United Nations. Well, let me say to you, sir—you are wrong again. We have had no pressure from anyone whatsoever. We came here today to indicate our willingness to discuss U Thant's proposals, and that is the only change that has taken place.

But let me also say to you, sir, that there *has* been a change. You—the Soviet Union—*has* sent these weapons to Cuba. You—the Soviet Union—*has* upset the balance of power in the world. You—the Soviet Union—*has* created this new danger, not the United States.

And you ask with a fine show of indignation why the President did not tell Mr. Gromyko on last Thursday about our evidence, at the very time that Mr. Gromyko was blandly denying to the President that the U.S.S.R. was placing such weapons on sites in the New World.

Well, I will tell you why—because we were assembling the evidence, and perhaps it would be instructive to the world to see how far a Soviet official would go in perfidy. Perhaps we wanted to know if this country faced another example of nuclear deceit like that one a year ago when, in stealth, the Soviet Union broke the nuclear test moratorium.

And while we are asking questions, let me ask you why your government, your Foreign Minister, deliberately, cynically deceived us about the nuclear build-up in Cuba?

And, finally, the other day, Mr. Zorin, I remind you that you did not deny the existence of these weapons. Instead, we heard that they had suddenly become *defensive* weapons. But today, again, if I heard you correctly, you now say, with another fine flood of rhetorical scorn, they do not exist, or that we haven't proved they exist.

All right, sir, let me ask you one simple question: Do you, Ambassador Zorin, deny that the U.S.S.R. has placed and is placing medium- and intermediate-range missiles and sites in Cuba? Yes or no? Don't wait for the translation. Yes or no?

[Zorin refused to answer, maintaining he was "not in an American courtroom."]

You are in the courtroom of world opinion. You have denied they exist, and I want to know if I understood you correctly.

I am prepared to wait for my answer until hell freezes over, if that's your decision. And I am also prepared to present the evidence in this room—now!

Zorin still did not answer and called on the representative of Chile to speak. Stevenson, however, retained the floor.

"I have not finished my statement," he declared. "I asked you a question, and I will now proceed, if I may, to finish my statement.

"I doubt if anyone in this room, except possibly the representative of the Soviet Union, has any doubt about the facts. But in view of his statements and the statements of the Soviet Government up until last Thursday, when Mr. Gromyko denied the existence of any intention in installing such weapons in Cuba, I am going to make a portion of the evidence available right now. If you will indulge me for a moment, we will set up an easel here in the back of the room where I hope it will be visible to everyone."

Stevenson then exhibited the incontrovertible photographic evidence.

After missile-carrying Soviet ships bound for Cuba had changed course, Kennedy and Khrushchev reached agreement on the removal of the weapons. A series of negotiations then took place between Soviet delegates, Stevenson and John J. McCloy, special United States negotiator on the Cuban issue. The crisis finally appeared to be at an end.

For Stevenson, however, it was the beginning of another crisis—a more personal one that deeply affected him and aroused the ire of his friends and associates.

In early December, an article appeared in *The Saturday Evening Post* purporting to be a reconstruction of meetings of the top-level National Security Council during the two tense weeks of the Cuban crisis. The article was written by Charles Bartlett, a reporter for *The Chattanooga Times* and a close friend of the President, and Stewart Alsop, *The Post's* Washington editor.

The article told of debate in a Council committee between the so-called "hawks" and "doves"—those advocating a tough policy and those favoring a more cautious approach. Eventually, the article said, a "rolling consensus" was reached in which everybody emerged as a "hawk" or a "dove." The consensus was for a blockade of Cuba, with other military measures, including possibly an air strike and even an invasion, to follow if the missiles were not removed.

The article said: "Only Adlai Stevenson . . . dissented from the . . . consensus." It added: "There is disagreement in retrospect about what Stevenson really wanted. 'Adlai wanted a Munich,' said a non-admiring official who learned of his proposal. 'He wanted to trade the Turkish, Italian and British missile bases for the Cuban bases.' . . . There seems to be no doubt that he preferred political negotiation to the alternative of military action."

The White House issued a denial of the story, but it only fueled the controversy. Press Secretary Pierre Salinger said: "I can state flatly . . . that Ambassador Stevenson strongly supported the decision taken by the President on the quarantine and brilliantly developed the United States position at the United Nations during the days which followed."

What the statement failed to make clear was whether before his ultimate support of the President's decision Stevenson advocated the views attributed to him by *The Post* article.

Stevenson himself dealt with that question almost immediately when, in a television interview, he called the article "wrong in literally every detail" and said that he had supported the idea of a blockade days before the decision was made. "What the article doesn't say is that I opposed . . . an invasion of Cuba at the risk of nuclear war until the peacekeeping machinery of the United Nations had been used."

As for the question of bases, Stevenson declared:

"I said that, if the United States started a negotiation about the elimination of the bases with Mr. Khrushchev, we would have to develop well in advance the content, the political content, of whatever our position would be. Among these would inevitably be the subject of bases which Mr. Khrushchev would raise."

Despite the statements by the White House and Stevenson, there was speculation that Stevenson might be on his way out at the United Nations and that *The Post* article was intended to grease the skids. Several days after the article appeared, Kennedy sent Stevenson a letter that voiced regret over the "unfortunate stir." He told Stevenson "how greatly we have admired your performance at the United Nations. . . . Your continued work at the United Nations will be of inestimable value," he wrote. "Meanwhile, it goes without saying you have my fullest confidence and best wishes."

It was noted, however, that the President voiced no opinion about *The Post* article's accuracy. Thus speculation persisted as to how the article was written, and, as nearly as can be constructed from reports, this is what happened:

Immediately after Khrushchev backed down, when a number of papers and magazines were putting together reviews of the crisis and the Administration's handling of it, Kennedy suggested to Bartlett that he should do an article, and Bartlett took on Alsop as a collaborator. While the President's suggestion may have created conditions for a favorable piece that would disclose a little more of the "inside story" than had been revealed to other reporters, there was no evidence that the President knew the content of the article in advance.

Despite the President's letter, Stevenson remained outraged. "This must be some kind of record for irresponsible journalism," he said at one point. "I hope the time hasn't come in the United States when it is considered better to advocate war to settle issues than peaceful means, because if that time should come the world is doomed. I think it's time to stop this childish talk about hard and soft lines among the advisers of the President. . . . "

Several days later he and Kennedy had a fifteen-minute meeting in Washington. That night they made their first public appearance together since the article at an awards dinner for scientists sponsored by the Kennedy family foundation.

As master of ceremonies, Stevenson introduced the President to the crowd as the "author, producer and star of Mr. Khrushchev's new play, 'A Funny Thing Happened to Me on the Way to Cuba.'"

Stevenson paused, glanced at the President and added: "I'm proud to have been a member of the cast."

Later in his speech, in an allusion to the magazine article, he quoted the late Joseph Pulitzer as having said: "Accuracy is to newspapers what virtue is to a lady, except that a newspaper can always print a retraction."

The house roared, the President applauded and there the matter appeared to end.

Stevenson was especially heartened in this period by a remarkably heavy and favorable amount of mail. The Gallup Poll also showed him to be popular across the country, and many diplomats and officials backed him publicly.

For Stevenson, the Cuban crisis and *The Post* article had come during an especially difficult time. His friend, confidante and adviser, Eleanor Roosevelt, had died in November and Stevenson was asked to deliver eulogies in the General Assembly and at a memorial service at the Cathedral of St. John the Divine. The eulogies, he later said, were as difficult and sad a task as he had ever been asked to perform. "Yesterday, I said I lost more than a friend; I had lost an inspiration. She would rather light candles than curse the darkness and her glow had warmed the world," he told the United Nations meeting.

In the early months of 1963 Stevenson traveled about the country for a series of speeches that were as humorous and as incisive as any he had ever delivered.

In New York on January 22, he told the tenth anniversary convocation of the Fund for the Republic's Center for the Study of Democratic Institutions:

I understand all these famous and wise men, foreign and domestic, have been dissecting democracy morning, afternoon and evening for two days. I wonder if the time hasn't come to leave the poor thing alone to recuperate!

And my discomfort isn't relieved by the subject Dr. [Robert] Hutchins has assigned to me: "The Prospects for Democracy Around the World"!

Have you no little questions, Dr. Hutchins? For I am neither prophet nor philosopher, but an ex-politician and a practicing diplomat, although many would doubtless dissent from both of these claims.

But if my qualifications for speaking to this exalted company are dubious, let me say that when it comes to faith in democracy, I refuse to take a back seat even for my distinguished predecessors on this platform. Because I believe in democracy and freedom, and I believe in their ultimate triumph with the fundamentalist fervor of a survivor of Valley Forge or a Presidential campaign—not to mention two! . . .

I suppose whether democracy can prevail in the great upheaval of our time is a valid question. Certainly, after 150 years of uninterrupted expansion of the idea of government by consent of the governed, it has recently met with mounting and formidable challenges all over the world from Fascist, Nazi, Communist authoritarians, and a variety of dictatorships. And we have good reason to know how clumsy, slow, inefficient and costly it is compared to the celerity, certainty and secrecy of absolutism.

But the important thing is that it *has* survived. The important thing is that even the absolutists masquerade as democrats; even the military and quasi-military dictatorships strive in the name of democracy to manage the public business. And all of them say that authoritarianism is only a necessary transition to democracy.

Why? Because it is the most popular form of government yet devised; because it is, as it always has been, not only the prize of the steadfast and the courageous, but the privilege of those who are better off; because, in short, as Jefferson said, it is "the only form of government which is not eternally at open or secret war with the rights of the people."

I have, therefore, no doubt that, distant as it may be for many people, it will ultimately prevail, that it will rewin lost ground, that it will expand its dominion—that it can withstand the mild winds that are blowing through the world—if, and I repeat if, we who are its custodians continually re-examine and adapt its principles to the changing needs of our changing times.

In February, at the fortieth anniversary luncheon of the Chicago Council on Foreign Relations, Stevenson said:

The United States has an aim in this world, an aim to build a community of nations, diverse, tolerant and genuinely independent—but bound together by a sense of common humanity and by a common interest in peace and progress. In such a community every nation and every man, strong or weak, will have the greatest chance to develop the unlimited possibilities of freedom. In such a community we Americans ourselves will have the greatest chance to hand down our freedom and prosperity to future generations. The growth of such a community, too coherent and too vigorous for Communism to undermine, therefore, is as vital a factor in our security—and for our future—as our armed power.

To build this community one of the instruments is the United Nations. It is not a magic lamp. Perhaps it is only a candle in the window. But its spirit is that of community, tolerance, give and take—without which there can be no peace. Its method is parliamentary diplomacy, debating, voting, the writing and rewriting of resolutions, days and nights of discussion and careful listening. We are successful at it, for both the spirit and the method are second nature to democracy.

But if democracy is to be nurtured in new countries, as well as preserved in the old, if the United Nations is to succeed, we must all have time—a time of peace. For it is peace which generates the factors most favorable to the growth of democracy: prosperity, stability, education, freedom of thought and the mutual trust which encourages free and fruitful communication between nations.

And in an address accepting the Tenth Annual Patriotism Award of the University of Notre Dame, Stevenson said in South Bend, Indiana:

We are Americans because we belong to a certain ideal, visionary type of political and social order. We can't point back to a long, shared civilization. It is true, most of us have Europe and the West behind us. But not all—and, anyway, it is a concept of the West that we create rather than inherit. And no one is standing on our necks keeping us down and together.

The result is a community, surely, whose instinctive, rooted, in-herited, taken-for-granted unity is much less than is normal in the world and whose intellectual, ideal, created and worked-at unity has to be all the more dynamic. If we are not dedicated to our funda-mental propositions, then the natural cement in our society may not be enough to take the strain.

I would agree that there are substitutes. When a President said that "The business of America is business," he told us something about the degree to which a standard of living can do stand-in duty for a way of life. But the question, "What manner of people are we?" cannot be everlastingly answered in terms of two-car families or split-level homes.

And if the gods of the market give no answers, neither, for us, do the gods of the tribe. We come back to our propositions. America is much more than a geographical fact. It is a political and moral fact—the first community in which men set out in principle to institutionalize freedom, responsible government and human equal-ity. And we love it for this audacity! How easy it is, contemplating this vision, to see in it—as Jefferson or Lincoln saw in it—"the last, best hope of man." To be a nation founded on an ideal in one sense makes our love of country a more vital and dynamic force than any instinctive pieties of blood and soil.

But it also demands a more complex and discriminating love. Will the fabric hold if the ideal fades? If the effort to realize our citizens' birthright of freedom and equality is not constantly renewed, on what can we fall back? As a going concern, we can no doubt survive many shocks and shames. It was Adam Smith who remarked that "There is a great deal of ruin in every state." But can we survive, as a great, dynamic, confident and growing community, if the essentially liberal thrust of our origins is forgotten, if we equate liberty with passive noninterference, if we exclude large minorities from our standards of equality, if income becomes a substitute for idealism, consumption for dedication, privilege for neighborly goodwill? ...

Societies based on blood ties can perhaps safely confuse conservatism and patriotism. People with long backward-looking traditions can perhaps do so. Countries under the heel of dictators must do so. But if the world's first experiment in the open society uses patriotism as a cloak for inaction or reaction, then it will cease to be open and then, as a social organism, it will lose its fundamental reason for existence.

Do not, therefore, regard the critics as questionable patriots. What were Washington and Jefferson and Adams but profound critics of the colonial *status quo?* Our society can stand a large dose of constructive criticism just because it is so solid and has so much to conserve. It is only if keen and lively minds constantly compare the ideal and the reality and see the shadows—the shadow of self-righteousness, the shadows of slums and poverty, the shadow of delinquent children, the shadow of suburban sprawls, the shadow of racial discrimination, the shadow of interminable strikes—it is only then that the shadows can be dispelled and the unique brightness of our national experiment can be seen and loved.

The patriots are those who love America enough to wish to see her as a model to mankind. They love her, of course, as she is, but they want the beloved to be more lovable. This is not treachery. This, as every parent, every teacher, every friend must know, is the truest and noblest affection. No patriots so defaced America as those who, in the name of Americanism, launched a witch hunt which became a byword around the world. We have survived it. We shall survive John Birchism and all the rest of the super-patriots—but only at the price of perpetual and truly patriotic vigilance.

Stevenson enjoyed speaking out of town, especially at colleges, and he enjoyed the social whirl of New York and the United Nations. He had complaints, of course, too. He once told a House Foreign Affairs Subcommittee that he tried to keep up with the United Nations parties to the limits of his "endurance and strength," but that it was getting to be onerous.

In addition to his United Nations responsibilities, he served as Chairman of the Field Foundation and the Eleanor Roosevelt Cancer Fund. "Then there are the social engagements," he told Martin Mayer in an interview in 1965 for *The Times Magazine*.

"You're honorary chairman of every darned thing that happens. The theater benefits. The World's Fair. The speeches before some organization. And there's been this development of the Award System; they grant awards to people these days for all manner of things. Somebody has to make a speech at the awards dinner, and eight or ten old friends beat hell out of you until you say you'll do it and then the speech has to be prepared."

As a marriageable celebrity, Stevenson was invariably mentioned in the social columns—far too frequently, he felt. "Over Christmas," he told Mayer, "I read a story about my glamorous social life. I was squiring Mrs. Kennedy, Ava Gardner, Lauren Bacall and some gorgeous dame I've never even met."

For relaxation, Stevenson sometimes slipped off for a country-house weekend or a little tennis at the River Club. He liked music, but he never got too much of a chance to attend concerts or the opera.

In his office, especially after a rough session, Stevenson enjoyed browsing through a big leather-bound scrapbook, "Dear Mr. Ambassador: Selected Writings from The Great American Public." Stevenson's correspondence rarely dipped below five hundred letters a week, and in such a week as the Cuban missile crisis the total rose to over three thousand.

There were proposals, pleas and denunciations, of course, but one of Stevenson's favorites was a letter that began:

"I really do admire you so much, but there's one thing you should know. Your posture at the Security Council is *negative*. Please sit up straight so you'll make a good impression on the neutral nations."

Stevenson was enormously popular at the United Nations.

"It's an odd thing to say," he commented once, "but everybody who has served at the United Nations has known me personally or by my writings or travel. And they were about 98 percent pro-Democratic during my campaigns. I've often said it was a damned shame I ran for President of the wrong country."

On the afternoon of November 22, 1963, Stevenson was attending a luncheon in a private dining room at the United Nations given by Luis Bossay of Chile for chief delegates. An aide brought the news that Kennedy had been assassinated in Dallas. Shocked, Stevenson excused himself and hurried back to his office.

Later that day, he said: "The tragedy of this day is beyond instant comprehension. All of us who knew him will bear the grief of his death to the day of ours. And all men everywhere who love peace and justice and freedom will bow their heads."

In the early days of the Johnson Administration, Stevenson was much closer to the new President than he had been to Kennedy. The two men had known each other since 1933, when Stevenson was a young lawyer in the Agricultural Adjustment Administration and Johnson was secretary to Representative Richard Kleberg, who wanted some help for his district from the AAA.

In late 1963 and early 1964, Stevenson plunged into a growing number of crises: United Nations financing, efforts to expand the organization's peace-keeping machinery, the bitter dispute between Greek and Turkish Cypriots, Vietnam.

"We are in Southeast Asia," Stevenson told the Security Council in 1964, "to help our friends preserve their own opportunity to be free of imported terror, or alien assassination managed by the North Vietnam Communists based in Hanoï and backed by the Chinese Communists from Peking."

At the time, Stevenson insisted that the United States' bombing of North Vietnamese torpedo boats in the Bay of Tonkin was an act of self-defense against attacks on United States destroyers on the high seas and was authorized by international law and the United Nations Charter.

Meanwhile, Stevenson was again mentioned as a candidate, this time for the Senate seat in New York held by Kenneth B. Keating. He declined, but he left the door open for a Vice Presidential nomination on Johnson's ticket. Although nothing came of this, Stevenson was heartened by the selection of Hubert Humphrey as Johnson's running mate, and in the waning weeks of the campaign he spoke with bite and vigor for the Johnson-Humphrey ticket.

With the election of Johnson, and the President's stated confidence in him, Stevenson began to feel more comfortable at the United Nations. Soon, however, escalation in South

Vietnam and the Marine Corps landing in the Dominican Republic raised new problems, or rather new versions of the ones that had plagued him during the Kennedy years.

These were a lack of involvement in the making of the Dominican and Vietnamese policy (at times he felt he was being simply ignored). Publicly, Stevenson echoed the views of the Administration.

For example, he told a convocation of the University of Toronto May 28, 1965:

In the Dominican Republic, while the Organization of American States force keeps them from each other's throats, we hope the embittered factions can agree on a government based on neither extreme of right or left that will keep the way open to genuine popular consultation as soon as possible. Then there must follow, I presume, economic redevelopment to launch education, diversify the economy, reform the agrarian structure and complete the revolution that began with the death of Trujillo. Meanwhile, perhaps it is reasonable for the skeptical to wait and see whether the United States Marines are simply repeating an old, melancholy and finished story. . . .

In Vietnam President Johnson has asked publicly and privately again and again for a peaceful settlement—to no avail. He has offered negotiations without preconditions—to no avail. It was said the North could not negotiate while the bombing was going on. So he suspended the bombing—to no avail. It must be apparent by now to even the most skeptical that it is not Saigon or the United States that won't negotiate, discuss or even meet, but Peking and Hanoï— as long as there is a prospect of winning.

For many of Stevenson's warmest supporters, including artists, writers and scientists, his public pronouncements were, quite simply, not to be believed.

In late June, 1965, as the Vietnam build-up continued, a group, Artists and Writers Dissent, sent Stevenson a declaration that said that Administration policies in Vietnam and the Dominican Republic had "clearly violated the United Nations Charter, international law and those fundamental principles of human decency which alone can prevent a terrifying, world-wide escalation of suffering and death."

"In the past," the artists' group wrote,

you have expressed your commitment to a world of law and to an honest, compassionate search for peaceful solutions to conflict. Therefore, we believe this must be a time of deep inner conflict for you, and we urge you to resolve that conflict in the interest of restoring sanity to this government's foreign policy. . . .

We urge you to resign as United States Ambassador to the United Nations and having done that, to become a spokesman again for that which is humane in the traditions and in the people of America. By this act, you can contribute immeasurably to the prospects of world peace. By remaining in your post—without speaking truth to power—you will have diminished yourself and all men everywhere.

The declaration shook Stevenson. It had been signed, he knew, by the very people who had been his strongest supporters, and he was troubled by the conflict between the intellectual, liberal community and the Johnson Administration.

Stevenson's associates called the proposed resignation an "inconceivable idea." They pointed to the numerous speeches he had made outside the United Nations upholding the government's position. A spokesman for Stevenson said that he would look on any resignation as a betrayal and that he was concentrating his efforts rather on "getting the United Nations back on its feet."

Following the declaration, which came on the heels of a meeting with seven members of the artists' and writers' group at the United States Mission, Stevenson flew to San Francisco for the twentieth anniversary celebration of the United Nations.

On the television program "Meet the Press," Stevenson was asked if he was opposed to the Johnson Administration's policies and contemplating resignation to speak his mind more freely.

"I don't want to leave the impression that I am opposed to this policy," he said. "I suppose every one of us would disagree on details about anything, virtually anything. I don't hesitate to say that as to every detail of the conduct of our policy I'm not always in agreement, nor I suspect are any of our responsible officials, and that's what you have a President for. He's the one who has to make the final decisions, however uncomfortable and distasteful they may be."

Shortly after the San Francisco meeting, he flew to Europe for a working vacation—meetings in Geneva of the United Nations Economic and Social Council. There he called for a search for a pattern of urban development that "will avoid the blight and misery so visible in many cities throughout the world."

"Rootless, hopeless, workless urban poverty is the greatest single cause of misery in the world," he said.

CHAPTER VIII

———◦◦◦———

THE INGREDIENTS OF GREATNESS

FROM GENEVA Stevenson started back for New York, with a stopover in London to see friends in the American Embassy and to engage in a dispute over television with some Britons about United States policy in Vietnam. The afternoon of July 14, with some free time on his hands, he decided to go for a walk. What happened was recounted in Anthony Lewis's dispatch:

Adlai E. Stevenson collapsed on a London street today and died.

The United States representative at the United Nations, twice Democratic candidate for President, was sixty-five years old. He had been in London since Saturday and had seemed in good health and good spirits.

Doctors declined to state the cause of death until a coroner's report was filed. The general assumption was that it was a heart attack.

Mr. Stevenson was walking along Upper Grosvenor Street, about fifty yards from the United States Embassy, at 5:10 on a warm, sunny afternoon. Mrs. Marietta P. Tree, his old friend and fellow member of the American delegation at the United Nations, was with him.

Suddenly he fell to the pavement. Mrs. Tree ran to the nearest building, the International Sportsmen's Club, and asked for a doctor. In a minute or two one appeared.

As the doctor attempted artificial respiration, Mrs. Tree knelt down and tried to revive Mr. Stevenson by breathing into his mouth. There was no response.

An ambulance took Mr. Stevenson to St. George's Hospital at Hyde Park, and attendants applied oxygen on the way. But he was pronounced dead on arrival.

An embassy official was on the telephone with a nurse, trying to find out how Mr. Stevenson was, when an unidentified doctor cut in at 5:35 and said: "I have just now signed the death certificate."

Mr. Stevenson was in London for what was termed a private visit. It mixed some diplomacy with the pleasure of seeing old friends. He was staying at the United States Embassy residence with Ambassador and Mrs. David K. E. Bruce.

On Saturday he went to Chequers and saw Prime Minister Wilson. Today he paid a call on the Foreign Secretary, Michael Stewart.

After the visit with Mr. Stewart he returned to the embassy, in Grosvenor Square, and taped a brief radio interview with the British Broadcasting Corporation. The tape, which represented his last public words, was broadcast after his death tonight.

In this interview Mr. Stevenson took pains to say that he stood with President Johnson in support of the United States' position on Vietnam.

"There has been a great deal of pressure on me in the United States from many sources to take a public position inconsistent with that of my government," he said.

"Actually," he went on, "I don't agree with those protestants. My hope in Vietnam is that resistance there may establish the fact that changes in Asia are not to be precipitated by outside force."

Last Monday Mr. Stevenson talked with British and American journalists for more than an hour. To some there seemed to be in him an undertone of unhappiness about aspects of American foreign policy, perhaps especially over the Dominican affair. But he said nothing directly critical of the President or his policy.

At a party last night in the embassy he was as gay as ever, and he looked a little leaner and more fit, if anything, than in recent years. At a dinner party afterward, one person said, "He went up the stairs like a bird."

His humor, which helped win him a strong personal following in the United States among those he christened "eggheads," also endeared him to the British.

They loved the skepticism and self-doubt that hurt him politically at home. They took to him right away in his first try for the Presidency, in 1952, and could never really understand why so intelligent and sympathetic a man was not elected.

Tonight the Foreign Secretary issued an official statement expressing the government's sympathy. It spoke of Mr. Stevenson's "liberality of mind and lucidity of expression."

"He will be remembered not only for what he did and what he stood for," the statement said, "but for the tolerant, humane way he acted.

"He will never be forgotten as a man because he was so much an individual, so humorous, so considerate and so firm and yet so gentle."

The Times of London, in an editorial, appraised the place of Mr. Stevenson in broader terms. It called him a "tragic figure" in American history "who was a prophet before his time, who received honor but not power" and who "died full of disappointments."

"Yet his life has left a mark that will not be eradicated," the editorial said. "Abroad he came to represent that aspect of his country that most sustains foreign confidence in the fundamental virtue of its intentions even when its actions seem wrong. . . .

"Through all the placid confidence of the Eisenhower era and the clumsy crusades of [Secretary of State John Foster] Dulles, he reminded the world that there was another America—sensitive, self-critical, thoughtful and visionary. At home he kept the light of intellect burning through a period when it was not fashionable to think."

Because of the time difference it was 1 P.M. when news of Stevenson's death reached the United States. President Johnson was just sitting down to luncheon at the White House with a group of Japanese Cabinet members. The President was stunned. To his luncheon guests he said:

A few moments before this luncheon began today I received word that the great and good man Adlai Stevenson had died in London.

Of course, my immediate reaction was to cancel this luncheon meeting. But after talking to some of the members of my own Cabinet and some of his friends they all realized that Adlai Stevenson would not have had us do any such thing. He would want us to continue because he was first, and he was foremost, concerned that the works of peace and the works of progress and, most important, the works of understanding, which have prevailed and predominated throughout this meeting, must go on.

So this, then, is our legacy from Adlai Stevenson—a charge to continue the quest for a decent world, for a better world order, for a life for man that is free of war and destruction and the oppression of his spirit.

So this is our pledge to the memory of this great man who is really, as all of you here know, a true citizen of the world—a pledge to devote our energies and our talents and our resources and our wills to the cause for which he died.

We realize that America lost its foremost advocate and its most eloquent spirit and one of its finest voices for peace in the world. The world of freedom has lost, I think, perhaps its most dedicated champion.

So I would like to ask each of you to stand with me in a moment of silent tribute to this great lover of peace, this great statesman, Adlai E. Stevenson.

Shortly after the luncheon Mr. Johnson went on nation-wide television for a more formal expression of his, and the nation's, sorrow. In slow and measured words he said:

The flame which illuminated the dreams and expectations of an entire world is now extinguished. Adlai Stevenson of Illinois is dead.

I am sending a delegation of distinguished Americans, headed by the Vice President, to London to bring his body back to America on the airplane of the President of the United States.

His great hero, Abraham Lincoln, said at the beginning of his political career that "I have no other ambition so great as that of being truly esteemed of my fellow men, by rendering myself worthy of their esteem."

And although his disappointments were many, in this, like Lincoln, he was vindicated.

Like Lincoln he was rooted in America's heartland, yet his voice reached across every boundary of nation and race and class.

Like Lincoln he was a great emancipator. It was his gift to help emancipate men from narrowness of mind and the shackles which selfishness and ignorance place upon the human adventure.

Like Lincoln he will be remembered more for what he stood for than for the offices he held, more for the ideals he embodied than the position in which he served, for history honors men more for what they were than who they were. And by this standard he holds a permanent place on that tiny roster of those who will be remembered as long as mankind is strong enough to honor greatness.

It seems such a short time ago that out of Illinois came that thoughtful eloquence summoning an entire nation back from its dangerous drift toward contentment and complacency. For an entire generation of Americans he imparted a nobility to public life and a grandeur to American purpose which has already reshaped the life of the nation and which will endure for many generations.

One by one he sounded the great themes of our times—peace and justice and the well-being of humanity. And many men will labor for many years toward the vision and high purpose which was the generous outpouring of this man's heart and skills.

He was an American. And he served his country well. But what he saw, and what he spoke, and what he worked for, is the shared desire of humanity. He believed in us, perhaps more than we deserved. And so we came to believe in ourselves, more than we had. And if we persevere, then on the foundation of that faith we can build the wondrous works of peace and of justice among the nations.

He will not see that day. But it will be his day still.

Let us, therefore, adversary and friend alike, pause for a moment and weep for one who was a friend and guide to all mankind.

Radio, television and the newspapers, meantime, had spread the news of Stevenson's death. Everywhere there was a pause, a sense of shock, simple sorrow. In New York flags at the United Nations were brought down to half-staff; at the Waldorf-Astoria where Stevenson lived, the huge flag on Park Avenue was lowered; and throughout the city, which he had adopted as a second home since 1961, mourning began. And amid the official expressions of grief there was a small unofficial one, a recollection of Stevenson's thoughtfulness—a characteristic that bound him to those who knew him as it did those who were only glancingly acquainted.

Norman Miller, a former information officer at the United Nations, stopped in his day's work to remember that in 1963 his eleven-year-old son had been ill of leukemia at Beth Israel Hospital. Stevenson and he, Miller recalled, had met only casually in the line of duty, yet one day when he heard of the boy's illness he quietly appeared in his hospital room one afternoon and spent fifteen or twenty minutes passing a pleasant time of day with the patient, leaving the hospital as unobtrusively as he had arrived.

Meanwhile Johnson's delegation headed by Vice President Humphrey flew to London to bring back Stevenson's body for a funeral service in Washington. This was held on July 16 in the National Cathedral, which was filled with friends in government. An old associate, Carl McGowan, who was Stevenson's aide during his governorship, delivered the eulogy, a simple statement that said:

We are a vast company, we friends of Adlai Stevenson. Only a few of our total number are met here in Washington today to mourn him. More will come together for the same sad purpose in his homeland in Illinois. But all taken together will be but a very small part of the whole.

This is because in his case the word friend has a staggering sweep. It comprehends those who have had the benison of his personal presence to delight as well as to inspire. But it also includes literally millions in this country and abroad to whom he is only a voice.

It is a voice, however, to which they have listened since he began speaking in the accents of reason to the American people and as he has continued to do to the peoples of the entire world in the United Nations.

These people have in all their sorts and conditions of life, of high and low degree, of varying color and religions, listened to that voice with unabated interest and with undiminished respect. They have heard in it the unmistakable intonations of friendship. They have responded with the gift of their affection to a man most of them have never seen.

They are of our company of friends today, as much as any one of us here. We have all heard the same voice.

That voice is still now. But its echoes are likely to be sounding down the corridors of history for a long time. For it is the essence of faith to believe that the world in its advancing age will set no less store than have we upon reason, upon intelligence, upon gaiety, upon charity and compassion and grace—all these things and more of and with which this voice has spoken to us so often and so clearly in the past.

We do not need now to be reminded of what we have lost. That hurt is deep and no one of us is too old to cry. We may better, then, give thanks for what we have had and rejoice in our recollections of how our good fortune came to be.

Many have asked how it was that a man of Governor Stevenson's sensibilities could have intruded himself into the dust and heat of politics. We may think, I believe, that it was simply his joyous response to one of his deepest instincts—that for public service.

He knew that the greatest opportunities for effective public service lie in elective office. The shattering disappointments that beset that way of life can also dissolve in the satisfaction of feeling the reins of political power in one's hands harnessed to good and just ends.

The disappointments were his in cruel measure. But the satisfactions were his as well. We need not fear that he ever looked back with despairing regret at the way the final balance was struck.

There was a strong family bent for politics, and Adlai Stevenson was of a generation of Princeton students who thrilled to the saga of Woodrow Wilson—that figure in our history in whom the contrasting worlds of the university and the precinct have had their most dramatic conjunction.

In this cathedral the spirit of Woodrow Wilson is always very close. Surely it has never been more so than at this moment. The youthful admirer has completed the course with honor and is at rest with the admired.

The two have often been compared; although there are obvious disparities in temperament, there are many similarities in political styles. Above all, they had a common vision of a just society at home and a peaceful one abroad. Both were agreed that the mobilization and direction of political power was a pursuit from which no man should turn away or of which he should be ashamed.

And who can say that the dream of the youthful Stevenson in terms of a world made safe for democracy did not include a happier ending, if only the rocky road to political power could be traversed once more by a man with the same vision.

Adlai Stevenson enjoyed politics. He relished the infinite variety of people he met there. He found them to be, as in other walks of life, of all descriptions, good and bad, and, more frequently, partly good and partly bad.

He had a particular liking for these last, for he knew that most of us, including himself, are in that group. He sensed that strain of sentimentality which is always just under the surface of political relationships and which binds together in a tacit brotherhood all those who live and die by the ballot box.

He brought to this highly emotional environment his own warm responses, shaped by those qualities which, beneath all the surface toughness and cynicism, it valued the highest, a cheerful lightness of spirit, a gift for undemanding frienship, a sympathetic understanding that most politicians have creditable reasons for worrying about the day after Election Day.

He had the expert political leader's sure instinct for trying to identify the other fellow's problems and pressures before passing judgment upon him. The Stevenson story has now become a legend. The glories of it are many, but none shines more brightly than the sight of him putting to work at the United Nations these very qualities which rocketed him to the foreground of domestic politics.

It was as if he were fated to move through personal disappointment to the very center of the problems that assail all people and upon which depend the survival of civilization itself.

His whole life had been a preparation for events of this scale of importance. And our sense of the fitness of things must be touched by this completely civilized man doing battle for the persistence of the very idea of civilization. For our biggest stake we put forward our best. And he met the challenge, to our and his eternal honor.

If there is reason to be despairing on this day, it is because this man has been removed from the important work of war and peace. But he who knew the perils ahead better than most was undaunted by them.

In virtually the last of his magnificent speeches he gave to the world he said: "For all our desperate dangers I do not believe in the words of Winston Churchill that 'God has despaired of His children.'"

Wherefore, then, are we now to falter and be faint of heart? We have lost a friend; but all the world has lost one. And that friend has left us in the fullness of his powers and secure in what he must have known to be a far-flung respect and affection.

He died as he would have wished, engaged in his country's business, and mankind's.

After the eulogy, the congregation stood and sang Julia Ward Howe's "The Battle Hymn of the Republic," Stevenson's favorite hymn. There were prayers; then the cathedral organ broke into the National Anthem and as its final notes faded, the great Bourdon bell in the tower began to toll.

Later that Friday Stevenson's body was flown to Spring-field, Illinois, where it lay in state in the gloomy rotunda under the Capitol's 361-foot dome. Reporting the event, Austin C. Wehrwein wrote:

He was honored here above all as the former Governor. The body was accompanied by his immediate family, along with a small band of close friends who always called him by his favorite title—"Governor Stevenson."

His simple wooden coffin covered with an American flag was placed on the same six-foot-long walnut table on which the coffin of Abraham Lincoln was placed when it was brought back to Spring-field from Washington a century ago last May.

Lincoln's memory was evoked, too, when the eighteen-car funeral procession passed through Oak Ridge Cemetery on its three-and-a-half-mile journey from the airport. The hearse and three cars bear-ing the immediate family detoured to pass the Lincoln tomb in that cemetery.

The procession began under a hot prairie sun after the Presiden-tial jet had arrived from Washington where world figures had paid tribute to Mr. Stevenson in the National Cathedral.

The scene here was plainer, though no less moving. A crowd of two thousand—women in summer dresses, men in shirt sleeves, many with children and some with cameras—lined the airport fence.

This was a silent, patient crowd unlike the jostling, shouting crowds that had seemed to make Mr. Stevenson so ill at ease when he was a candidate for public office.

Out on the green airport field, the 33d Infantry Division of the Illinois National Guard fired a nineteen-gun salute with a howitzer. At the foot of the steps that had been rolled to the side of the jet, Governor Otto Kerner solemnly met the debarking party led by Adlai E. Stevenson 3d.

From the other side of the four-engine jet, the coffin was carried by National Guard pallbearers commanded by Lieutenant Lemon Works of the 178th Infantry, a tall, broad-shouldered man who towered over his men.

The 399th Army band from Fort Leonard Wood, Missouri, played four ruffles and flourishes, followed by "The Stars and Stripes Forever" in a slow cadence. The band then played a hymn and the coffin was placed in a hearse provided by the Smith Funeral Chapel, which had supplied the Lincoln coffin.

In Springfield outside the silver-domed Capitol, three hundred more persons watched as the coffin was carried into the rotunda. The Capitol, closed to any business, was as hushed as a church. . . .

In the mourning party with Adlai E. Stevenson 3d and his wife were Mr. Stevenson's two other sons, Borden and John Fell, and Mrs. John Fell Stevenson.

Also in the party was Mrs. Marietta P. Tree, the U. S. representative on the United Nations Trusteeship Council who was with Mr. Stevenson when he died in London Wednesday; Secretary of Labor W. Willard Wirtz and various other friends, relatives and former associates.

Then on Monday Stevenson was buried in Bloomington after a service in the town's Unitarian Church in which the Rev. Robert Reed, the pastor, read brief selections from Stevenson's writings. These included one from his last speech in which Stevenson said of this "little spaceship," the earth, that "we cannot maintain it half fortunate, half miserable, half confident, half despairing, half slave to the ancient enemies of man, half free in a liberation of resources undreamed of until this day."

Fifty-four thousand persons saw the funeral procession to Evergreen Memorial Cemetery and President Johnson's arrival and departure.

As Stevenson was being buried in Illinois, a memorial service was held at the United Nations Building in New York. Raymond Daniell reported:

In the great green-and-gold hall of the General Assembly where his voice will be long remembered, more than two thousand admirers of Adlai E. Stevenson gathered this afternoon to pay their respects to his memory.

Among them were delegates from many lands, including a large number of dark-skinned men and women from the new countries of Africa and Asia, who regarded him as an understanding friend. . . .

Four speakers addressed the memorial gathering, which was presided over by Francis T. P. Plimpton, acting head of the United States Mission. They were Dean Rusk, Secretary of State, U Thant, Secretary General of the United Nations, Archibald MacLeish, the poet, who was an old friend of Mr. Stevenson, and Dr. Carlos Sosa-Rodríguez, former president of the General Assembly. . . .

Referring to him as "a universal man," Mr. Rusk said that Mr. Stevenson's "universality did not rest upon his being a prince among plain men, but upon his being a plain man even among princes."

Mr. Thant spoke feelingly of the deep friendship and understanding that existed between him and Mr. Stevenson. . . .

"It has often been said," he went on, "that in war the first casualty is truth. The cold war is also capable of inflicting the same casualty. The weapons designed and utilized to crush and mutilate the human mind are as potent as any of the weapons designed for physical destruction.

"The weapons of the cold war contaminate our moral fiber, warp our thinking processes and afflict us with pathological obsessions. These are the invisible but, nevertheless, the most devastating effects of the cold war on humanity. I believe Adlai Stevenson, in his innermost thoughts, realized these truths."

Mr. MacLeish spoke of Mr. Stevenson as a man "whose life had a particular singleness, an unusual wholeness, its own law."

"And it is here in this room," he said, "I think, that that wholeness best appears. For the United Nations, though it knows and suffers from our contemporary trust in power, is dedicated to another end: the subordination of power to the hope for peace—which is to say the hope for humanity."

The official encomiums did not, of course, advert to Stevenson's growing sense of unease about the Johnson Administration's foreign policy and his increasing feelings of frustration in his United Nations post. Nor did the eulogies mention that he was contemplating resigning and had told former Senator William Benton of Connecticut, a close friend, that he would quit after the 1965 session of the General Assembly. Nonetheless, in the last few months of his life Stevenson was actively debating his future with himself and with his friends.

When Stevenson accepted his appointment to the United Nations he had told Norman Cousins of *The Saturday Review* that "I don't want to be a lawyer arguing a case whether he believes in it or not." At about the same time he was voicing doubts to Harry Ashmore, the staff director of his 1956 Presidential campaign, who recalled them in *The Arkansas Gazette* after Stevenson's death. "The point is that Jack Kennedy is going to make his own foreign policy, as he should, and there simply isn't enough in his record to indicate how much of it I might agree with," he said. "And yet, if I accept this appointment I am committed to support him this side of treason or madness. There is no way for a man as prominent as I am to quietly step down. If I were to resign, no matter the excuse, it would signal a major break over United States policy."

Stevenson agreed in the end to go to the United Nations in part because he was given Cabinet rank and assurances that he would be consulted on policy. These, however, were so vaguely worded that he couldn't cash them in when indeed he was consulted as a formality after policy had been fixed. Stevenson minded very much the demeaning job of being an errand boy, and it hurt very badly when it was reported after the Bay of Pigs episode that Kennedy had referred to him as "my official liar." Yet he stayed on.

"I'm a team player," he once remarked to Edwin L.

Lahey, a friend and columnist for *The Chicago Daily News*.

Stevenson publicly insisted, however, to the last day of his life that he did not disagree with the objectives of the Johnson policy in Vietnam nor with the aims of United States intervention in Santo Domingo nor with the over-all thrust of foreign policy. But he was less positive in conversation with his friends and in letters to them.

"Everything has not been to my liking of late," he wrote James Wechsler of *The New York Post* shortly after Marine Corps members landed in Santo Domingo and the issue had been raised in the United Nations.

In another letter he confessed that "the constant role of 'debater' instead of 'creator' " was "awkward" for him.

This was a theme that Stevenson touched on shortly before his sixty-fifth birthday in an interview with Martin Mayer for *The Times Magazine*. "This job has been a terrible drill," he said, adding: "In my own life I've been accustomed to making policy. I've sometimes been a little restless in this role of executing and articulating the policies of others.

"There is a disadvantage in being anywhere other than the seat of power. And every issue that comes to the United Nations has its antecedents before it gets here. The State Department has been involved in the negotiations, and now the situation has become insoluble, so it gets dumped onto us."

In private conversations Stevenson often used the word "blunder" to describe the Administration's execution of foreign policy. He was appalled by what he regarded as the Johnson Administration's "corn pone." These attitudes encouraged a number of his friends and old associates and admirers to press him to resign in protest over Johnson's Vietnam policy and to lead a national drive against it. Their importunings increased after Johnson scrapped the draft of a speech Stevenson had prepared for him late in April for the twentieth anniversary of the founding of the United Nations. He had wanted Johnson to refrain from attacks on Communist China and to give some real assurance of a solution to the unpaid dues issue in the General Assembly, but Johnson declined.

At the San Francisco gathering Stevenson, according to Donald Grant of *The St. Louis Post-Dispatch*, was "a sobered man, his face twisted with inner pain." He knew then, Grant wrote, that Johnson "had rejected his suggestions."

The Dominican Republic crisis was another blow. According to David Schoenbrun, a foreign correspondent, Stevenson had complained to Ambassador Harriman about the "massive blunder" in Johnson's armed intervention there and remarked that its defense in the Security Council "took several years off my life."

"I could not believe in some of the things I had to say," Stevenson was quoted as having told Harriman.

Still, Stevenson at his death was not prepared to oppose the course of policy in Vietnam and in the Dominican Republic or toward the Soviet Union. Indeed, he was in full agreement with these policies; his dissents were tactical not strategic; and he could not understand how it was that so many persons he respected, especially in the academic and literary world, opposed them.

In preparation for resigning the United Nations post, as he

had decided to do, Stevenson was planning a series of public statements clearly enunciating his support of basic policies.

"How can I honorably and decently leave this United Nations job?" he had asked Eric Sevareid of CBS, shortly before his death. With Sevareid Stevenson seemed wistful and tired, but not bitter; and looking to the future he had sighed and said: "Oh, what I would really like is just to sit in the shade with a glass of wine in my hands and watch the dancers."

Apart from the implications that could be read into a resignation at a time when Administration policy was under acute attack, there were other explanations for Stevenson's holding onto his post. "It's easy to reconcile a sense of duty with this job," he told Mayer; and Stevenson did feel duty-bound, for he was a man intensely loyal to his commitments. In addition, he did like the diplomatic life and the parties and the pretty women he escorted to the theater or to dinner. These served as anodynes to his inner hurts and they helped assuage his feelings of loneliness.

Nonetheless, there were times when he was moody and gloomy. At one party at which he was the host, he was found alone munching a sandwich and staring at his scuffed shoes. At times he described himself as "a battered, beat-up bureaucrat" and spoke of the "oblivion" that the United Nations had become for him. Some of these remarks were in keeping with the self-deprecatory stories that he liked to tell about himself, but others seemed to express a certain joylessness about himself, as though he were an indentured servant waiting only to return to his farm at Libertyville and to enjoy his grandchildren.

Stevenson was moody and introspective to a greater degree than was generally realized; not that he took to funks or was a solipsist, but that he was sensitive about himself. "Give me the benefit of your candor and your criticism," he told friends assembled for his sixty-fifth birthday party at the River Club in New York, "but please keep your doubts to yourself, because I have enough of those of my own."

Some of this sensitivity was there for all to see—the endless scribbling and rewriting of speeches, as though he couldn't settle on a definitive phrasing. Some of it came out in his stories or remarks about himself, in which he invariably was the comedy character who made a hash out of things. Some of it was expressed in the form of doubts as to whether he was pursuing the best possible course of conduct. And some of it was shown in private brooding. Stevenson could tell the guests at a dinner in his honor that he was there, too, to pay tribute to himself, the man whose ideas, particularly on nuclear testing, had cost him three million votes.

Or he could let his hair down with a friend. One such was Norman Cousins of *The Saturday Review*, an adviser in the 1952 campaign who went to Springfield to work with the candidate.

"Not far outside the city there's a hilltop," Stevenson told Cousins in a moment of self-revelation. "It's not more than a couple of hundred feet high, but you can look out over a great panorama of the American plains.

"You can see long vistas from mountaintops or skyscrapers, but you won't have a stronger feeling about America than you can get from this particular lookout. When Abe Lincoln was in Springfield he used to come to this hilltop alone, spend hours there and let thoughts come to him. . . .

"After I became Governor I would go out to that hilltop

by myself; sometimes I would stay out there eight or ten hours at a time. It helped me. It helped me a great deal."

Another friend, Kenneth S. Davis, noticed that Stevenson would sit for hours alone in the yard at Libertyville, "looking far out across the [Des Plaines] river and then writing now and again on the long yellow pad of ruled paper in his lap, writing . . . notes for a speech on which he wanted help."

Stevenson's self-sensitivity was akin to his loneliness, which was accentuated after his divorce in 1949. Often he was so lonely that he couldn't bear to be still; at other times, when he was living in the Executive Mansion in Springfield, he would implore his friends to visit him for the weekend; and sometimes he was just silent.

To many of his friends in his last years Stevenson appeared weary and tired. They noticed lines in his face deepen. They saw that he was touching up his hair. His speeches at times lacked their former verve and they contained, moreover, whole paragraphs from old speeches and lines that had lost their sparkle from overuse. He was eating too much, and this showed in his figure; for Stevenson was indifferent to exercise.

"Adlai loved good food, perhaps a little too much," Representative Jonathan B. Bingham recalled. "In a restaurant, he would try to order sensibly in terms of calories, but when the food arrived he was apt to check up on what everybody else ordered and to complain that he had got the worst of it."

On the tennis court, Bingham said, Stevenson was "a delight." "He explained that his purpose in playing tennis was to get as little exercise as possible. He loved to stand at the net and, if the ball came within reach, dispose of it neatly with a nicely angled shot that would hardly bounce."

Stevenson had many friends. A particular one was Eleanor Roosevelt, with whom he worked so closely to revitalize the Democratic Party. Talking about her to the party convention in Atlantic City in 1964, he told the delegates:

She has passed beyond these voices, but our memory and her meaning have not. She was a lady—for all seasons. And, like her husband, she left "a name to shine on the entablatures of truth—forever."

There is I believe, a legend in the Talmud that in any period of man's history the heavens themselves are held in place by the virtue, love and shining integrity of twelve just men. They are completely unaware of this function. They go about their daily work, their humble chores—doctors, teachers, workers, farmers (never, alas, lawyers, so I understand), just ordinary, devoted citizens—and meanwhile the rooftree of creation is supported by them alone.

There are times when nations or movements or great political parties are similarly sustained in their purposes and being by the pervasive, unconscious influence of a few great men and women. Can we doubt that Eleanor Roosevelt had in some measure the keeping of the party's conscience in her special care? . . .

She thought of herself as an ugly duckling, but she walked in beauty in the ghettos of the world, bringing with her the reminder of her beloved St. Francis, "It is in the giving that we receive." And wherever she walked beauty was forever there.

Because Stevenson had so many devoted friends, it may seem a contradiction to suggest that he did not have the common touch, but with him it was forced. His inability to express his compassion was a source of great concern to his advisers.

"I remember riding behind his open campaign car [in 1952] with James Reston, who pointed out the contrast between Adlai's diffident wave and Ike's spread arms flung overhead in V for victory," Harry Ashmore recalled in *The Arkansas Gazette*.

There was, God knows, a mighty effort to change the image. Professionals from Madison Avenue and volunteers from Hollywood and Broadway and the upper reaches of television flocked in to plead with him to watch his timing, take his laughs and project for the camera. City ward heelers and county bosses gave him instruction in handshaking, bagel-eating and the proper tilt of a cowboy's Stetson.

He tolerated advice on these matters and he may even have listened to it. Once when we were whistle-stopping down the spine of Florida in the 1956 primary, he turned to me as we drove out of a little town and asked how he had done. "Well," I said, "it wasn't bad. But when you are shaking hands in a supermarket and a little girl in a starched dress steps out of the crowd and hands you a stuffed alligator, what you say is, 'Thanks very much, I've always wanted one of these for the mantelpiece at Libertyville.' What you don't say is what you did say: 'For Christ's sake, what's this?' "

He was delighted and recounted our conversation at the next stop—and probably lost a hundred votes to Estes Kefauver, who was born knowing how to react to an outthrust alligator.

Stevenson tried harder in 1956 to put on a traditional political show, but it wasn't really in him. He liked people in small quantities, but in the aggregate he found them difficult to get on with. It was not so much that he was remote or aloof as it was that political blarney was alien to his nature. He wanted ideas and ideas alone to be persuasive. Kennedy, coming afterward, was able to build on Stevenson's example —and on his mistakes—for Kennedy not only projected ideas, but he also knew how to glad-hand.

A characteristic that set Stevenson apart in American politics was his possession of a sense of history as a process. That is to say he thought of the United States as an evolving and developing nation with a past, present and future, and of other nations in the same terms. And he understood that a political system that served the American people well could not be exported to serve another people equally well. Yet Stevenson's intelligence (which accounts in large measure for his popularity among those in the professions) was not intellectualism; for he was by no means widely read, nor was he an original thinker.

Stevenson, to his credit, did not pretend to scholarship nor to being a savant. He preferred being a student—a characteristic attitude that he demonstrated amusingly in an incident in 1959 that involved his interest in abstract art. Gay Talese wrote the story under the headline, "Stevenson Studying Abstract Art":

Although he once bought ebony heads in Nigeria and owns a Picasso or two, Adlai E. Stevenson has never been regarded by either party as a connoisseur, and nobody ever thought he would battle Governor Rockefeller for the Art Students League vote.

But Mr. Stevenson said yesterday that he had become interested in abstract expressionism. And he therefore stands opposed to President Eisenhower, who likes realistic painting; to Governor Rockefeller, who likes modern painting; and the former Governor W. Averell Harriman, who prefers easy-to-understand French painting.

In fact, Mr. Stevenson visited three New York studios last Friday to learn more about such abstract-expressionists as Mark Rothko, a creator of wild shapes; Adolph Gottlieb, who paints large and expensively; and Franz Kline, who now can make $7,000 a painting but who, in 1952, painted "Vote for Adlai" posters for nothing.

"I have been interested in art for a long while," Mr. Stevenson said by telephone from Chicago yesterday, "but I've had very little opportunity to study the nonobjective painters. I've never quite understood it, so I tried to understand it better."

"Mr Stevenson seemed very keen, very keen in my studio," Mr. Gottlieb recalled yesterday. "He was very curious when I showed him a painting of mine called 'Counterpoise,' which is nine feet high and seven and one-half feet wide, and has a big, round form on top, and an irregular shape at the bottom. Mr. Stevenson asked, 'What do these forms mean?'

"And I said, 'Well, it has nothing to do with science fiction, or celestial bodies; these are disparate images. But I can't control the association—the circular form at the top can represent the female element, like an egg; the irregular form at the bottom, which is rugged-looking, could represent the male.'

"Mr. Stevenson nodded," Mr. Gottlieb said. "But he didn't pretend to know anything he didn't know. He was quite keen."

Mr. Stevenson said he was especially interested in talking to Mr. Kline, who had volunteered to paint campaign posters. "I tried to find out what ever happened to those signs," he said.

"Did you?" he was asked.

"I never found out," he said.

"Did you buy any paintings?"

"I wish I could afford to," he said. "Mr. Kline did give me a nice little picture he did in 1947, when he was a little objective."

"Did you learn anything from your visit?"

"Yes," Mr. Stevenson said. "I think I learned a good deal. I can't say that I have completed my education, however. I'm a diligent student."

Stevenson borrowed heavily from his friends in the intellectual community, and what serious reading he did, he did thoroughly and well, but he was not bookish. The distinction between intelligence and intellectualism is important because it goes far to explain why Stevenson was the despair of some of his academic friends over Vietnam and the Dominican Republic. They challenged the basics of Johnson's foreign policy and expected that Stevenson would do the same. And of course he did not. In turn, he could not understand, or accept, the criticisms of foreign policy fundamentals that issued from the Vietnam teach-ins, nor the moral overtones that Vietnam generated.

That Stevenson's mind was less probing than it seemed is demonstrated by a rereading of his speeches. Their phrasing is brilliant, often inspired, but developed argument is frequently lacking. He excelled in giving swift impressions, at stating visions and goals, at calling to greatness, at denouncing the obscurantism of McCarthyism, at evoking man's higher instincts; yet his argumentation was loose. His mind, however, was in the right place, and he desperately wanted intelligence to be brought to bear on problems. He strove to make people think, to achieve mastery by their brains, to act with reasoned temper; and so it may perhaps be beside the point to inquire too closely behind the luster of his speeches and the magic of his words. That they stimulated thought and led to action is perhaps tribute enough.

Stevenson had a way of learning from people. Not only was he an intent and absorbed listener and an eager questioner, but he also paid those with whom he talked the ultimate compliment of being interested in them as persons. He was quick to grasp what was said to him and was never patronizing. He talked to all manner of people at home and abroad from the high to the humble. This was one reason he was so well informed, especially about the new nations with whose representatives he spent much time. It also accounts for the uniformly high esteem in which he was held, for he treated his friends as his equals.

One example of this capacity for engendering friendship was a long trip Stevenson took through Latin America in 1960 with former Senator Benton. He was sought out and conversed with by all elements of society. He talked with the poor, the students, the disaffected, the wealthy; and from each he gained an understanding of the social and economic restlessness of Latin America. To them he was the conscience of the United States because he invited their confidences.

Stevenson was peculiarly the beau ideal of his country

abroad, especially among the new nations. This was partly because he was known to believe that the world was in the twilight of imperialism and colonialism and partly because he was not censorious about the struggles of the once colonial peoples for nationhood. He did not, for instance, count it against them that they sought economic aid from the Soviet Union or that their politics were not conducted according to American principles. He gave the impression of sympathetic intimacy, but above all he was sensitive to their pride. It was significant that he treated his African friends at the United Nations as his distinguished colleagues, and he saw to it that they received the same attention and respect accorded, say, the British Ambassador.

Although Stevenson's ambassadorial role at the United Nations was not so concerned with policy as he would have liked, there is no doubt that he was convinced of the necessity of the world organization and its paramount place in adjusting international differences and in keeping the peace. He recognized it as an organization that the great powers could and should employ for their common advantage; yet he was quite realistic about the fact that this was not always the case.

Talking one day to J. Robert Moskin of *Look* magazine about the United States in the United Nations, Stevenson said:

"It is getting harder and harder to dominate the scene. We must depend more on persuasion and moral force. This is the way it should be. We must insist that the Soviet Union not have its way by intimidation or threat or bluff. This will require great vigilance and sacrifice. We must be willing to pay the price.

"We are in the twilight of imperialism, and the death of

every imperialism has been followed by a new one. Our imperialism is dying, and the Russian is rising. It is, in effect, a form of Roman imperialism—a universality of authority. It has the force of military power and the great force of an ideal especially attractive to the underdeveloped countries.

"The conflict is: Is the Soviet Union going to prevail, as the new imperialisms always have? What we are experimenting with now is whether we can make a transition from the old imperialism to a new era without imperialism. This is really what the United Nations means. Can it enable us to pass from this imperialism to a new order without a new imperialism and new violence?"

In this respect, he told Moskin, "I feel it's useful work I'm doing." And Stevenson believed profoundly that history would vindicate his "useful work."

The United Nations that Stevenson had helped bring into being, nurtured and served was one expression of his service to the United States and his countrymen. But what of his contributions to American public life? In the film *Dr. Strangelove* many believe he was mercilessly caricatured as Merkin Muffley—high-minded and ineffectual. And this is an estimate, without the caricature, that seems so easy to make about Stevenson—too easy, for it does not fit.

The vigorous existence of Stevenson Democrats attests one example of his effect. These are the men and women who shunned politics until 1952—the academics, the college-bred, those in the professions—until they were summoned to it by the sound of his voice enunciating a highhearted vision of public life. Suddenly they found themselves licking postage stamps, ringing doorbells and attending grubby meetings. And once in politics as participants (rather than as spectators and voters) they remained there.

Moreover, it was not merely as Democrats that this new group was significant; many of them entered public life as officeholders and administrators, thus opening politics on a wide scale to men of intellectual talent. True, there had been brain trusters with Roosevelt, but with and because of Stevenson large numbers of men of brains and dispassion exerted a sustained influence in the United States.

This contribution of Stevenson's (along with some others) was aptly summed up in a *New York Times* editorial, "The Legacy of Adlai Stevenson," published the Sunday after his death. It read:

Power is ephemeral; and once-vivid memories of great deeds and stirring events eventually fade. But the moral force of personal example—for good or bad—inevitably endures, for it enters the minds of contemporaries, shapes the way in which they see and judge reality, is passed on to posterity and becomes part of history and of the historian's measure.

The death of Adlai E. Stevenson this week left a unique void because through his deeds, words and mode of life he had set an unusually compelling example to the practitioners of politics. It is possible to misunderstand the nature of that example. Although he was well read and interested in ideas, he was not an intellectual seeking to live the life of the mind. He was indisputably a public man who understood politics and sought power. To see Stevenson solely as a preacher of high ideals or as a literary figure miscast in the brutal world of politics is to miss the main force of his career.

The essence of Stevenson's example was that he demonstrated that moral values are relevant to politics. In 1952 he took over the leadership of the Democratic Party, which, despite many great accomplishments, had grown fat, careless and corrupt. He reorganized the party's national headquarters, recharged the party's sluggish idealism and gave it a new tone and direction. Four years later in his much undervalued second campaign, he set forth in his "New America" program most of the intellectual basis for the later New Frontier and Great Society.

Largely because of his leadership, the Democratic Party in the 1950's provided a viable alternative. Senator Eugene McCarthy did not exaggerate when he told his fellow partisans at the 1960 convention that Stevenson was "the man who made us proud to be a Democrat." Nor is it an exaggeration to say of him that he had a more profound and lasting effect on his party as an opposition leader out of power than his successful Republican opponent had on his party in power.

To the problems of foreign policy, Stevenson brought his admirable gifts of tact, timing, patience, incisive eloquence and skillful maneuver. His clear moral insight guided him through the ambiguities and indirections of diplomacy. He recognized that peace is not only an end which most men seek, but it is also a means for reaching that end, which many men tend to forget. Stevenson bequeathed to the nation in foreign affairs not a plan or a policy, but a reminder that moral self-restraint in the use of power is a source of strength.

Stevenson knew defeat and disappointment, but he never knew vulgarity, panic or despair. He was no stranger to ambition, but he remembered that win or lose he had to live with himself after Election Day. To the public dialogue of his time he brought intelligence, civility and grace. We who have been his contemporaries have been companions of greatness.

History is full of Cleopatra's noses and horseshoe nails. Speculation about Stevenson is equally idle. Would he, like Lincoln, have grown in the Presidency? Or would he have been the Merkin Muffley of *Dr. Strangelove?* It is more tempting to think of the man as he was and to assess his failures and his successes.

Stevenson, on the record that he wrote, seemed to want the Presidential office, although he denied that it was a gnawing ambition. But he wanted it on his own terms, as he had wanted and received the governorship of Illinois, little understanding the lupine ways by which power is achieved and, in any event, holding off from them. Power in

American politics is almost as much the working out of single-minded purpose by the candidate as it is the gift of the electorate. Stevenson, being of several minds at once, lacked the decisiveness to gain power. By contrast, Roosevelt, Truman, Kennedy and Johnson had that single-mindedness.

Stevenson's inability to grasp the nettle of power was accounted a blemish. He himself was rueful about it and even made jokes about the funny things that happened to him on the way to White House, so that it seemed at if he almost treasured his public losses more than his personal triumphs.

If that is in any measure true, it may be because the personal qualities and successes—integrity, probity, class, intelligence, soaring vision, friendships, infusing politics with a new spirit, lifting men's minds above the petty and the mean —often seem less to the eye of history than do bills and treaties and laws and the direction of government. Yet this is perhaps the ultimate illusion about history; for if men in the long run make their own history, they must make it not only out of the stuff at hand but also out of their own potentialities. To these potentialities Stevenson made a splendid contribution.

A great man does not have to be unflawed, nor is he ever. It is sufficient that, flaws and all, he try to help mankind light its way onward.

INDEX

237; contest with Kefauver (1956), 138-40; conversations with Khrushchev, 183-86, 190-92; criticizes Eisenhower Administration, 107, 112, 116ff, 156ff, 174-75; criticizes McCarthy, 96, 115ff; and Cuban crisis, 219-21, 227, 238ff; death of, 255ff; and death of Ruth Mary Merwin, 15-16; declines Presidential candidacy (1952), 48, 50, 52, 54ff; defeat in 1956, 6, 168ff; defeat in 1952, 2-3, 6ff, 104-5; in defense of Truman, 117; on democracy, 33-35, 45, 246-247; disarmament speech (November 15, 1961), 232-33; discusses public issues, 4-5; dislike for Kennedy, 201-2; divorced from Ellen Borden, 18; early education, 15; on education, 5, 136, 181; egghead label, 5; and Eisenhower-Taft limerick, 97; elected Governor of Illinois, 9, 27-28, 29; elected managing editor of *The Daily Princetonian*, 16-17; on employment for older persons, 157-158; with Encyclopaedia Britannica Films, 174; endorsed by Truman for 1956 campaign, 132; England's regard for, 257; farewell report as Governor of Illinois (January 8, 1953), 107; on Federal aid, 140-41; foreign policies, 36-40, 49, 57, 112ff, 120, 148, 152, 160, 163ff, 175ff, 216ff, 252, 254, 255, 267ff; funeral of, 264ff; Godkin Lectures, 119-20; on goodwill tour of South America, 228-29; as Governor of Illinois, 29-63 *passim;* Gridiron Club speech (December 13, 1952), 8-12; at Harvard Law School, 17; and Hiss trial, 46, 88; humor, 4, 5-6, 8ff, 55, 66, 83, 86-87, 89, 92-93, 96, 97, 139, 179, 197-99, 205, 224, 244; hydrogen bomb issue, 163ff; inaugural address (1949), 30-31; on isolationism, 36-40, 113, 125; joins *The Bloomington Pantagraph*, 17; joins Cutting, Moore & Sidley (law firm), 17; joins Quadrangle eating club, Princeton, 16; on Kennedy's death, 250; Korean War issue, 81-82, 102-104; lack of pomposity, 6; lack of self-pity, 6, 8; lauds U Thant, 231; as lawyer to Frank Knox, 20ff; literateness, 4, 5-6, 9-10, 93; loses Truman's nomination (1956), 143ff; McGill University speech, 188-89; marries Ellen Borden, 18; meeting with Roosevelt, first important, 20-22; on "Meet the Press," 254; moderateness, 31, 136, 143; on national neurosis, 121ff; on national wealth, 123; on negotiations with Soviet Union, 114; and New America program, 150-52, 157, 280; nicknamed Laddie, 15; nicknamed Rabbit, 17; nominated for Presidency (1952), 62, (1956), 141, 149; at Northwestern University, 17; on patriotism, 67, 69ff; with Paul, Weiss, Rifkind, Wharton & Garrison (law firm), 174; practices public speaking, 18-19; on the press, 11-12, 74; press opposition to, 4, 10, 74; at Princeton University, 16-17; public's devotion to, 4-5, 7; reforms made in Illinois, 31; returns to politics, 112; and Eleanor Roosevelt, speaks of, 273; shoe-with-a-hole trademark, 83-84; on Social Security, 30, 123-24, 158; speculation of Stevenson-Kennedy ticket, 197-98; forename Adlai, source of, 13; and Taft-Hartley Law, calls for repeal of, 83, 194; tour of Europe and Asia (1958), 182-88; travels around the world (1953), 109; on unilateralism, 113; United Parents Association speech, 181; urged to seek third nomination, 200ff; urges test ban treaty, 231; veto of Broyles bill (1951), 42-46; on Vietnam crisis, 251ff

Stevenson, Borden (son of Adlai E., 2d), 186, 265

Stevenson, Ellen Borden (wife of Adlai E., 2d), 17

Stevenson, Helen Davis (mother of Adlai E., 2d), 12

Stevenson, John Fell (son of Adlai E., 2d), 186, 265

Stevenson, Mrs. John Fell, 265

Stevenson, Lewis Green (father of Adlai E., 2d), 12, 14

Stewart, Michael, 256

Stratton, William G., 106

Strout, Richard Lee, 6

Supreme Court, United States, 136, 137, 143, 146